# HAND-BOOK
## OF
# COLLOQUIAL TIBETAN

# HAND-BOOK OF COLLOQUIAL TIBETAN

A PRACTICAL GUIDE TO THE LANGUAGE OF CENTRAL TIBET

IN THREE PARTS

BY

GRAHAM SANDBERG, B. A.,
AIN, M. M. BENGAL GOVERNMENT; AUTHOR: "MANUAL OF SIKKIM-BHUTIA."

GYAN

*Published by*

GYAN

Gyan Publishing House
5, Ansari Road
Daryaganj, New Delhi-110002
Phone: 011-47034999, 9811692060
E-mail: books@gyanbooks.com

*Distribution Network*
gyanbooks.com
India, USA, Canada, UK, Australia, France



ISBN : 978-81-212-4415-2 (PB)
First Published, 1894

2nd Impression 2020

*Printed at:* Gyan Press, Delhi.

# HAND-BOOK

OF

# COLLOQUIAL TIBETAN.

A PRACTICAL GUIDE TO THE LANGUAGE OF CENTRAL TIBET.

IN THREE PARTS.

BY

GRAHAM SANDBERG, B. A.,

CHAPLAIN, H. M. BENGAL GOVERNMENT; AUTHOR: "MANUAL OF SIKKIM-BHUTIA."

Calcutta:

THACKER, SPINK AND CO.

1894.

# PREFACE.

The present work is designed to afford not only a complete guide to the Vernacular of Tibet Proper, but also considerable technical information to the traveller in that little-explored land. The Tibetan territory is computed to hold a population of six millions, sparsely distributed over some 650,000 square miles; and the time is said to be approaching when these extraordinary regions will be laid open to the enterprise of the explorer, the missionary, and the trader. In the days, then, that are to come, a knowledge of the idiom of the inhabitants will be a necessity.

Up to the present date, no grammar of the colloquial language has been placed before the public. Jäschke, indeed, in his learned works, has fully dissected the old classical language; but the modern speech differs so materially from the literary vehicle, both in vocabulary and in grammatical structure, that a proficient in the latter might in vain attempt to hold converse with the native of to-day. The famous Moravian linguist, however, has brought together in his Dictionary great store of facts concerning the spoken tongue, particularly the Western; and that store has proved a treasure-hoard to myself in these pages.

It is the *lingua franca* of the Tibetan Empire which has been analysed and codified in this Handbook; not the dialectic forms spoken in corners of the country, as in Ládak, Lahul, and Sikkim, but the general Vernacular current in the heart of the land, and which will carry the traveller from west to east and from north-east to south. Besides availing myself of materials already published, I have had the advantage of close intercourse with two men formerly resident in Lhásá. Those two I freely consulted. A stay of three months in Darjiling last year, where I made the acquaintance of Tibetans from various districts, afforded much further help.

Three Parts are here attempted. First; the grammatical circumstances of the colloquial have been minutely set forth, with copious examples on every page. Secondly; a body of useful conversations has been prepared with especial view to the peculiar incidents of Tibetan travel. To these have been added many technical lists, bearing on the Religion, Natural History, and Geography of the land; and, as much of these collections is new, it is hoped they may prove valuable. Thirdly; the Compendious Vocabulary, in Tibetan and Ládaki, contains an assortment of such words and expressions as it was thought would prove most useful and useable. Alternative renderings have been generally avoided as productive of bewilderment. A long illness, let me add, has caused the postponement of the publication of this work, but the result of the delay has been a complete revision of the whole.

SUBÁTHU: PANJÁB, *August*, 1894. GRAHAM SANDBERG.

# TABLE OF CONTENTS.

## PART I.

### GRAMMAR OF THE COLLOQUIAL.



## PART II.

### PHRASES—CONVERSATIONAL EXERCISES—TECHNICAL LISTS.

# PART III.

## VOCABULARY.



# APPENDIX.

# PART I.

## GRAMMAR OF THE COLLOQUIAL.

# TIBETAN GRAMMAR.

## CHAPTER I.

## SOUNDS AND SYLLABLES.

The pronunciation of Tibetan words differs greatly from the orthography, and in the chief colloquial idioms there are many letters and combinations of letters which have lost their primitive sounds. That in earlier times the words were generally sounded as they still continue to be spelt seems plain, from the fact that at the present day, in the remotest fastnesses of Tibet, and, curiously, where the populace cannot read, the spoken language adheres more or less closely to the original spelling. This is the case in Skardo, north of Kashmir, as well as in the wild mountainous tracts of Amdo on the Chinese border, provinces 3,000 miles apart. The decay or change of pronunciation is to be found principally in letters occurring as initials or finals, as well as in letters compounded, as are Sanskrit characters, out of two or three others.

Our present treatise deals solely with the speech in general use. Accordingly, in these pages, all words shall be spelt as they are now sounded; and therefore, also, there can be no need here to explain the rules for the pronunciation of words written in Tibetan characters.

2

The sounds occurring in the main colloquial are the following:—

## VOWELS.

*a*: the short *a*, heard usually as the English *u* in "sun," though in some words approaching to the *a* in "man," "sand," &c.

*á*: the longer *a*, which shall always be marked, pronounced as *a* in "father."

*ā*: the prolonged *a*, sounded almost as a double or iterated *a*, both with the Italian sound; perhaps as the second *a* in our "papā."

*e*: generally carries the short sound of an English *e* in such words as "ten," "mend;" but when the final letter of a syllable, it is heard, not like our English *e* in "he," &c., but as the Italian *e* in "ché," answering to our *ai* in such a word as "praise."

*i*: frequently as the English short *i* in the word "pin." Thus we hear in Tibetan *rin* "price," *min* "is not." But as a final, it takes the orthodox sound of the letter *i* as heard in most European languages, namely, that of English *e* in "he," "me," &c.

*o*: usually as our *o* in "tone," "polo," &c.; and rarely as our *o* in "pond," "lot," &c., except in words ending in *ng*, as *song* "went," *tsong* "onion," sounded as in our word "song."

*ō*: long *o* occurs only as an initial in Tibetan. Its sound, like the long "ā," is somewhat peculiar, and as if two separate pronunciations of the single vowel followed one another, and were almost slided the one into the other. Perhaps *ō-ōh* might represent the sound, but often heard as *wo*.

*ö*: when *o* is immediately followed by either *n* or *d* in the original spelling, it assumes this half-tone, a common sound in German and Danish, and heard in such French words as *peu*. As the *d* of the original is generally dropped at the end of a syllable, the *ö* in our orthography will be frequently found as the terminant letter in colloquial Tibetan words. Ex: *yö'* "is," *nyö'-chhung*, "fragile."

*u*: always sounded as the English "oo." As an initial is prolonged.

*ü*: another half-tone, occurring immediately before the letters *n* or *d*, the latter consonant as a final being then often hardly audible. May be popularly described as the letter "u" pronounced in an affected, mincing manner; but it is, of course, a regular vowel sound in several continental languages: heard in *Müller* in German, and in *feu* in French.

## CONSONANTS.

*k*: as in "kettle."

*kh*: as the aspirated *k* in Hindustani; and in many parts of Tibet it is sounded as the *ch* in "loch," or as the Russian X.

*g*: always hard in sound, as in "gone." As a final sounds as *k*; and wherever in these pages we have printed *g* as final, let it sound *k*.

*gh*: nearly as *k* in ordinary talk, and will be understood always if so sounded. But we shall discriminate its occurrence; defining it as *gh* in the English "ghastly." As initial only. Ex: *ghá-pa* "where" (mostly heard as *ká-pa*).

*ng*: a nasal *n*. Is a single letter in Tibetan and is common as the initial letter of words. To attain the pronunciation of *ng*, when used as initial, first sound the English word "hunger," and then try to say the *nger*, without the *hu*, eliminating much of the *g* sound. As final, *ng* is very short and abrupt.

*ch*: as in "church."

*chh*: an aspirated form of *ch*, as in "reach hither."

*j*: as the English *j* in "judge."

*jh*: aspirated as in "Jhansi," but often sounded as *ch*.

*ny*: uttered like the initial sound in our words "neuter," "nawt."

*t*: the dental *t*, as in "tumble."

*t'*: aspirated *t*, not as our *th*, but as *thana, thora*, in Hindustani.

*d*: dental *d*, as in "dunce." As a final, is in pronunciation nearly always dropped. However, in these cases, we shall indicate its place by an apostrophe: thus *tö'pa* for *tödpa*, *yö'* for *yöd* "is."

*dh*: aspirated *d*. In practice we advise the sound of an ordinary unaspirated *t*, which is sufficiently correct.

*n*: as in "nut." Both *n* and *d*, when either occurs as final in any syllable, modify the preceding vowel; changing *a* into *e*, *o* into *ö*, *u* into *ü*. Thus *pün* "brother," *nyen yong* (for *nyan yong*) "will hear."

*p*: as in "port." As final often for *b*; while on the contrary, as initial, in Eastern Tibet is changed into *b* occasionally.

*p'*: not heard as English *ph* (*f*), but with distinct aspirate sound.

*b*: as in *bone*. As final letter generally sounds *p*.

*bh*: had best be pronounced as our *p*; but really slightly different and different in Tibetan orthography. Thus *bhe-u* "a calf" sounds *pe-u*, and *bhu-mo* "girl" sounds *pu-mo*. We shall generally print *bh* where it occurs, while advising the sound of *p*.

*m*: as in "mat;" where it occurs before *p* it really represents *n* in the original spelling.

*ts*: only an initial, and heard as the *tes* in our words, "plates," "rates."

*ts'*: the same letter aspirated; as in our "cats' heads."

*dz*: a rough *z*, sounded with *d* as in the English "adze."

*y*: as in "yell," *w*: as in "wander."

*r*: as in "rather," but is never rolled.

*l*: as in "lamb." Where we have placed it as a final, it is often inaudible, and always changes a preceding *a* to *e* and *u* to *ü*. In the capital of Tibet, the *l* as final is said to be always heard.

*lh*: heard really as *hl*, or as the Welsh initial *Ll*. Thus *Lhása* sounds *Hlása*. However, we print *lh* in these pages in order to coincide with the Tibetan spelling.

*sh*:, *s*: these letters take the ordinary pronunciation; but the depth of tone with which they are sounded differs in different words and affects the whole word. See pp. 15, 16.

*h*: the ordinary aspirate; never a silent letter.

*ky* : sounded as written, and as this is theoretically, and often in practice, the correct pronunciation, we shall always print it as *ky*; but frequently it is heard as if *ṭy*.

*khy* : to be printed thus, but often sounded *t'y*.

*gy* : to be printed thus, but often sounded *dy*.

*chy*, *chhy*, and *jhy* : these occur as initial sounds in those words which in the written language begin with the letters *py*, *p'y*, and *by*, respectively. They represent the modern pronunciation of the latter combinations. The *y* sound is generally distinctly heard after the *ch*, *chh*, and *jh* in all such words; e. g., *jhye'pa* "to make," "do," *chhyir-tu* "for," "because of."

In some parts of Tibet the *p*, *ph*, and *b* sounds prevail in these words, and not the anomalous *ch*, *chh*, and *jh* sounds; the only change being the omission of the *y*. All over Tibet *p'imo* is as commonly heard as *chhyimo*, *p'ila* as *chhyi-la*; whilst *P'i-ling* "an Englishman" is in much more frequent use than *Chhyi-ling*.

## CEREBRAL LETTERS.

We find *t*, *t'*, *d*, and *dh* occurring as cerebrals, and pronounced, not against the teeth as the ordinary forms, but with their sound thrown up against the roof of the mouth. The *t* in our English words *torn* and *talk* is really a cerebral and differs from the *t* in *ten*, &c. As is customary, these sounds in the following pages will be printed *ṭ*, *ṭ'*, *ḍ*, and *ḍh*. They only occur in those words which in the written language have initials bearing a subscribed *r*; e. g., *bras* "rice," sounds *ḍai*. However, according to the Appendix to Mr. Rockhill's "Land of the Lamas," it would seem that *ṭr* and *t'r* are in use in Lhasa. Of this use I am partly satisfied.

---

## THE TONE-PITCH IN TIBETAN.

As in Burmese, Annamese, Chinese, &c., certain "tones," that is, a certain pitch of voice, have become recognised as attached to the pronunciation of words.

In many instances the different pitch, or *tone*, serves to discriminate words which otherwise would be sounded alike.

In Tibetan the *tone* depends altogether upon the particular letters which happen to occur in the original spelling as the two or three initial letters of any word. Though the letters, particularly the first consonant, may bė silent in pronunciation, their presence or absence in the Tibetan spelling regulates the *tone* and is thus really felt.

In our transliteration we cannot exhibit the spelling or note the unpronounced initial consonant or consonants, but we shall, where requisite, mark the *tone* of a word resulting from such spelling.

In Tibetan there are properly three *Tones.* These are the High-pitched, the Medial, and the Low Resonant.

As the majority of words are uttered in a fairly high key, we shall not as a rule distinguish the High-pitched from the Medial or ordinary *tone ;* but where useful for discrimination in words commencing with certain letters, we shall make use of the sign ◡ above the first letter of the word to mark the higher pitch. The Low Resonant *tone* will be identified by the superscribed sign ⌒ on the initial.

The High-pitched *tone* is rendered by an elevated treble or feminine style of voice, continuously sustained at one pitch; and the Medial being scarcely lower, that must be the key in which the ordinary flow of words ought to run, merely subduing the voice to the Low Resonant *tone,* which is guttural in character, whenever a word or words proper to that *tone* are introduced. If one is on the alert to notice the variation of *tone* while listening to two natives in converse, the exact distinction of voice will be at once distinguished and can be readily applied and reproduced.

The initial invariably gives the *tone* for the whole word. Taking three different words, each according to our colloquial mode of representing sounds spelt precisely alike, we may note that, being shewn with the same initial, the only way of indicating the *tone* in print will be by the use of the above-given signs. Thus, we have *ser* "says," *ser* "a nail," and *ser* "gold." In the original spelling there is the following distinction in these words: *zer* "says," *gzer* "a nail," and *gser* "gold;" and that spelling determines in truth the present *tone* in use for each.

*ŝer*, "says" is pronounced in Low Resonant tone
*šer*, "a nail," „ „ „ High-pitched tone
*ser*, "gold" „ „ „ Medial ordinary voice.

Nevertheless, as already remarked, the general flow of talk is high-pitched; and it is in fact only in the case of words commencing with s or sh that any additional elevation of *tone* is distinctly audible. Accordingly, only on words beginning with these letters shall we hereafter denote the High-pitched *tone* whenever, in words so beginning, it happens to occur. When words commencing with s or sh have no *special* elevation of voice required, no mark will be superscribed, save, of course, when they are low-pitched and require the Low Resonant sign.

Low Resonant Tone.—Words commencing with gh, jh, dh, ḍh, bh, or r, are invariably guttural and low-pitched; and accordingly no mark will be superscribed, as it will be known that the Low Resonant pronunciation is required for *all* such words.

Words having as initial letter either ng, ny, n, m, w, y, l, dz, sh, or s, being variable in *tone*, we shall whenever the word is a Low Resonant one—but only then—indicate the *tone*, except in the case of the pronouns *n̂ga* and *n̂garang*, the auxilliary verbs *ŷin*, *ŷö'*, and the negative particles *m̂a*, *m̂i*, which, it may be said at once, are always sounded in the Low Resonant *tone*, but which recur too often to have the *tone* indicated by sign. Capitals, also, cannot be marked.

Words commencing with either of the vowels o or u are likewise heard in the Low Resonant *tone*.

Examples: *ŵoma* milk, *n̂gempo* bad, *n̂yinmo* day, *n̂áts'á* sickness, *ŝampa* a bridge, *ŷangmo* light (not heavy), *l̂eb-l̂eb*, flat, *m̂e-tok* flower, *šhá* hat.

But *wang* power; *ngömpo* blue, *nying-top* courage, *num* oil, *sampa* thought, *yangts'e* clay cup, *yang-lü* hide or skin, *lung* wind, *marpo* red, *sha* flesh.

All words beginning with the letters kh, chh, p', and t', are high-toned in a pronounced degree.

## SYLLABLES AND PARTICLES.

1. Primarily the language of Tibet is a monosyllabic tongue, every syllable being ordinarily a word of definite meaning. However, in later times, a decided tendency to polysyllabism has been steadily developing itself. Besides new coinages for the purpose of expressing new and complex ideas, which have been formed by linking two or more monosyllabic words so as to make an artificial polysyllable, the tendency has been exhibited in another way. For all things in common use there existed and do exist simple names, each a word of one syllable. Nevertheless, the colloquial has by degrees grown (so to speak) dissatisfied with these primitive designations, and has succeeded in expanding a large number of them into words of two syllables. More curious is this predilection, because apparently the original names were in most cases amply sufficient to discriminate the various objects indicated. And the phenomenon of the modern tongue preferring the longer words seems still more incongruous, when we find even in modern *writings*, the old plain monosyllables generally adhered to. Doubtless the change in the pronunciation of the simpler forms has had something to do with these accretions. In the written language, words which are now sounded alike, are spelled differently. At the beginning and end of words are still written certain letters which formerly were pronounced but now are silent. These additional letters (in the case of initials, now styled "prefixes") imparted a distinction in sound to words which from the second or third

letter onwards were identically spelled. The process of attrition which has been going on in the pronunciation of the language, whereby time has gradually worn away the sound of the letters beginning and terminating words, has approximated to one another the sound of innumerable words, which in spelling and in former pronunciation were sufficiently discriminated.

Another element of confusion arises from the fact that certain collocations of letters have lost their original sounds and are now pronounced as if they were spelled with letters totally different. Thus the letters *by, py, p'y,* are now heard as if they were *jhy, chy, chhy.* We cannot in this place enter further into the subject; nor need we illustrate our remarks by examples. Nevertheless enough has been said to make plain that two processes, directly opposed to one another, have been long operating in this remarkable language. By wear and tear and carelessness, and for the saving of trouble which would result from the avoidance of sounding difficult combinations of consonants, words originally sufficiently distinctive have been reduced to such shadows and skeletons of their former selves as to be in many cases indistinguishable the one from the other. On the other hand, in order to counteract this process of denudation, and to escape from the inconvenient consequences of it, further syllables have been tacked on bodily to the older and half-wasted forms. Thus, while the syllables have been attenuated down to a minimum, rendering sufficient variety impossible, compensation has been sought, and confusion to some extent eluded, by conjoining syllables and producing by this combination the variety which the denuded monosyllables no longer afforded.

So it comes to pass, through the foregoing or other causes, that the Tibetan colloquial is no longer monosyllabic but MOSTLY MADE UP OF WORDS OF TWO SYLLABLES. One example: In written Tibetan *Sná* is "the nose," *Rná* is "the ear;" but, as initials, S. and R. are no longer sounded; and thus *Ná* becomes the word for each of two very different facial features. To prevent confusion in speech, *Ná* "ear," takes the particle *wa*. But *Ná-wa* means also "to be sick." Accordingly, at length, in the modern colloquial, *Ná* "ear" has developed into *Námchhok*. Nevertheless in *writing* the word "ear" we should still use the older forms *Rna*, or *Rna-wa;* while for such compounds as "ear-ring" we still hear *ná-kor*, not *námchhok-kor*. Analogously *Ná* "nose," has at length been developed into *Náḳu*, and even *Námts'ul*.

In words of two syllables the accent or stress is laid upon the second syllable, except when such second syllable is one of the servile particles *pa*, *wa*, *po*, or *wo*, or when the denominative affix *ghu* or *bhu* is appended, or even *chha* or *tse*. In these latter cases, the first syllable carries the accent. Thus we hear *dáwa* "the moon," not *dawá*.

2. In Tibetan we find a large number of primitive monosyllabic words to which have been affixed certain short syllables, each consisting of no more than two letters, which short syllables seem removable often at pleasure without altering the meaning of the word affected. To nouns and verbs one of two of these short syllables may be added, either *pa* or *wa*. When affixed to the root of a noun, the particle does not usually change the meaning of the word; but when an adjective is conjoined with the nouns, we frequently find the particle dropped. In the colloquial language the particle is not so often dropped as it is in the book language. However, when a compound word is created by combining two nouns, the particles (if any), are invariably omitted. The particles *ma* and *mo*, by custom, seem not removable. When either *pa* or *wa* is added to a verbal root, it may indicate either the Infinitive mood of the verb or a verbal noun, or else the participle. Thus the root *jhye*

takes the particle *pa;* and *jhye'pa* can mean "to do," or "the making," or "doing," according to circumstances. The employment of these servile particles, on the other hand, with ordinary nouns and adjectives, has come to be governed by pure custom and to be subjected to no general rule. With certain nouns and adjectives they are always heard; whilst with others they have come to be either optional or else neglected entirely. Finally, many substantives are pure monosyllables to which no particle or other syllable is, or has ever been, annexed.

NOTE ON PRONUNCIATION.—In Tibetan a final letter usually undergoes some modification. Where a syllable ends with the letter "g," it mostly takes the sound of "k," though in the following pages we have printed this final sometimes "g" and sometimes "k." So also with the letter "b," which as final sounds as our "p." Where "d" is the last latter it is nearly always inaudible and thus we have invariably omitted it, but at the same time this elision has been everywhere indicated by the use of an apostrophe. Thus *jhyed-pa* "to do" is invariably heard as *jhye'pa,* and so in these pages do we print it. Both "k" (g) and "p" (b) as finals are also often elided; thus *pák-lep* "bread" is usually heard as if *pá'le'*.

Final "s" is never heard in Tibet Proper, where it is either bluntly dropped or (and generally) assumes the sound of a quick "i." Thus the name of the chief province of Tibet is written DBUS. The "d" and "b" are held to annihilate one another, leaving the word as US only. Now, in Central Tibet the name of the province is heard as UI, in Southern Tibet as Ū, and in Ladak only is the final letter sounded and the name pronounced US. It should be noted, however, that if the letter preceding the final "s" is a consonant, the "s" is simply dropped and no "i" sound heard.

When the first syllable of a dissyllable ends in "n" and the second syllable begins with "p" or "b," the "n" sounds as "m."

Lastly, all vowels, save those marked long, are sounded very short: *men* as our "men;" *rin* as our "pin."

# CHAPTER II.

## THE ARTICLE.

1. In the Tibetan colloquial, both of the so-called Articles are to be heard in constant use.

The Indefinite Article, "a," "an," is represented by the word *chik*, placed immediately after the substantive or adjective to which it belongs; and in those cases where the word which it thus follows terminates with any vowel, except *o*, or with one of the letters *m*, *r*, or *l*, the *chik* is changed into *ŝhik*. In common practice the final *k* of the Article is hardly audible; so we may say *hlam ŝhi'* a boot, *m̂i-po chi'* a man, *kyermén chi'* a woman, *khyi ŝhi'* a dog.

When this Article occurs with a noun of any other case than the Nominative, it is in conversation generally dropped. Thus we hear *Pu-tsá ŝhi* a boy; but in the genitive *Putsá-yi* of a boy. Also when the noun is uninflected in the Accusative case, the Article is still unheard: *Pu-tsá khur shok:* Bring a boy!

This Indefinite Article likewise carries the signification "one;" and, strangely enough, has at times the meaning "some," being even used with numbers in such phrases as "some four boys." (See Chap. V, 3 γ.)

2. The Definite Article is rendered *di* "the," and is very much used in the colloquial, contrary to the literary custom. It is not an uncommon practice in general talk to place *di* before the noun to which it belongs; though properly, like *chik*, it *always ought to follow* the noun or adjective. Where

any singling out of a thing is desired, the Article may be placed both before and after the noun, as *Di jhyá di,* the bird.

When reference is made to anything just previously mentioned *di* is changed into *dhé.* Thus, supposing some man had been mentioned as appearing and we went on to say: "when the man came up, &c.," the Article used with "man" in this second and in subsequent *immediate* allusions, would be *dhé.*

Should the noun belonging to it stand in the genitive or other case, *di* is not necessarily dropped; and if it follow an inflected word the *di* would receive the inflections instead of that word.

# CHAPTER III.

# NOUN SUBSTANTIVES.

## A.—FORM AND ETYMOLOGY.

**1.** As to form, noun substantives are of two classes—simple and compound.

**2.** The simple forms are primitive monosyllables, to which in many cases custom has attached an additional syllable partaking of the nature of a servile particle. This class therefore comprises words of one and two syllables; but where a second syllable occurs it is a mere expletive which sometimes indicates the gender of the noun and which frequently can be dropped without obscuring the meaning of the word. At times, however, the appended particle serves to discriminate words analogously spelt, moreover affixes other than *pa, wa, po, wo,* are never dropped.

We will first quote a short list of monosyllabic substantives to which particles are never appended and which are always used as they are here given:—

| | | | | | | | |
|---|---|---|---|---|---|---|---|
| *Khyi:* | dog. | *Pün:* | brother. | *Jhá:* | tea. | *Hlam:* | boot. |
| *Mik:* | eye. | *Ḍom:* | box. | *Gáng:* | hill. | *Khyim:* | house. |
| *Me:* | fire. | *Lung:* | wind. | *Ming:* | name. | *Luk:* | sheep. |
| *Chhu:* | water. | *Do:* | stone. | *Ḍul:* | journey. | *Ṭi:* | knife. |
| *Shing:* | tree. | *Jhyá:* | bird. | *Lak:* | hand. | *Ḍhu:* | boat. |

The above are naturally some of the simplest and most commonly occurring words in the language.

Of the particles found conjoined with the roots of nouns the first variety are *pa, wa,* and *a.* These may hardly be said to be used or not used at pleasure; but when any adjective is employed with the noun, the particle belonging to the noun is *sometimes* dropped, though its retention is always permissable :—

| | | | | | |
|---|---|---|---|---|---|
| *Sam-pa:* | bridge. | *Kang-pa:* | leg. | *Gom-pa:* | monastery. |
| *Mū-pa:* | mist. | *Dá-wa:* | the moon. | *Ngur-wa:* | red duck. |
| *P'or-pa:* | cup. | *Kyá-wa:* | oar. | *To-wa:* | victuals. |
| *P'ák-pa:* | pig. | *Chhar-pa:* | rain. | *Ṭö-pa:* | belly. |
| *Tŭ-pa:* | smoke. | *Rdu-a:* | a fence. | *Chhu-pa:* | over-coat. |
| *Khau-a:* | snow. | *Ko-a:* | hide-boat. | *T'o-a:* | hammer. |

Another series of substantives assume a second syllable in *po, wo,* and *bo*—affixes which in composition are occasionally dropped :—

| | | | |
|---|---|---|---|
| *Le-po:* | a basket. | *Ḍhá-wo:* | buck wheat. |
| *Te-po:* | an axe. | *No-wo:* | younger brother. |
| *Ṭok-po:* | a friend. | *Chhu-wo:* | a river. |
| *Gyal-po:* | a king. | *Re-wo:* | yak-skin canvas. |
| *Ting-po:* | a pipe. | *T'eb-bo:* | the thumb. |
| *Tang-po:* | a beggar. | *Dá-o:* | comrade. |

Provincially the affix *po* is frequently heard as *bo*; e. g., ***Pai-bo*** for *Palpo*: a Nipal man; *pömbc* or even *bömbo* for *pömpo*: any official or head man—used also as form of address: *Pömbo* "Officer," "Sir!" Again, *wo* often seems to lose the *w* sound, as *no-o* for *no-wo,* and *pá-o* for *pá-wo* "dare-devil." Many nouns in *po* denote distinctly the male sex. Added to the participle, *po* expresses the doer of an action: *lab-pa-po,* "the speaker."

Certain substantives take *ma* or *mo*—a non-removable affix :—

| | | | | | |
|---|---|---|---|---|---|
| *Nyi-ma:* | the sun. | *Jhye-ma:* | sand. | *Táb-mo:* | a fight. |
| *Lo-ma:* | a leaf. | *Chi-ma:* | a tear. | *Long-mo:* | alms. |
| *Wo-ma:* | milk. | *Zi-ma:* | eyelashes. | *Rol-mo:* | music. |
| *Lá-ma:* | chief monk. | *Dhe-mo:* | the elbow. | *Gong-mo:* | evening. |
| *Ping-kyu-ma:* | a kite. | *Yor-mo:* | a sail. | *Chong-mo:* | thimble. |

In general, be it noted, *mo* indicates a feminine noun; but the above examples are not of that class—a class to be illustrated hereafter.

Other sets of particles, similarly attached, are *ká*, *khá*, *ghá*, *tse*, *chha* :—

| | | | |
|---|---|---|---|
| *Chhá-ká* or *Chhá-la* : | a thing. | *T'ang-ghá* : | picture (on cloth). |
| | | *T'ok-tse* : | table. |
| *Le-ká* : | work, a task. | *Chem-tse* : | scissors. |
| *Yar-ká* : | summer. | *Yá-tse* : | a duck. |
| *Gün-ká* : | winter. | *Dzé-tse* : | smoke-hole. |
| *Log-ká* : | lightning. | *Ken-za* : | staircase. |
| *Lam-khá* : | pathway. | *Pé-chhá* : | book. |
| *Long-khá* : | guts. | *Lap-chhá* : | talk, a chat. |
| *Pang-khá* : | a shelf. | *Sel-chhá* : | details, particulars. |
| *Kang-serkhá* : | crevasse. | *To-chhá* : | food. |
| *Ya(l)-ghá* : | a bough. | *Lá-chhá* : | sealing wax. |
| *Khyo-ghá* : | husband. | *Lo-chhá* : | woman's chatelaine. |

To these may be added examples of words taking appendices regarded as diminutive affixes, though the effect in question is not always apparent :—

| | | | |
|---|---|---|---|
| *P'u gu* : | a child. | *Tong-bhu* : | a hole. |
| *Lu-gu* : | lamb. | *Sham-bhu* : | cap. |
| *Ang-gu* : | pigeon. | *Sing-bhu* : | mare's milk. |
| *Nyu-gu* : | pen. | *Dhung-bhu* : | love. |
| *Ung-gu* : | lamp. | *Ts'il-lu* : | fat. |
| *Dzug-gu* : | finger. | *Kyal-lu* : | cloth bag. |
| *Ts'i-gu* : | kernel. | *Ts'ál-lu* : | a cock. |
| *Á-ku* : | uncle. | *Tur-ru* : | a foal. |
| *Ts'ang-khu* : | cradle. | *Khye-u* : | infant. |
| *Ná-ku* : | the nose. | *Le-u* : | chapter. |
| *Wo-ku* : | the chin. | *Pe-u* : | calf. |
| *Ḍhil-bhu* : | bell. | *A-yu* (or *a-yo*) : | puppy. |

3.—Originally a monosyllabic language, the modern style would seem to prize compound forms. Thus the second or compound class of nouns, including dissyllables and trisyllables, is being continually augmented. Such words are either direct compounds of two or more distinct words crudely conjoined to express some complex thing or derived idea; or else they are mere paraphrases and euphemisms, signifying simple things, which have at length crept into ordinary use, superceding the ancient and more direct monosyllables. In the subjoined examples we shall not discriminate between the regular compounds and the paraphrases, merely adding that some of the latter are of ancient lineage, and that no simpler word for the thing indicated in such cases has been ever apparently in use:—

| | | | |
|---|---|---|---|
| *Nám-chhok* or *Am-chhok*: | the ear. | *Mé-tok*: | flower. |
| | | *Shom-dap*: | leaf (large). |
| *Nám-ts'ul*: | the nose, muzzle. | *Jhi-tsi*: | rat. |
| *Mendá*: | gun. | *Tsi-tsi*: | mouse. |
| *She-dang*: | anger. | *Káng-ŝak*: | a pipe. |
| *Shá-nye*: | lead. | *Ḍang-rok*: | neighbour. |
| *Shá-kar*: | tin. | *Men-shar*: | girl. |
| *Ge-long*: | monk. | *Shüm-mar-pa*: | lamp. |
| *Am-chhi*: | physician. | *Lek-bham*: | a volume. |
| *Lok-nyo*: | spoon. | *Shing-ta*: | cart. |
| *O-mo-su*: | stocking. | *Sá-lep*: | brick. |
| *Nang-mik*: | room. | *Pák-lep*: | loaf of bread. |
| *Ḍhong-khyer*: | town. | *Gye-kar*: | window. |
| *Yul-ts'o*: | village. | *Mik-yang*: | generosity. |
| *P'ur-nyi*: | trap. | *T'a-má-khá*: | tobacco. |

The derivation of some of these, and other compound words is very quaint. Such are *m̂e-tok* "fire-button" (flower), *khang-mik* "eye of the house" (room), *m̂ik-yang* "broad eye" (generosity), *sá-lep* "flat earth" (brick), *ts'o-lak* "lake's hand" (a creek), *n̂yi-ŝer* "nail of the sun" (sunbeam), *sem-chen* "possessed of mind" (an animal), *p'ák-suk* "secret push" (bribery).

Deliberate compounds are of course very numerous, and no instances need be specified; however, as a general rule, it may be accepted that every syllable of a compound word in Tibetan has a distinct meaning. This rule may be even extended to proper names and the names of places. Thus Pemiong-chi monastery in Sikkim is really *Pema Yangtse* "the offering-bowl of lotos-flowers."

4.—Gender. A large number of nouns possess both a masculine and a feminine form. The discrimination of gender is generally indicated by the variation in the servile particle; although at the same time it must not be forgotten that the mere presence of an affix, significant usually of male or female sex respectively, does not in Tibetan invariably convey the notion of any particular gender. Many substantives terminate with the feminine particle *mo* which have none save a common gender:—

| | | | |
|---|---|---|---|
| *Mi :* | a man. | *Mo :* | woman (general term *bhü'me'*). |
| *Khyo-po :* (or *Khyo-ghá.*) | husband. | *Khyo-mo :* | wife (usual term *kyer-mén*). |
| *Pu-tsa :* | boy. | *Pu-mo :* | girl. |
| *Jhá-pa :* | cock. | *Jhó-mo :* | hen. |
| *Lang-to :* | bull. | *Bhá-mo :* | cow. |
| *Á-p'á :* | father. | *Á-má :* | mother. |
| *Yáb :* | father. | *Yum :* | mother (honorific terms). |
| *Ná-wo :* | host. | *Ná-mo :* | hostess. |
| *Gü'po :* | father-in-law. | *Gü'mo :* | mother-in-law. |
| *P'o-yak :* | male yak. | *Ḍimo :* | female yak. |
| *Gyal-po :* | king. | *Gyal-mo :* | queen. |
| *Yi-pa :* | male lad, offspring. | *Mo-yi :* | female child, girl. |
| *Réi-po :* | an old man. | *Réi-mo :* | an old woman. |
| *Gur-po ;* | a crooked man. | *Gur-mo :.* | a crooked woman. |
| *Tá-po :* | horse. | *Tá gö'ma :* | mare (also *gö'-ma* alone). |
| *Chyil-pa :* | male dweller in a thatched hut. | *Chyil-ma :* | female ditto. |
| *Bhe-to :* | bull-calf. | *Bhe-mo :* | cow-calf. |
| *Pál-po-pa :* | man of Nipal. | *Pál-po-ma :* | woman of Nipal. |
| *Bhö'pa* or *Bhö'mi :* | Tibetan man. | *Bhö'mo :* | Tibetan woman. |
| *Ming-po :* | brother of a girl. | *Sing-mo :* | sister of a man. |
| *Shar-pa :* | young men. | *Shar-ma :* | young women. |
| *P'oré :* | male kid. | *Mo-re :* | female kid. |
| *P'á-pe'* (ཕ་སྤྱད) | father and his offspring. | *Má-me'* (མ་སྨྱད) | mother and her offspring. |

---

## B.—DECLENSION OF NOUNS.

1. In the Tibetan tongue the relationship of the noun to other words or, in grammatical phraseology, the different cases of the noun, must be expressed by means of short syllables styled *Postpositions,* placed immediately after the word to be declined. A Noun Substantive may be thus arranged in the form of a Declension:—

*Kyermén chi'* : A wife.

| | | |
|---|---|---|
| Nom: | *Kyermén chi'* : | A wife. |
| Gen: | *Kyermén kyi* : | Of a wife. |
| Dat: | *Kyermén la* : | To a wife. |
| Accus: | *Kyermén* or *Kyermén la* : | A wife. |
| Locative: | *Kyermén na* (or *tsáne*) : | On or at a wife. |
| Ablat: | *Kyermén ne* (or *le*) : | From a wife. |
| Agentive: | *Kyermén kyī* : | By a wife. |

(*N. B.*—This common word is often heard sounded as if it were *Kimmen.*)

A slight variation is made in the affixes attached in the Genitive and Agentive cases when the word declined ends in the letter *k* or *ng*. Thus *ghyok chi* : "a cannon :" becomes *ghyok-ghi* : "of a cannon," *ghyok-ghī* : "by a cannon." So also *chháng* : "beer;" *chháng-ghi* : "of beer;" *chháng-ghī* : "by beer." Where the substantive terminates with a vowel, the same two cases are also affected, as in the subjoined example:—

*Mábjhá shi'* : A peacock.

| | | |
|---|---|---|
| Nom: | *Mábjhá shi* : | A peacock. |
| Gen: | *Mábjhá yi* or *Mábjhé* : | Of a peacock. |
| Dat: | *Mábjhá la* : | To a peacock. |
| Accus: | *Mábjhá* or *Mábjhá la* : | A peacock. |
| Locat: | *Mábjhá na* (or *tsána*) : | On or At a peacock. |
| Ablat: | *Mábjhá ne* : | From a peacock. |
| Agentive: | *Mábjhá yī* : | By a peacock. |

To the cases made use of above, Jaeschke adds what he terms the Terminative case, implying "into," "unto;" but we have not met with it in colloquial idiom.

In those words in which the final vowel is *o*, we have the Genitive *oi*, as *jo-mo* : "a milch-yak," *jo-moi* : "of a milch-yak." If the word end in *i*, the Genitive usually takes *yi*, but in words of two syllables ending in *i*, we often hear *kyi* : e. g., *khyi* : "a dog," *khyi-yi* : "of a dog;" *gyá-ṭ'i* : "a chair," *gyá-ṭ'i-kyi* : "of a chair." With a final *e* the Genitive requires *yi*, while the vowel *u* takes *i* alone, as *m̂e*: "the fire," *m̂é-yi*: "of the fire;" *p'u-gu*: "a child," *p'u-gu-i*: "of a child."

The Article *di* when it follows the noun makes a Genitive in either *yi* or *kyi*. We frequently hear *di-kyi*: "of the."

The Vocative case differs from the other cases, in that it is preceded by an exclamatory syllable and requires no post-position—*Kye lámá*: "O lama!" *Ho-kye kyapgön*: "O protector! *Wé ṭok-po*: "O friend;" "Well, friend!" Accent or stress is usually laid on the last syllable of the noun in the Vocative. Often the prefixed syllable is dropped in quiet address: *Lhachám, t'u'je chhe*: "Thank-you, lady!"

2. THE PLURAL NUMBER is not always formally expressed in Tibetan. Whenever the substantive is accompanied by any numeral or by such adjectives as "some," "all," "many," the use of which naturally implies a plural signification, then the singular is invariably heard. Otherwise the Plural affix may be added to the word either as *ts'o* or as *chá* (*chák*) and sometimes as *nam*:—

*P'i-ling-ts'o*: "Englishmen."

| | | |
|---|---|---|
| Gen: | *P'i-ling-t'soi*: | Of the Englishmen. |
| Dat: | *P'i-ling-ts'o la*: | To the Englishmen. |
| Accus: | *P'i-ling-ts'o la*: | The Englishmen. |
| Locat: | *P'i-ling-ts'o na*: | In the Englishmen. |
| Vocat: | *Wé P'i-ling-ts'o*: | O Englishmen! |
| Ablat: | *P'i-ling-ts'o nai* or *ne*: | From the Englishmen. |
| Agentive: | *P'i-ling-ts'ö*: | By the Englishmen. |

As to the alternative affix *chá*, it is added mostly to inanimate nouns—*toktse*: "table," *toktse-chá*: "tables."

3. USE OF THE CASES.—*a*. The Genitive is employed to signify both possession and quality, and when it is in any way a part of the subject of a sentence the word in the Genitive stands first in the order of words in the sentence. As expressive of Possession we find the usual construction,

*i. e.*, "the boy's dog" is "the dog of the boy," and yet the Tibetan rendering is in form closely like the English order; *Putsá-yi* (or *Putsé*) *khyi di*: "of boy the dog."

*β*. Where the Genitive is a Genitive of quality it assumes the character of an adjective. This Genitive also invariably precedes the noun which it describes. Ex: *ngul-kyi kuten*: "a silver image;" *shing-ghi khyim*: "a wooden house;" *Bhö'kyi lha*: "a Tibetan god." In these cases, it frequently happens that the Genitive affix is dispensed with; and thus we hear such forms as *ngul kuten*: "silver image;" *ts'ar ŝam* for *ts'ar-kyi ŝampa*: "cane-bridge;" *nyuk khyim* for *nguk-ghi khyim*: "bamboo house;" *ser ţ'eng* for *ser-kyi ţ'engwa*: "golden chain;" *ser-dok* for *ser-kyi dog*: "gold-colour."

These phrases can also be expressed by means of adjectives formed from the respective substantives (Chap. X, 4 *a*).

*γ*. The Genitive seems, furthermore, to be resorted to in order to indicate a less obvious relationship than that of mere possession. Thus "an ear-ring" is *ná-kor*, contracted from *ná-yi kor*; a "water-tub" or tub for water is *chhu-ŝom*; a "day's wage," is *n̂yin-lá* from *n̂yin-kyi lá*; *num-kong* from *num kyi kong* = "an oil basin;" *n̂ák-bhum* from *n̂ák-ghi bhumpa* ("flask of ink") = "inkstand;" and so forth. In this manner in fact a large number of compound terms are constructed.

*δ*. The Dative with *la* is found after verbs of giving, shewing, and speaking. Thus we hear:—

| | |
|---|---|
| *Khyi-la chhu ter*: | Give the dog water. |
| *Mi-la l̂am di teng-nang*: | Shew the man the way. |
| *Kho-la jámpo lap*: | Speak to him gently. |
| *Kusho-la khyörang-ghi m̂ing lap*: | Tell the Sahib your name. |

In the foregoing examples we must note *khyi-la* "to the dog," *mi-la* (or *mi-po-la*) "to the man," *kho-la* to him, *kusho-la* "to the Sahib."

Motion towards is seldom expressed colloquially by the Dative. The ordinary style is with some compound post-position (the Tibetan preposition) such as *t'ukpa* "unto," "up to," or *tsá-ne* meaning "near;" the use of the latter being precisely analogous to the use of *pas* in Hindustani and being linked like *pas* to the noun by the Genitive affix. (See Chap. VIII, 3. Examples). However in such phrases as these *la* is frequently heard :—

*Gompa-la song :* Go to the temple.
*Khyim-la song :* Go home, (*vulg.*, "Nang-la song.")

Further remarks upon the use of *la*, as a Locative rather than a Dative affix, will be found in Chapter VIII, 2.

ε. The Accusative requires no affix in sentences having a remote as well as a proximate object; e. g.—

*Ngárang-la ŵoma nang :* Give me the milk.

(*Woma* is here the proximate object placed in the Accusative. *ngárang-la* = to me.)

Again where the remoter object is unexpressed :—

*shing khur shok :* Fetch the wood.
*tá-po di ṭ'i :* Lead the horse.

However the Accusative, when it is the object of any direct action, takes the affix *la :* e. g.—

(1) *Kho-yi tā-la dung-ki-du' :* He is beating the horse. (Lit: *Kho-yi* by him, *tá-la* the horse, *dung-ki-du'* is beating).

(2) *Dhe-la lákpa ma t'uk :* Don't touch it, (*Dhe-la* = "it.")

Or where it is the object of any passive feeling :—

(3) The mother loves the son: *Amá-yi pu-la tse-dung jhe.'* (*tse-dung jhe'pa* = "to love").

(4) Remember me : *Ngá-la sem-la ngei !* (Lit: *Ngei* be sure, *sem-la* in mind, *ngá-la*, as to me).

But we hear

(5) *Go di gyák :* Shut the door.

**x. The Agentive case ought to be used instead of the Nominative with all transitive verbs whether the verb be in the Present, Past or Future tense. This important rule (see (1) and (3) of the last four examples above) is fully explained in a later chapter.**

---

# CHAPTER IV.

## ADJECTIVES.

1. The adjective almost invariably follows its noun in the common speech of the people. Very frequently in literary Tibetan, however, we find it placed before the noun it qualifies and, when in that position, instead of agreeing with the noun as to Case, it invariably takes the Genitive Case. To place the adjective immediately preceding the noun is also pefectly allowable in colloquial Tibetan, but such order of the words is only occasionally resorted to, though *when it is practised* the adjective must then be heard in the Genitive.

2. When the adjective—as indeed it nearly always does—follows the substantive, it receives the inflexions which would, otherwise, belong to the substantive. In other words, the case-signs are then attached to the adjective instead of to the noun-substantive which it is qualifying. Thus :—

*Nám mün-po chi'* : A dark night.
*Putsa tsok-pa-i ɩák di* : The hand of a dirty boy.

(Note : The order of the words in these sentences is exactly the reverse of the English orders : e. g. " Boy dirty of hand the.")

*Ḍhe'-mó chhempo di-yi mik serpo di* : The yellow eye of the large bear.

(Here the adjectives used are *chhempo* and *serpo*. The definite article *di* being used with the adjective *chhempo* " large," the article and not the adjective receives the Genitive affix. As in Tibetan composition the Genitive-words generally stand first in the sentence, we have here also in the Tibetan an exact reversal of the English order of the words :—" Bear great the of eye yellow the." This reverse order does not obtain in all or even many instances.)

*Di lo-ma lenchen-kyi sá-la shö'-dhu di* : The leaf down on the wet ground.

(Here *lenchen* " wet," the adjective qualifying *sá* " the ground," is placed before its noun and therefore stands with the Genitive affix. Note, also, the article belonging to *lo-ma* is repeated so as to lock in with it all direct enlargement or expansion of the subject.)

3. When it is necessary that the plural number should be expressed otherwise than by implication, the plural particle *is attached to the substantive* and not to the adjective : *Mik-cha serpo* " yellow eyes ;" *Mi-ts'o hampachen* : " greedy men ;" *ta-po-ts'o ñakpo karpo* " black-and-white horses ;" *tá-po ñak tá-po kar* : " black horses and white horses."

4. Nearly all adjectives in the colloquial which are not derived from substantives are found with the particle *po* attached. Sometimes this termination may be dropped as in the last-quoted example ; but this elision is more frequent in the written than in the spoken language. In certain particular adjectives the affix *po* is varied to *mo* when used with a feminine noun ; but frequently no notice of the gender is taken and the adjective in *po* is coupled with a feminine substantive. On the other hand, a number of adjectives used indiscriminately with either masculine or feminine nouns carry the affix *mo* which then bears no sexual signification.

The following adjectives are known to vary the affix according to the gender of the noun to be qualified :—

| | | | |
|---|---|---|---|
| *Marpo—mo* : | red. | *Chhorpo—mo* : | handsome. |
| *Nákpo—mo* : | black. | *T'o-o T'omo* : | angry. |
| *Karpo—mo* : | white. | *Ringpo—mo* : | tall, long. |

5

*Chhyukpo–mo:* rich.
*Sarpo–mo:* young, fresh, un-polluted.
*Rilpo–mo:* round.
*Sháwo–mo:* lame.
*Dhungpo–mo:* cautious, retiring.
*Chholpo–mo:* licentious.
*Sharwa–mo:* blind.
*Ulpo–mo:* poor.

But these adjectives, terminating in *mo*, are common in gender :—

*Gá-mo:* middling.
*Le-mo:* good.
*She'mo:* strong.
*Yangmo:* light (not heavy).
*Démo:* well, happy.
*Ts'emmo:* hot.
*Ḍhömmo:* warm.
*Ḍhongmó:* cold (also *ḍhongwa*).
*Dhalmo:* calm, quiet, still.
*Lámo:* easy (of a task, &c.)
*Bolmo:* soft, yielding.
*Sra-mo:* hard, solid.
*Sem-kyo-po:* disappointed.
*Ship-mo:* thorough, minute.
*Ngo-yangmo:* gay, sportive.
*Sab-mo:* smart, spruce.
*Ḍen-mo:* naked (also *jem-pa*).
*Dhak-mo:* clean (also *dhakwa*).
*Silmo:* cool.
*Kyurmo:* sour.
*Ngarmo:* sweet.
*Gharmo:* thick, dense (of fluids).
*Tamo:* thin (also "powdery," "finely divided.")

5. There are many adjectives which do not take the affixes *po or mo.* All derivative adjectives are simple roots with such paraphrastic syllables as *chen:* "possessed of," *chhok,* "fit for," annexed. (See Chap. XI, 4 *a* and *β*.) Those formed from substantives by annexing *chen* make a lengthy list; and if the opposite qualification has need to be expressed the syllable *chen* is replaced by *me'*, which signifies "without," "free from" :—

*Shengchen:* broad.
*Shengme':* narrow.
*Si-chen:* brilliant.
*Si-me':* dull, obscured.
*Nyö'chen:* durable, well-made.
*Nyö'me':* fragile, flimsy.
*Rin-chen:* precious.
*Rin-me':* worthless.
*Khoi-chen:* important.
*Khoi-me':* unimportant.
*Gyákchen* or *gyákshá:* fat, stout.
*Gyákme':* thin, meagre.
*Ts'ulchen:* just.
*Ts'ulme':* unjust.
*Ts'erchen:* uneasy, anxious.
*Ts'erme':* not anxious, easy.

6. Another series of adjectives, colloquially much favoured, are re-duplicated forms, which generally express continuous or flowing action, or qualities of that easy or undulating nature :—

| | | | |
|---|---|---|---|
| *Lhap-lhup* : | loose, unconfined. | *Seng-seng* : | weak (of tea, &c.) |
| *Ril-ril* : | oval. | *Leb-ǐeb* : | flat. |
| *Kor-kor* : | round. | *Ts'im-ts'im* : | dazzled. |
| *Hrab-hrip* : | dim, glimmering. | *Yor-yor* : | aslant. |
| *Jám-jám* : | smooth. | *Gop-gop* : | stiff, powerless. |
| *Sam-sum* : | low (in sound). | *Wále-wále* : | clear, distinct. |
| *Shong-ŝhong* : | hollow, excavated. | *Gur-gur* : | crooked. |

7. When the adjective is used as an attribute, the affix *po* is occasionally omitted :—

| | |
|---|---|
| The pomegranates are fresh : | *Sendu di sar yin* (*sar*, not *sarpa*). |
| The flower is red and yellow : | *Me-tok di mar dhang ser yin.* |
| The dog is large : | *Khyi di chhe yin* or *khyi di chhempo yin.* |
| The price is small : | *Gong di chhung yin* ("price" is also *rin*). |

8. The adjective can be rendered more intense by various words or syllables placed before it: *háchang*, much, very, too; *rab-tu* very, especially; *tsa-wa-ne*, quite :—

| | |
|---|---|
| The path is very narrow : | *Lamkhá di háchang ṭ'á-po re'.* |
| The horse is too fat : | *Tá-po di rab-tu gyakpá yin.* |
| The bridge is very slanting : | *Sampa di háchang yorpo yin.* |
| The knife is perfectly blunt : | *Ṭi di tsa-wa-ne no-me' du'.* |

Sometimes the word *há-chang* like *tsa-wa* assumes the ablative affix *nai* or *né* :—*Khorang há-chang-ne chhor yin* :— He is very handsome.

Other intensives to the adjective are *ril* (meaning "round") and *chhe* (meaning "much," "great"). These, however, follow the adjective :—

| | |
|---|---|
| A horse quite white : | *Tá-po kar ril.* |
| Very muddy water : | *Chhu nyokpo chhe.* |
| The pass-top is very indistinct : | *Laptse dhe hrab-hrip chhe du'.* |
| A perfectly flat plain : | *T'ang ǐeb-ǐeb ril chi'.* |

I am quite lame and very tired: *Ngárang la khong ril dhárung háchang-ne t'ang-chhe-po jhung.*

*Note.*—The last sentence runs literally: "to me has arisen (*jhung*) to be quite lame and very tired."

## 9.—COMPARISON OF ADJECTIVES.

*a.* The expedient for making comparison of the quality of things is akin to the method of the Hindi language to the south of Tibet, and to that of the Mongolian language to the north of Tibet. It is brought about by means of a certain arrangement of the words of the sentence and by the introduction of the postposition *le,* meaning "than." To give an example:—

Tibet is larger than Sikkim: *Dái-jong le Pö'yul chhem-po du'.*

Examining the Tibetan we find it runs: *Dái-jong le* "than Sikkim," *Pö'yul* "Tibet," *chhempo* "large," *du'* "is."

This order of words must be strictly observed, otherwise the comparative intention will not be evident. Another example:—

The sun is more brilliant than the moon: *Dá-wa le nyima di ši-chen du'.*

Again, the order runs: Than moon, the sun, brilliant is.

This stirrup-strap is longer than the other: *Zhem-ma le yop-t'ák di ring* (or *ring-po*) *du'.*
He is honester than you: *Khyörang le kho sháma du'.*
To-day is finer than yesterday: *Dang-le dhering le'-pa du'.*

When the comparative degree occurs apart from any compared object, the words *Dhe-la,* "than that," may be introduced for the sake of perspicuity:—

A firmer ice-ridge: *Khyak-sam dhe-le tempo chik*
A more honest priest: *Lama shá-ma lhak chi'*

*β*. The superlative degree is usually paraphrased into an universal comparative. So in the sentence: "He is the tallest," we should hear, "Than all he tall is." But "than" would be now rendered by *nang-ne* instead of by *le*.

This peak is high; that peak is higher; that other peak is the highest: *Di zoktse di t'o-a du'; dhe-le di zoktse di t'o-wa du'; ts'angma nang-ne zoktse šhèm-ma di t'o-shö du'.*

*N. B.*—*Di* means "this," or "that" according to Tibetan phraseology, if it represents the *present* object of reference. Any *past* object of reference is denoted by *dhe*, whether we in our English colloquial style it "this" or "that." *ts'angma nang-ne* means "than all."

Another popular mode of indicating the superlative degree is compassed by adding the syllable *shoi* or *shö* to the adjective. And this is often used without introducing "than all." Thus:—

| | |
|---|---|
| That temple is the most famous in Tịbet: | *Di gompa ḍi Pö'-kyi-yul kyi rák-chen-shoi du'.* |
| This animal is the smallest: | *Dhüd-ḍo di chhung-shö du'.* |
| Lhása is the greatest city: | *Lhásá dhong-khyer chhe-shoi du'.* |
| That sheep is the whitest: | *Luk dhe kár-shö du'.* |

*Note.*—When *shoi* is appended, the affix *po* of the adjective is always omitted. Also, the arrangement of the words in the sentence is not of importance when *shoi* is employed. Akin to *shoi* is the word *chhok*, often confounded with it, which means "the best." *Chhok* is also added to adjectives to form an emphatic superlative. In comparing, however, *yakpo* = "good" and *yák-shö* or *ṭák-shö* = "best."

*γ*. For such comparisons as involve the connexion "so—as," *e. g.*, "so great as," "so good as," "as far as," see *post*, Chap. VII, 4, iv. *γ*.

## ADJECTIVES WITH SUBSTANTIVES.

| | |
|---|---|
| *Chhu-pa lönpa :* | a wet coat. |
| *Shuten bolpo :* | a soft seat. |
| *Pu-mo ya'po :* | a good daughter. |
| *Ná-ku marpo :* | red nose. |
| *P'ugu nying-jhémo :* | darling child. |
| *Chö' pe' kyurmo :* | sour lemon. |
| *Shim-shim ḍhö'chen :* | delicious sweetmeats. |
| *Láma chhempo :* | great lama. |
| *Go chhung-ngu :* | small head. |
| *Mo-yi chhung :* | little girl. |
| *Menshar khe'pa :* | clever maiden. |
| *Chhu ḍhang-mo :* | cold water. |
| *Chhu dhang-po :* | clear water. |
| *Lam tön-khen yerpo :* | cautious guide. |
| *Solwa nyukchen :* | ceaseless prayers. |
| *Khyákpa bömpo :* | thick ice. |
| *Sokma kampo :* | dry straw. |
| *Kyermen ṭ'o-mo :* | angry woman. |
| *Mi-po ṭ'o-o :* | angry man. |
| *Lamkhá ŝhengme' :* | narrow path. |
| *Me-tok kar-po :* | white flower. |
| *Khau-á ling-po :* | firm snow. |
| *Pe-chhá numtsi :* | greasy book. |
| *Shei-hor rinchen :* | costly hookah. |
| *Putsa hurpo :* | sharp boy. |
| *Ngá-ra dukchen :* | poisonous air. |
| *Jol-t'a dzepo :* | pretty jolmo (a bird). |
| *Jhá karbo :* | strong tea. |
| *Tukpa chutchen :* | strong soup. |
| *Woma rul :* | putrid milk. |
| *Tá yipchen :* | fine (shapely) horse. |
| *Ṭi ŝhimpo :* | a sweet smell. |
| *Gyá-o ringpo :* | a long beard. |

# CHAPTER V.

## CARDINAL AND ORDINAL NUMERALS.

1. In Tibetan the numbers, both cardinal and ordinal can be used either as adjectives or as substantives. Used in the adjectival sense, the numeral invariably follows the noun which it qualifies; and, if there happens to be any ordinary adjective likewise attached to the noun, then the numeral is placed after such adjective :—

*A-yu kyong-po sum* : Three expensive puppies.
*Wá-pák-kyi ŝhámo ngá* : Five fox-skin hats.

[Here *wá pák* is a substantive placed in the genitive; the literal meaning being "five hats of fox-skin."]

*Lama ŝhi-gyá-ŝhip-chu lep jhung* : 440 lamas are present.
*Ang-ki di ţé-ts'o-sum dhang tong-t'a gye' dhang re-sum yö'* : The number is 38, 063.

[Here *ang-ki di* means "the number;" while 38, 063 is thus expressed: Three ten thousands and eight thousand and sixty-three. *Yö'* is the auxiliary.]

2. Such forms as "the four," "the two," "or both," &c., may be expressed by adding *ka* or *po* to the number: *ŝhi-ka, nyi-ka*. Fractions by annexing *chhá*, as *dün-chhá* "the seventh." Multiplies by prefixing *len*, as *len-nyi* "twice," *len-ngá* "five times."

3. The ordinals annex *pa* to the cardinal, except "the first" which is *dhang-po*, as *sum-pa* "third." However, "thirty-first" is *sum-chu chikpa*, &c., not *sum-chu dhangpo*.

In conversation it is usual not to employ the bare ordinal alone, but to prefix the word *ang-ki* to each. Thus "the eighth" is expressed as *ang-ki gye-pa*:—

*Mi dhe khang-pa ang-ki dhang-po la dö' gi-yö'*: That man lives in the first house.

*Su ang-ki dhang-po lep t'up yong; toi-dhang*: See! who can get first.

It is even prefixed to *juk-shö'* or *ŝhuk-ma* "the last":—

*Mi šhem-ma dhe khangpa ang-ki juk-shö'la dö'-gi-yö'*: That other man lives in the last house.

4. General Remarks.—*a.* When two, three or more persons or things have been mentioned, it is a common custom to add the exact number of individuals or things thus enumerated. For example we might have such a sentence as: "The father, mother, with two sons and a daughter arrived at the town;" and, most probably if such were spoken in Tibetan, after the last person mentioned the numeral "five" would be introduced as indicating the total number of persons referred to: *Pu nyi pumo dhang yab yum ngá ḍhong-kyer la p'ep jhung* (lit: "Father, mother, with two sons daughter five arrived at the town"). Again, when the number would be otherwise obscure: "The woman and her husbands (four) were turned out." This, the exact rendering of the Tibetan would indicate, not that the woman had four husbands, but that she and her *three* husbands, making together four, were ejected. So, also, if a woman and her *two* children were to be mentioned: in Tibetan, we should say *kyermen dhang p'ugu sum* = "Woman and her children three," meaning that together the whole numbered three. This habit of speech causes Tibetan enumerations to be not always obvious. Another instance: *ŝáng-bhu chhem-po chhung nyi*: "large small degchies, two," *i. e.*, "two degchies, a large and a small."

*β*. When alternative estimates of numbers are made, the conjunctions are omitted: *e. g.* *Sum šhi khur shok* "Bring three or four."

*γ*. It is a frequent practice to add the numeral *chik* "one" to any specified statement of numbers.

Thus we might hear: *Ḍhu-khá Chák-šam-la Tang-tong Gye-poī chhorten gyá-tsá-gye chik tsik-pa re'* meaning "At the Cháksam ferry Tang-toug Gyalpo built one hundred and eight chhortens," but literally "built one (or "a") one hundred and eight chhortens." Again: *Láma sok-nyi chik p'ep jhung* "One (or "a") thirty-two lamas have come." The conclusion is that the best rendering of this superfluous *chik* is by our indefinite pronoun "some." However *chik* indicates a definite and not an indefinite number; accordingly when any doubt as to the exact number exists, the word *tsam* follows the numeral with the meaning of "about" or "almost;" *e. g.*, *luk sumchu tsam* "about thirty sheep."

## 5.—CARDINAL NUMERALS.

1. Chik གཅིག་
2. Nyi གཉིས་
3. Sum གསུམ་
4. Shi བཞི་
5. Ngá ལྔ་
6. Ḍhuk དྲུག་
7. Dün བདུན་
8. Gye' བརྒྱད་
9. Gu དགུ་
10. Chu-t'ámba བཅུ་ཐམ་པ་
11. Chuchik.
12. Chunyi.
13. Chusum.
14. Chupshi.
15. Chongá.
16. Chuḍhuk.
17. Chudün.
18. Chopgye'.
19. Chupgu.
20. Nyi-shu.
21. Nyer-chik.
22. Nyer-nyi.
30. Sum-chu-t'ámba.
31. So-chik.
32. Sok-nyi.

33. Sok-sum.
34. So-shi.
40. Ship-chu-t'ámba.
41. She-chik.
42. She-nyi.
50. Ngá-chu-t'ámba.
51. Ngá-chik.
60. { Ḍhuk-chu-t'ámba; or Khe-sum.
61. Re-chik.
62. Re-nyi.
70. Dün-chu-t'ámba.
71. Dön-chik.
80. Gye'-chu-t'ámba.
81. Gyá-chik.
82. Gyá-nyi.
90. Gu-chu-t'ámba.
91. Go-chik.
100. Chik-gyá-t'amba གཅིག བརྒྱ་ཐམ་པ་
101. Gyá-dhang-chik.
102. Gyá-dhang-nyi or Gyá-tsá-nyi.
200. Nyi-gyá.
201. Nyi-gyá-tsá-chik.
210. Nyi-gyá-dhang-chu-t'ámba.
220. Nyi-gyá nyi-shu.

300. Sum-gyá.
340. Sum-gyá-ship-chu.
1000. Tong-t'a chik.
1001. Tong-t'á chik dhang chik.
2000. Tong-t'á nyi.
2161. Tong-t'a nyi dhang chik-gyá-dhang-re-chik.
2780. Tong-t'á nyi dháng dün-gyá-tsá-gye'-chu-támba.
5500. Tong-ngá dhang ngá-gyá.
10,000. Ṭ'i-ts'o chik.
20,000. Ṭ'i-t'so nyi.
36,000. Ṭ'i-ts'o sum dhang tong-t'a ḍhuk.
100,000. Bum-chik.
300,000. Bumts'o sum.
1,000,000. Sá-ya.

A Score: Khe-chik.
A Hundred: Gyá-ṭ'ák.
By Threes: Sum sum.
By Fours: Shi shi.
Two each: Nyi-re-nyi-re.
Six each: Ḍhuk-re ḍhuk-re.
Twice: Len-nyi.
Thrice: Len-sum.
100 times: Len-gyá.

# CHAPTER VI.

## THE VERB.

### SECTION A.—FORMATION.

1. In the language of the books we find the different modifications or tenses of the Verb expressed in two ways. Sometimes the structure of the verbal root itself is altered in order to produce these modifications, the spelling being changed according to the tense exhibited. At other times the required shade of meaning is brought out by means of additional syllables—one or more—appended to the simple root. Such affixes are either mere particles or else the various parts of some auxiliary verb. In the colloquial, this treatment with syllables affixed to the root seems to be almost the sole way of dealing with the various phases of the verb. The practice in the literary language of forming the tenses by changing the spelling of the simple root is in a few instances, however, resorted to in the colloquial.

The simplest form of the verb is, naturally, the bare root unattended by any affix. However if we are to resort to the ordinary European practice of presenting the Infinitive as the primary shape, we must in Tibetan set forth each root with a particle already adjusted.

The particle thus added to the verbal root for the production of the Present Infinitive is invariably either *pa* or *wa*, the former being affixed where the final letter of the root is any consonant save r or l, while *wa* is used after those consonants and after a final vowel. So many of the final letters being dropped in the colloquial, the application of this rule will therefore be not always observable in these pages, our present scheme being the representation of the words not as written but only as they are sounded. Thus we have :—

*Jhye'pa :* to do; *Lū-pa :* to be left, to remain.

These are words which in the written forms have *d* and *s* respectively as final letter of the root, and not as here a vowel, and which therefore take *pa* instead of *wa.* The specified rule, nevertheless, is easily traceable in the examples subjoined :—

| | | | |
|---|---|---|---|
| *Yong-wa :* | to come. | *Lok-pa :* | to read. |
| *Ḍo-wa :* | to go. | *Lap-pa :* | to speak. |
| *Nyo-wa :* | to buy. | *P'ab-pa :* | to take down. |
| *Sher-wa :* | to measure, appraise. | *Nyen-pa :* | to hear. |
| | | *Chhin-pa :* | to arrive. |
| *Jál-wa :* | to measure (length, &c). | *Dzing-pa :* | to fight. |
| | | *P'ep-pa :* | *honorific term* for either "to come" *or* "to go." |
| *Sá-wa :* | to eat. | | |
| *P'ul-wa :* | to give (*hon.*) | | |

2. To view the elements of the formation of the verb in the regular course of its development and elaboration we shall properly deal next with the

## SUBSTANTIVE VERBS.

Of these there are several forms in use, namely :—

YINPA (sounded *Yimpa*) *:* "to be"—the mere auxiliary.

RE'PA : "to be"—another auxiliary.

YÖ'PA : "to be," "to exist," "to be present" (in a place.)

DU'PA (really *Dukpa*) *:* "to be," "to exist,"—most common in Western Tibet.

CHHI-PA : (མཆིས་པ་) "to be," "to exist"—polite form.

LÁGS-PA (generally sounded *Lā-pa*) "to be"—auxiliary employed instead of *Yinpa* addressing superiors.

ME'PA: "to be not"—negative form of *Yö'pa.*

MÖ'PA: "to be indeed"—intensive variety of *Yö'pa.*

MIN-PA: "not to be"—the negative copula.

*a.* The Present tense, Indicative, of all these verbs is the respective root of each standing alone; and this root is employed for all persons and both numbers:—

Thus: *yin* = am, art, is, are.
And so with *Yö', Re', Du', Lā.*

*Yin,* however, is restricted in use to the connection of the noun with an attribute whether adjective, noun or pronoun, and to its duties as auxiliary affix to ordinary transitive and intransitive verbs:—

| | |
|---|---|
| *Khyak-pa dhe tempo yin:* | That (*or* The) ice is firm. |
| *Ming di Dondup yin:* | The name is Dondub. |
| *Ngárang Pö'kyi mi yin:* | I am a Tibetan. |

However, when *yin* is conjoined, as it often is, with *Du'pa,* we frequently hear such combination used to express existence in a place, but chiefly in negative and interrogative sentences:—

*Pe-chha di dhe-pa min-du':* The book is not there.

The auxiliary *Re'* is very popular and heard commonly, but not exclusively, in negative sentences. Its general use is as a copulative, like *yin:*—

| | |
|---|---|
| *Khyi di ngarchen ma re':* | The dog is not fierce. |
| *Di ngai ma re':* | This is not mine. |
| *Di-ni Pö'kyi pe-chha re':* | This is a Tibetan book. |

Nevertheless we have

| | |
|---|---|
| *Ghande re':* | How are you? |

*N. B.*—*Yin* is more commonly used with the 1st person, *re'* with the 2nd and 3rd persons.

In positive sentences we find *re* as a pleonastic addition to the verb *yö'pa:*—

*Khorang má-gi-la yö'pa re':* He is down there.

*Su yö'pa re'* : who is here? *Kho-pa ghâru yö'pa re'?* Where are they?

We can employ *Yö'pa* more frequently than any other of this series, and both *Yö'pa* and *Du'pa* (though primarily verbs of existence) may always take the place of *Yin-pa* in attributive sentences, though *Yin-pa* cannot be substituted for them:—

| | |
|---|---|
| *Khopa Gyang-tse-la yö'* : | They are at Gyangtse. |
| *Ngá-la dhe-pa ṭokpo s̄hi' yö'* : | I have a friend there (*i. e.* To me there a friend is). |
| *Di s̄himpo du'* : | This is nice. |
| *Há-lai-pa yö'* : | It is astonishing. |
| *Yam-ts'empo du'* : *kho ge'po min-du'* : | It is wonderful: he is not an old man. |
| *Dzá-ra di-la shu-gu mi yö'* : | The shrew has no tail. |

*N. B.*—*Yö'* is more commonly used with the 1st person, *du'* with the 2nd and 3rd persons.

*β*. INTERROGATIVELY, the use of the Substantive Verbs is as follows:—

| | |
|---|---|
| *Yimpe* or *Yinná* :<br>*Du'ká* or *Yindu'* or *E du'* :<br>*Yö'pe* or *Yö'dhá* or *E yö'* : | } Is it, is he, are you? |
| *Di-la ghanḍe é yö'* : | Why are you here? |
| *Mi-ts'o su yimpe* : | Who are the men? |
| *Di-pa khyi ḍa du'ká* : | Are there any dogs here? |
| *Nyi'la lukts'o khâshe yö'dhá* : | Have you some sheep? |

If *re'* is the verb chosen (as it is often), then the interrogative tone of voice is sufficiently significant:—

| | |
|---|---|
| *Khyi di s̄ang-khyi re'* : | Is the dog a real mastiff? |
| *Torma-yi kargyen di ghá re'* : | Where are the torma butter-ornaments? |
| *Khyö' la há-lai-pa re'* : | Are you surprised? |

The negative question forms are *mindu'*, *ma re'*, *me'pe*. Alternative interrogatives are frequent; and the most common of these are the phrases *du'ka mindu'* and *yin-du' mindu'* (usually *'indu' mindu'*) meaning "is it or not?" Also *yinnam mannam* and *re'tang ma re'*, the latter attributively :—

| | |
|---|---|
| *Pe-chha di choktse wokla du'ka mindu'?* | Is the book under the table or not? |
| *Khyi ḍa du'ká mindu'; toi shok*: | Are there any dogs or not; see! |
| *Di-pa 'indu' mindu'*: | Is (he) here or not? |
| *Sap-ŝap re'tang ma re'*: | Is it deep or not? |
| *Di-ni ngái re'tang ma re'*: | Is this mine or not? |

Emphatically *re'* is annexed to *yö'pa*, as in :—

| | |
|---|---|
| *Di lá di tengla khau-a yö'pa re', me'pa re'*: | Is there snow on the pass or not? |
| *Khyörang-la di-ka yö'pa re', me'pa re'*: | Have you it or not? |

Also *re' ma re'* and *yö'pe me'* are other forms, the former being only used with attributes :—

| | |
|---|---|
| *Dhenḍa re' ma re'*: | Is it so or not? |
| *Gömpe nangla pechha-ts'o yö'pe me'*: | Are there any books in the gompa or not? |

γ. The Past tense of all these auxiliary forms can be represented by either *yö'pa yin* or *chhī du'* :—

| | |
|---|---|
| *Khyi-yi dok di nák-po yö'pa yin*: | The colour of the dog was black. |
| *Ngárang mi ngempo ŝhik song*: | I have been a bad man. |
| *Kho dhe-tü šhön-šhön yö'pa yin*: | He was young then. |
| *Pé-chha ŝhik diru chhī du'*: | There was a book here. |
| *Ngá-la khá-tsang á-lich yö'pa yin*: | I had a little yesterday. |
| *Na-ning Dok-ghur ḍá sá-chhá la yö'pa yimpe*: | Were there any nomads' tents in this place last year? |

Naturally for our "has been," "have been," the past tense of "to go" is employed, which is either *chhinpa yin* or *song*:—

*Khyörang ghäru song*: Where have you been?

But of events *yö'pa yin* is rightly employed, and "was" in the assertive sense is rendered by that or by *chhī·du'* or *chhī yö'*; as in *di chhī yö' kyang, tanda ma yö'*: "though it was, now it is not," &c. Again, *yin lā* is another perfect auxiliary as in *Dák-la kap yin lā* "I have had the opportunity." (*Lit.* "To self opportunity was.")

However the Tibetan idiom seems to avoid as much as possible the resort to preterite tenses in the substantive verb when the latter would stand alone. Nevertheless, although the past tense of the verb "to be" when unsupported is very infrequent; yet, in combination with other verbs, as auxiliaries such forms are common and indispensable.

δ. Where the Future tense of the verb "to be" is called for, *ḍo-wa* "to go" and *yong-wa* "to comē" are used as bearing the additional meaning "to become;" also *jhung-wa* "to arise":—

| | |
|---|---|
| *Dharing ts'á-po yong*: | It will be hot to-day. |
| *Khyörang yákpo yong-gyu-yin*: | You will be good. |
| *Ngárang dher jhung-yong*: | I shall be there. |

"Will be" is also rendered by *yong lā* (*lágs*).

Such constructions can often be put as the ordinary future of an impersonal verb. Thus in the sentence "I shall be sick" we resort to the future of the verb "to suffer by sickness" (*ne'kyī širwa*) using the dative of the personal pronoun. So also "I shall be hot" can be transformed into "Heat will come to me": *ngárang-la ts'á-wa yong-gyu·yin.*

## SECTION B.—THE VERB ACTIVE.

I. Present Tense.—*a.* This tense is expressed in its simplest form by just the root of the verb deprived of all particles, saving of course in compound or connected sentences when there is annexed—as explained hereafter—some continuative particle (Infra. XIII, § 3.)

Ex: *Gyuk-pa*: to run: PRES. TENSE: *gyuk*: runs.

The modern colloquial has in most cases adopted for use, both as infinitive and as indicative present, the perfect root of the verb as it occurs in the written language. Thus *sdod-pa* and *sdod* are the literary forms of the verb "to stay, to remain," in the infinitive and present; but the colloquial has taken the past tense *bsdad* for these purposes, and has *dadpa* and *dad* for "to stay" and "he stays," pronouncing them however in accordance with the modern rule *de'pa* and *de'*. (See: Chap. I, *Note.*)

*β.* But when we come to place before the present tense (or other tenses) of a transitive verb some pronoun or any other noun, we find there is in Tibetan no such thing as a nominative case governing a verb and no such construction as a nominative being used with a transitive verb. In fact our conception of an ordinary simple sentence with subject, predicate, and object, has properly no place in the Tibetan mode of speech.

That which in European languages would be regarded as the subject and which would be placed in the nominative case is regarded in Tibetan as the agent by which a certain action or condition is brought about and is placed in the Agentive or Instrumental case, whilst the verb assumes almost the signification of a participle or a verbal noun to which, in the tenses other than the simple present, some auxiliary verb is added. The object is put as with us in the accusative. Thus the sentence: *He wears a cap* would in Tibetan be turned in this way: *By him a cap a wearing is.*

However, as Tibetan grammarians regard "a wearing is" as the present tense of the verb "to wear" and would not render the verbal noun "a wearing" always in this same manner, our theory of construction may be a mere speculative nicety, nevertheless we should translate our sentence into Tibetan *Khorang-gī ŝhámbhu ghön ;* and from thence merely deduce the practical rule that with a Tibetan transitive verb the nominative must be rendered by the agentive case.

Moreover—as if to render our remarks still less important—it must be admitted that in loose easy speech the agentive affix is frequently dropped and the noun or pronoun appears as though it were the ordinary nominative. Where the pronoun is not important to be expressed, it is altogether omitted : *Shámbu ghön :* "he wears a cap." Furthermore, with verbs of coming going or thinking the agentive case is not used.

γ. Another form of the Present tense and one perhaps in more common employment than the mere verbal root is produced by the addition of the syllables *ghi yö'* or *ghi du'* to the root. This is a sort of narrative present which, with a view to distinguish it from the simple indefinite present, we term Definite Present tense. It is as common with us as with Tibetans, under the form : "I am—ing."

Ex : *Sá-wa :* to eat : *ŝá-ghi-du' :* he is eating.

The similar forms *ghi yin'* or *ghi re'* are nearly as frequent ; and in Eastern Tibet the use with *re'* supersedes that of *du'* completely. Framing sentences with these appendices, we say :—

| | |
|---|---|
| *Ngárang Norbhu-gang máru ḍo-ghi-yin :* | I am going down to Norbhu-gang. |
| *A-ḍhung-ghī ḍhe-po ṭol-ghi-du' :* | The sa'is (horse boy) is unfastening the mule. |

Of this tense we may subjoin a specimen in orthodox form, using the pronouns in the Agentive, as the verb "to beat" is a transitive one.

### INDICATIVE MOOD.

*Definite Present Tense.*

| Singular. | Plural. |
|---|---|
| *Ngárang-ghī dung-ghi-yö'* (or *yin*): I am beating. | *Ngáts'o-ghī dung-ghi-yö'* (or *yin*): We are beating. |
| *Khyörang-ghī dung-ghi-du'* (or *re'*): Thou art beating. | *Khyöts'o-ghī dung-ghi-du'*: You are beating. |
| *Khorang-ghī dung-ghi-du'*: (or *re'*): He is beating. | *Khopái dung-ghi-du'*: They are beating. |

8. A third kind of Present Tense is likewise in vogue. It appears to be resorted to in order to indicate that an action is just on the very point of being carried into operation. It seems appropriate to class this notion as a Present rather than as a Future action; the idea being that it is too imminent to be considered in any sense as what is "about to be"—the motion and its announcement, as it were, starting simultaneously. We style the expression of this idea the Present Imminent Tense. Perhaps it signifies "I am just doing so-and-so," quite as frequently as it means: "I am on the point of doing so-and-so." The Tibetan equivalent is expressed in two ways:—

(1) By the addition of the word *kap* to the root of the verb and annexing thereafter *yin* or *yö'* for the first person and *re'* or *du'* for the other persons.

(2) By affixing the syllable *găng* (really བསྐང) to the genitive of the Infinitive of the verb, annexing also auxiliaries similarly as in (1).

In Lhása (2) has superseded in the colloquial the first method which, however, continues to be followed in epistolary composition. *Kap* (really *skabs*) = "chance," "means," "opportunity."

### Present Imminent Tense.

Singular.

*Ngá ḍo-wai găng yin* : I am just going.
*Khyö' ḍo-wai găng re'* : Thou art just going.
*Kho ḍo-wai găng re'* : He is just going.

Plural.

*Ngá-ts'o ḍo-wai găng yin* : We are just going.
*Khyö'ts'o ḍo-wai gang re'* : Ye are just going.
*Kho-pa ḍo-wai găng re'* : They are just going.

The precise meaning of *Ngá ḍo-wai gang yin* or *Nga ḍo kap yin* would therefore be "I am starting":—

| | |
|---|---|
| Bring the horse up to the door : | *Tá di gya-go t'uk ṭ'i shok !* |
| I am just bringing it : | *Di ṭ'i kap yö'.* |
| The sun is setting : | *Nyima gai-pai găng re'.* |
| The milk is on the point of boiling over : | *Woma lü'pai găng re'.* |
| Make tea : The water is about to boil : | *Soljha sö chik : Chhu di khol kap du'.* |
| I am just doing some work : | *Ngá le-ka jhye'pai găng yin.* |
| Are they starting now or not : | *Khopa tanda ḍo-wai găng re' ma re'.* |

(*N. B.*—The *ai* in *ḍo-wai, gai-pai*, &c., is sounded nearly like *ay* in our "way.")

## PAST TENSES.

(1) There appear to be several ways of expressing the more or less perfected form of any action and the exact shade of meaning indicated by the different methods employed is not ascertainable from native informants. The more frequent shape which the past tense assumes is the root of the verb with either *jhung* (sounded *chung*) or *song* annexed as an affix. Certain verbs prefer *jhung ;* others

*song ;* and no rule seems to determine the affix chosen, custom deciding the usage with each particular verb :—

| | | | |
|---|---|---|---|
| *Shi-wa :* | to die ; | *shi song :* | died. |
| *Ts'ar-wa :* | to finish ; | *ts'ar song :* | finished. |
| *T'ong-wa :* | to see ; | *t'ong jhung :* | saw. |
| *T'ọb-pa :* | to receive, obtain ; | *t'ob jhung :* | received, got. |

(2) The more emphatic sense, or perhaps what the French would style the Past Indefinite, is best rendered by another form, namely, the participle with *yin* annexed for the first person, and *du'* or *re'* for the second and third : *e. g., chhyin-pa-yin :* I did go ; *chhyin-pa-re' :* he has departed ; *dzang-pa-re' ;* has sent ; *t'ob-pa-du' :* did get. Choice of past forms often depends on the person involved. Thus neither *jhung* nor *song* seem used with a 1st person ; so, "I arrived" is *Ngá lep-pa-yin* and never *Ngá lep jhung ;* but "he arrived" might be *Kho lep jhung.*

(3) Other forms seem to indicate rather a Passive meaning, though often used for more emphatic expression of the perfect tense active :—

*a.* The root with *yö'* or *du'* added : *dzang du' :* was sent, has been sent ; *to ŝai yö'* (ལྟོ་ཟས་ཡོད་) has been eaten.

*β.* Sometimes *du'* is annexed in addition to *song : shi song du' :* has died, is dead :—

| | |
|---|---|
| *Loma t'amché shing-ne bok song du' :* | The leaves have all dropped from the tree. |

*γ.* To the gerund in *nai* (*ne*), yö' is added. This appears to require a rendering approaching our Imperfect Tense : *Ḍul-ne-yö' :* I was walking, have been walking.

*δ.* Final completion of any operation is expressed where necessary by the addition of *ts'ar du'* or *zin du'* to the root of any verb :—

*Pumo di le-zhu khor kyap zin du' :* The girl has done spinning.

| | |
|---|---|
| *Khopa to sái ts'ar du'* : | They have finished eating. |
| *Dhá-rung kho to sái t'sar mi du'* : | He has not yet finished eating. |

*Ts'ar-pa-yin* (1st person); *ts'ar-pa-re'* (2nd and 3rd) are occasionally heard here instead of *ts'ar du'*; also, negatively, *ts'ar-pa-me'*.

(4) There exists in Tibetan a regular form of Imperfect Tense, but which is not resorted to on all occasions when we should use that tense. It is a curious circumlocution, but is, I am assured, in common use in Lhasa. It is formed by adding to the verbal root the expression *go-sám-jhung* or *go-sam song* meaning literally "did think must." Ex: *Khorang shing la dzak go-sam song-te mar šak song*: As he was climbing the tree, he fell down.

A lengthier form is *go-sam-nai chhyin-pa*: e. g. *Tumling la ḍo go-sam-nai chhyin-pai nge pui-mo dap jhung*: In going to Tumlong, my knee was hurt.

(5) Sometimes a perfect inflection of the verbal root is current; it is then generally conjoined to *pa yin*: e. g. *šai-pa-yin* has eaten; *n̂yoi-pa-yin* has bought.

## FUTURE TENSE.

There are two particular forms for this tense both in common use; either *yong* or *gyu yö'* (*yin* or *du'*) may be added to the root of the verb: *n̂yo yong* "will buy;" *n̂ang-la ḍo-gyu yin*: "I will go home;" *khyö di-la ts'ong-gyu-du' ka mindu'*: "will you sell it or not?" *kho tanda gyel-gyu-yö'*: "now he will slip."

Sometimes the Infinitive alone is employed, as in:—

| | |
|---|---|
| *Ngá-ts'o la chhá-ghang nyo-wa* : | What shall we buy? |
| *Khyö'la ghang jhye'-pa* : | What will you do? |

But, it will be seen, the nominative changes to the dative case.

Very commonly we notice the Present Narrative taking the place of the Future, e. g. *Ḍo-ghi-du'* used for *Ḍo-gyu-du,* as is the English practice also.

The negative form takes *me'* as the final syllable; occasionally we have *min* :—

| | |
|---|---|
| *Má-gi-la tö ma dhang; dhenḍa khyö'rang gyel-gyu-me'* : | Don't look down; then you will not fall. |

With the affix *yong* the negative particle is *mi* :—

*Kyapgön di dhárang ge-long-ts'o la jalkhá nang mi yong* : The Protector (*i. e.*, Grand Lama) will not give audience to the ge-longs this morning.

*N. B.*—The rule, generally so rigid in Oriental speech, that if the dependent clause of a conditional sentence have the future construction so also shall the antecedent clause, is not commonly observed in Tibetan colloquial. Take such a sentence as this: "If you always read at night, you will certainly injure your eyes." In Hindustani every native would turn the first part of the sentence "If you always shall read, &c." Contrariwise, the Tibetan would express the future only in the second clause as we do in English, thus :—

*Ke-si khyö' ts'en-la takpa-reshi ŷige dok na, nenten m̂ik-la ŝük gyak-gyu-re'.*

## IMPERATIVE MOOD.

*a.* The simplest form is the mere root, which in some cases has the central vowel altered. Occasionally we find a special word is in vogue. To the root, whether altered or not, may be always appended *chik* or *shik,* sounded quickly This is the more imperative style of demand. However the traveller will do well to remember that Tibetans are not so amenable to curt commands as are the natives of India. A real order, nevertheless, requires *chik.*

*β.* Several politer forms are used among equals and these are by aggregation rendered still more precative when addressing superiors. Thus the following alternative appendices may be added to the root in lieu of *chik* :—

(1) *Ro;* (2) *Ro chik*—often contracted into *Roch;* (3) *Ro nang;* (4) *Ro dzö';* (5) *Nang chi';* (6) *Ro jhyi-shik!*

These all imply the sense of our word "please."

In Western districts, instead of *chik*, the word *tong* is used, and instead of the polite forms a second word *zhu* is appended. *Ro zhu* is also heard in lieu of the *Ro nang* of Central Tibet.

Examples :—

| | |
|---|---|
| Wash the horse: | *Tá-po di ṭui ŝhik.* |
| Lay the child down on the cushion: | *P'ugu ch'u'ten-la nya'ne ŝhok!* |
| Give me two rupees for the dog: | *Ngá-la khyi-i chhyirtu gyá-tam nyi nang ro nang!* |
| When your work is done, come to me: | *Rang-ghi le-ka ts'ar-ne nge tsar p'ep ro chi'!* |
| Please shew me the way: | *Lam di ten ro dzö!* |
| Please send three rupees without delay: | *Gyá-tam sum tanda l̂amsang tang roch.* |
| Come with me the whole way: | *Ngá dhang nyampo l̂am kang-gá la p'ep nang chi'!* |

*Ro* alone added to the verbal root is generally enough; or *zhu* in the West and in Ladak. The causative verb *jhye'pa* is frequently added to the Imperative to give emphasis: *Shing luk jhyi':* put on wood.

γ. With certain verbs we find the Imperative formed by annexing *tang* or *dhang* (really "and") to the verbal root or the Imperative word; e. g. *Di to ŝo dhang:* Eat this; *Tö tang:* See! Look!

With other verbs, *shok* ("come") makes the Imperative.

δ. As already stated, a number of verbs retain in the colloquial the special inflected forms which are to be found in the literary language. The principal are these :—

| | | | |
|---|---|---|---|
| *Do-wa :* | to go | imperative : | *Song !* |
| *Yong-wa :* | to come | „ | *Shok !* |
| *Shákpa :* | to place | „ | *Sho !* (guttural) ! |
| *Kkyakpa :* | to carry | „ | *Khyok !* |
| *Tá-wa :* | to see | „ | *Tö dhang* or *Tö shok !* |
| *Jhye'pa :* | to do, to make | „ | *Jhyi* (pr. *chyi*) *!* |
| *Kyelwa :* | to convey | „ | *Kyal !* (or *kyö shik*) *!* |
| *Khur yong-wa :* | to bring | „ | *Khur shok !* |
| *Khur ḍo-wa :* | to take away | „ | *Khur song !* |
| *Ṭ'i-wa :* | to lead | „ | *T'i shok !* |
| *To ŝá-wa :* | to eat | „ | *To ŝo* or *ŝo dhang !* |
| *Dze'pa :* | to do, make (*honorific*) | „ | *Dzö' !* |
| *Chhák-pa :* | to break | „ | *Chhok chik !* |
| *Tang-wa :* | to let go, send | „ | *Tong !* |
| *Dzek-pa :* | to climb | „ | *Zok !* |
| *Táb-wa .* | to strike | „ | *Top !* |
| *Ták-pa :* | to tie | „ | *Tok !* |
| *P'áp-pa :* | to put down, adjust | „ | *P'op !* |
| *Yar lang-wa :* | to rise up | „ | *Yar long !* ("Get up") |

It will be observed that in the majority of the above, the Imperative is merely the verbal root with the central vowel altered into " o."

## PARTICIPLES.

*a.* There are two forms used to represent the participial mood; but there seems to be no distinction made between the present and past participle, either form being employed whatever the time of action. The more correct form is identical with the Infinitive, being expressed by the root of the verb with the affix *pa* annexed, or after vowels and final *r* or *l* the kindred affix *wa* :—

| | |
|---|---|
| *Ngárang gyel-wa la t'á-nye-po yö'pa yin :* | I was nearly falling (*lit :* was near to falling). |

More often, however, the colloquial adopts the affix *khen* instead of *pa* or *wa*.

*β*. These participles are employed in composition precisely after the fashion of adjectives; being used in the nominative case when placed after the noun to which they are related, or in the genitive when preceding the noun :—

| | |
|---|---|
| *Nám kang-gá hab-khen kyi khyi di:* | The dog barking all night. |
| *Shi-wai lang-to t'ong jhung:* | I observed the ox dying. |
| *Mi-po ngá-la dung-khen dhe sampai t'e'-lam la gyuk song:* | The man who struck me ran over the bridge. |
| *Ngárang gyel-ne di pui-mo ngön-ts'e dung-khen dhe-la dap song:* | I fell down and bruised the knee which was formerly struck. |

The *di* is introduced in order to to mark off the participial clause more clearly; but this usage is optional.

Where the conjunction "that" would be resorted to in English, a participial construction is often found in Tibetan :—

| | |
|---|---|
| I did not see that the water was frozen: | *Chhu di khyak-pa t'ong-pa-me.'* |
| I knew that he was coming: | *Nga-í kho yong-pa she jhung.* |

From the foregoing examples it will now be evident that the whole participial clause can be handled and moved about bodily as if it were a single adjective qualifying the substantive. Thence we are brought to the most important function of the participial construction in Tibetan.

*γ*. All relative clauses are expressed without the use of relative pronouns by the substitution of the participial for the relative construction. In these cases the verb is made to take the form of a participle and the whole clause becomes one gigantic adjective qualifying the antecedent of the relative clause. As before the whole clause being terminated by the participle it may be handled and shifted as any other adjective, the participle being inflected according to its position with respect to the antecedent and the sense to be conveyed.

Thus such a sentence as—

"The butcher who brought the sheep to the door of this house stole my boots."

Must be rendered somewhat in the style of—

"The bringing-the-sheep-to-the-door-of-this-house butcher stole my boots."

"Bringing-the-sheep-to-the-door-of-this-house" is, as it were, the gigantic adjective qualifying the noun "butcher;" and the whole sentence in Tibetan stands thus:—

*Khyim di-yi go t'uk luk khyer-wái shempa dī ngárang-ghi lham kui-ne khur song.*

As the verb in every clause or sentence invariably occurs as the final word, the participle in these cases alone receives inflection. In the foregoing example, the relative clause might just as readily be placed after the antecedent *shempa*, the participle taking the nominative in lieu of the genitive case. The article in this arrangement often occurs twice, standing both before the noun and after the gigantic adjective or relative clause, thus:—

*Di shempa khyim di-yi go t'uk luk khyer-wa di*, &c.

Let another example be taken:—

"The boy to whom I gave the dog was clad in a yellow coat." Before attempting to translate this sentence, it may be conveniently transposed as follows—

"The boy who by me was given a dog was clad in a yellow coat." We can now shape our gigantic adjective as "The by-me-given-a-dog" and place it before or after the antecedent noun "boy," rendering the sentence thus:—

*Ngárang-ghī khyi ŝhik ter-khen kyi potso dhe-yī ko-lok serpo ghyön-pá-du'.*

Analysing our example, we have the relative clause with its terminative word the participle *ter-khen* appearing in the genitive case because of the position of the clause before the qualified noun *potso*. Then we have *potso di* appearing in the agentive case as the subject of the main clause (Ch. VI, § B. I. β,) and the verb *ghyön-pa-du'* the nearest approach to an imperfect tense which would seem the most appropriate to the general meaning of the sentence. *Ko-lok 'serpo* "yellow coat" might be also *dukpo ser*.

Another example:—

I praise the girl who did this: *Ngárang-ghī menshar di-ni jhye'-khen dhe-la tö'-ra tang-ghi yö'*.

*N. B.*—Here *di-ni jhye'khen* is the quasi adjective following its noun *menshar* a girl, and interposed between the noun and its article *dhe*.

But such a sentence as the following is correlative rather than relative and requires the relative pronoun:—

I praise whichever girl did this: *Ngárang-ghī su yang di-la jhye'-khen-kyi menshar lá tö'-rá nang*.

Or perhaps less cumbrous would be the alternative form—

*Ngárang-ghī menshar su yang jhye'khen la*, &c.

δ. Other participial forms will fall more conveniently under subsequent illustratious of gerundial construction.

## 6.—GERUNDS AND SUBORDINATE CLAUSES.

*a. Gerunds of Occurrence.*—Short dependent clauses indicating the time or occasion of some general or particular statement in a principal sentence are ruled by a subordinate verb which in English takes the form of a gerund, or else is a simple verb introduced by the pronoun "when." In Tibetan such dependent clauses are terminated by the simplest form of the verb to which the affix *la* or *na* is annexed. Sometimes the Infinitive with the same affix is resorted to in these cases.

Several examples will exhibit the usage with gerunds of this kind :—

| | |
|---|---|
| On approaching the horse, it kicked violently : | *Tápo dhang t'á-nyépo ḍo la, ḍhákpo dok-t'o p'ul jhung.* |
| On hearing the voice, he looked back : | *Drá di nyen-pa la, kho chhi-lok tai jhung ;* or *kho drá di nyen-pa la, chhi-lok,* &c. |
| When he stepped on the bridge, it broke : | *Sampa-i tangla dok bor-la, chhák jhung.* (*dok bor-wa* = to place foot). |
| When you fire the rifle, I will run towards you : | *Mendá gyak la, khyörang-ghi t'ekya shor yong.* |

(*N. B.*—The pronouns are frequently omitted, as *ngarang* "I" is omitted here).

ii. A less obvious use with *la* is in short copulative sentences where in Hindustani we should employ the past conjunctive participle; *e. g.* Go and pick it up : *Song la ruk shik' !* Go and fetch the girl : *Song la menshar di khur shok !* Wake up and light the fire : *nyi' sö'la mé bhar nang chi' !*

This is evidently only a derived use, as the *la* is annexed to the verb in its imperative form, and therefore is hardly analogous to the Hindustani idiom : *Jakar dekho ; kadam uthake jao,* &c.

iii. Frequently in accessory clauses commencing with "when," instead of the gerund in *la,* we hear used the verbal root with the adverb *tü* or *tui* "at the time of" annexed. Sometimes also in those cases the participle in *khen* in the genitive with *ts'e-na* added serves the same purpose : e. g. *Leb-khen-kyi ts'ena, ke tang jhung* "When he arrived, he shouted out ;" or *kho leb tui, ke tang jhung.*

*β. Gerunds of Mode* or the verbal use in accessory participial clauses. Properly the Gerund is mainly an expanded advert explaining the accessory circumstances accompanying any action ; and thus we do right to class as gerundial all those clauses which are an enlargement or explanation of the principal predicate. These clauses are in English interposed in sentences with the aid of the participles in "ing" or "having—ed." Such clauses in colloquial Tibetan are rendered by using a gerund consisting of the verbal root and the particle *nái* (sounded almost as *ne*). Examples:—

| | |
|---|---|
| He remained all day thrashing the corn: | *Kho, ḍu yur-le jhe'ne, nyin-kang gor song.* |
| Putting out his tongue, the Tibetan ge-nyen saluted me: | *Ché jung-ne* (or *tön-ne*), *Pö-kyi ge-nyen di ngá-la chham-bül ŝhu jhung.* |
| Having abandoned father, mother, and his younger brother, this man dwells alone in the cave: | *Mi-po di yab yum no-o pang-ne, chik-pu ṭak-p'uk nangla dé.* |

ii. Many sentences composed of co-ordinate clauses may be reduced into forms akin to the foregoing gerundial construction and are usually rendered by the aid of the gerund in *ne*. Thus such a sentence as "I will climb up the tree and fasten the rope," being adapted for translation into the form "Climbing up the tree I will fasten the rope," is easily rendered: *Shing-la dzag-ne, t'ák-pa di dam-gyu yin.*

In fact it should be borne in mind that THIS IS THE ONLY CORRECT WAY OF RENDERING ALL SUCH SENTENCES:—

| | |
|---|---|
| He took up the gun, crossed over the bridge, and has not yet returned: | *Khorang mendá len-ne, ŝampa la galne, tanda par lokne leb ma jhung.* |
| I will hold the bridge and then you can easily pass over: | *Ngárang-ghi ŝampa-la zin-ne, khyörang le-lá-po-la gal chok.* |

iii. The passive form of these gerundial clauses is equally to be translated by the gerund in *ne*, e. g.:—

| | |
|---|---|
| Having been found stealing, I dismiss you: | *Ngé khyö'rang ku-ma ku-khen la nye-ne, gong-pa ter-ghi-yin;* or *Ngárang khyö'rang ku-ma ku-pa dhang ṭ'e' jhung-ne, khyö'rang-la ṭol ter.* |

iv. In copulative sentences, akin to those in *a*, ii, *ne* is likewise employed :—

| | |
|---|---|
| Go and see; is it so or not: | *Khyö' song-ne dheṅda yinnam mannam ; tö' shok !* |

γ. Minor interpositions in gerundial clauses often take a gerund of another form. This is composed of the root, to which the particle *ching* or *shing* is annexed, e. g. :—

| | |
|---|---|
| The Chinaman having departed uttering vain abuse, the Tibetans laughed loudly : | *Gyá-mi di lap-she dhön-me' la gyak-ching song-ne, Pö-pa-ts'oi há-chha gyak song.* |
| The argali, as it ran away bleeding, fell down into the gorge : | *Nyen di ṭ'ák nang-ching* (or *ṭ'ák tar-ching*) *shor-ne ḍokpo-i t'engla ḍil jhung.* |

δ. *Gerunds of Sequence.* The clauses governed by gerunds of this class imply some result directly proceeding from and dependent upon their statements, and we often find such clauses introduced in English by the preposition "by." The particle *pai* or *pe* annexed to the verbal root is in Tibetan the form for this kind of gerund, and it may be employed in all clauses which allege a reason for something which is asserted immediately as a result therefrom. Thus "by doing so-and-so," "because he did this," &c., all require the gerund in *pe*. As before, the usage may be best indicated by examples :—

| | |
|---|---|
| By leaving the milk on the fire, it has boiled over : | *Woma di m̃e-la lāi-pe, lü'song.* |
| You left this stick, so I have brought it now : | *Khyörang-ghī di yuk-pá di bor-pe, tanda ṅge di-la khyok jhung.* |
| Send the oxen first, they will trample down the snow : | *Ngáma lang-ts'o dzang-pé, dhe-ts'oī khau-a dzi yong* (or *dok dung yong*). |
| He ran away to Dongtse, because he was afraid : | *Khorang ŝhe'-pé, Dongtse t'ukpa la shor-jhung.* |

| | |
|---|---|
| Having lost my baggage in crossing the river, I have neither tent nor bedding: | *Chhu-wo gal-ching, rang-ghi chhá-lák ghö'-la song-pe, ngá-rang-la ghur malchhá me'.* |

ii. As will have been noted in the foregoing sections, the use of the ordinary copulative "and" is in Tibetan generally avoided. Where in English two sentences, not necessarily subordinate to one another, are linked together by the conjunction, in transfering them into the Tibetan tongue we must resort to the gerundial or participial construction. The same practice obtains in those compound sentences when the second clause is in any way to be interpreted as a consequence of the first; and, although such conjunctions as "because," therefore," "but," &c., have their equivalents in Tibetan, they are only seldom heard. *Pe* denotes always the consequential construction and is used even when the conjunction is expressed as well. For disjunctive clauses with "but," see the chapter relating to conjunctions in general. A few more examples are added :—

| | |
|---|---|
| The father pursued them and regained his daughter: | *Á-p'á di kho-ts'o-la nyak-pe, rang-ghi bhumo yang lokne nye jhung.* |
| Meeting the Chinaman in the ravine, the brave Tibetan fired his gun and the Chinaman fled: | *Hrak-la Gyá-mi dhang ṭ'e'-pe, Pö'pa pá-o dī menda gyap-pe, Gyá-mi ḍoi song.* |
| I beat the dog for biting the traveller: | *Ngárang-ghī khyi-la, bhé'pa di so t'ap-pai lén-la, dung song.* |
| I engaged the man because he is honest: | *Ḍhángpo yimpe á-ŝuk mi-po dhang dzin ŝhak jhung.* |
| Being intent on reading, the appearance of the bear frightened me: | *Ḍok-pa m̃ang-po-la ten-pe, ḍhe'-mo jhung-ne, ngá-la ḍhe'pa jhye' du'.* |

Literally: "By being held in much reading, the bear appearing (*or* 'there being an appearing by the bear') to me a frightening was made."

7. SUPINES.—This part of the verb, properly speaking, is always an appendix to some other verb, being in truth nothing else than an "extension of the predicate." It is chiefly annexed to verbs of seeing, coming, going, and wishing. In Tibetan colloquial we find various methods of expressing a supine.

α. Sometimes in offhand speech the mere Infinitive or even the bare root:—

| | |
|---|---|
| The rain has ceased to fall: | *Chharpa di bap chhé song.* |
| I want to go: | *Ngarang-la ḍo goi-pa-yö'.* |

Literally: "To me there is a wanting to go,"—*ḍo* tallying with the supine "to go."

β. More frequently we meet with *la* annexed to the root or infinitive, especially after verbs of motion:—

| | |
|---|---|
| I go to make ready the victuals: | *Ngá to-chha ṭ'al-ḍik jhe'pa-la ḍo.* |
| I came to see the monastery: | *Di gompa t'ong-la yong jhung.* |

Supines here are *ṭ'al-ḍik jhe'pa-la* and *t'ong-la.*

| | |
|---|---|
| The beggar is coming to beg: | *Pang-go di long-la yong-ghi-du'.* |

γ. Most correctly with *gyu* or else by means of *dhöndhu* and the genitive participle:—

| | |
|---|---|
| Marpa, having heard it said that Dolma was coming, went to meet her: | *Marpa-yī Ḍolma yong-ghi-du' ŝer-gyu t'oi-nai, dong t'uk-pai dhön-dhu song.* |

*N. B.*—Here we have two supines "said" or "to be said" expressed by *ŝer-gyu*, and *dong t'ukpai dhöndhu* meaning "to meet," *dong t'ukpai* being the genitive of the participle. Literally we may translate the Tibetan: "Marpa (in agentive case) having heard to be said 'Dolma is coming,' went in order for meeting (her)." Pronouns where obvious are omitted.

| | |
|---|---|
| He gave it me to eat: | *Khö ngá-la di ŝá-gyu ter-pa-re'.* |
| As the sun is sinking, you will see me approaching from over the mountain: | *Nyi-ma nup nup la, khyö-kyī ngá-la ri-kyi teng-nai jön-gyu tá-gyu yin.* |

*N. B.*—"As" "while" are expressed by *la* with the repeated verbal root.

In place of *dhöndhu*, we frequently hear *dhönla* (*tön-la*) and *dhön dhák-la* (*tön-ták-la*):—

| | |
|---|---|
| I shall stay at home to read books: | *Ngá pechhá dok-pai dhön-dhák-la nang-la gor-gyu-yin.* |

δ. Frequently, in expressing the supine, *la* is attached to *gyu*; and in fact that is the commoner usage with *gyu*:—

| | |
|---|---|
| I am longing to eat these puffs: | *Ngárang mo-mo di-ts'o ŝá-gyu la ŝhem-ki-yin.* |
| I promised to thresh the corn to-morrow: | *Ngárang sang-nyin ḍu-la ge' gyap-gyu la khe lempa yö'.* |

But, equally, we hear

| | |
|---|---|
| I wish to go home: | *Ngá nang-la ḍo-gyu ḍö'-ghi-yö'.* |
| Have you learned to write: | *Khyö' ŷi-ge ḍi-gyu shei jhung-nga?* |

ε. The practice with the *Inchoative Verb* is to place *gyu* in the genitive:—

| | |
|---|---|
| He began to build the new wall yesterday: | *Kho khá-sang tsik-pa sarpa di gyap-gyu-i go-dzuk song.* |
| I am beginning to speak Tibetan a little: | *Ngárang Pö'-ke' tik-tse chi' lap-gyu-i go-tsuk-ghi-yö'.* |
| Always begin to work at once: | *Dhü-gyün le-ka jhye'gyu-i go-dzuk t'el-t'el-la.* |

*N. B.*—"At once" is sometimes for convenience placed after the verb; see also this construction in other cases where two adverbs might occasion confusion.

Sometimes, however, the usage with *gyu-la* is observed with an inchoative; e. g.:—

| | |
|---|---|
| He began to eat an hour ago: | *Kho to ŝa-gyu-la go-tsuk-ne chhu-ts'ö' chik song.* |

(*Literally*: "From he beginning to eat, one hour has gone.")

*N. B.*—*Go-dzuk-pa* and *go-tsuk-pa* "to begin" are both in use.

*z.* In such expressions as "Tell him to go," "Order him to send it," &c., the supine would never be employed; but instead two Imperatives—"Tell him-go!" &c.

8. Negative forms.—i. There are two negative auxiliary verbs correspondent to *yö'pa* and *yim-pa,* namely *me'pa* "to be without," "not to exist," and *min-pa* "to be not," the simple connective of the attribute. The former may also be used as the negative connective.

| | |
|---|---|
| I am without food: | *Ngá-la to-chhá me'* ("To me there is not food.") |
| The dog is not savage: | *Khyi di ngarpo min.* |

Sometimes *du'* is annexed in the latter case:—

| | |
|---|---|
| The girl is not pretty: | *Menshar di chhormo min du'.* |

Here is an example of the negative in a participial or relative clause:—

| | |
|---|---|
| Chinese are men without pity (*lit*: "Chinese are men who are without pity:") | *Gyámi-ts'o di nying-je me'pa-yi mi-ts'o yö'.* |

ii. Two negative particles are in use with ordinary verbs either in the case of the simple root of a verb or with the compound forms:—

*Mi* is employed with the Present Tense and Future Tense.

*Ma* with the Past Tenses and the Imperative Mood.

These negative particles in the case of compound verbs should be introduced just next preceding the last syllable of the compound:—

| | |
|---|---|
| I shall not eat meat to-day: | *Dhe-ring shá ŝá mi yong.* |
| The men have not perished: | *Mi-ts'o lák ma jhung.* |
| I do not see him: | *Ngá kho-la m̂ik mi tá.* |

Where one member of the compound is *yin* or *yö'*, we may substitute in negative forms *mén* or *me'*:—

| | |
|---|---|
| It will not be necessary: | *Goi-gyu-men.* |
| He will not do the work well: | *Le-ka ŷákpo jhyá-gyu-me'.* |
| He is not running now: | *Dhá-de kho gyuk-ki-mén.* |

iii. *Important.* In the negative Imperative, the Present Indicative form of a verb, and not the ordinary Imperative is used. Thus, "Don't come" is *ma yong*, not *ma shok;* "Don't eat" is *to ma ŝá*, not *to ma ŝo!*

9. INTERROGATIVES.—*a*. The simple interrogative form of the verb is the same as that in literary use; *i. e.*, the final letter is re-duplicated and the syllable *am* affixed thereto: but the final *m* is usually silent:—

| | |
|---|---|
| *Lep jhung-ngá:* | Has he arrived? |
| *Yong-gyu-yinná:* | Will he come? |
| *Dhárung khyö' to ŝai ts'ár-rá:* | Have you finished eating yet? |

*β*. Where an interrogative pronoun is introduced, the additional syllable is unnecessary (though sometimes used), and the pronoun is then generally placed immediately before the verb:—

| | |
|---|---|
| *Khyö'kyi singmo ghá-ru ḍo-ghi-yö':* | Where is your sister going? |
| *Di su yin:* | Who is this? |
| *Di-pa su yö':* | Who is here? |

*γ*. In a sentence of past signification, in which an interrogative pronoun occurs, the verb is always used as in the Infinitive Mood Present Tense:—

| | |
|---|---|
| *P'orpa di su-la ter-pa?* | To whom did you give the cup? |
| *Khyö' nam leb-pa yim-pa?* | When did you come (arrive)? |

A curious construction is resorted to in sentences of present and future signification the gerundial affix *pas* (sounded *pai* or *pe*) being appended to the auxiliary terminants of those tenses:—

| | |
|---|---|
| *Khyö'-kyi singmo ghá-na ḍo-ghi yö'pai?* | Where is your sister going? |
| *Khyö' ŷi-ge ṭi-gyu shin-ghi-yö'pe:* | Are you learning to write? |
| *Dhering ḍo-gyu-yimpe:* | Shall we go to-day? |
| *Khyö' la ghang jhung-wai:* | What is the matter with you? |
| *Khorang-ghī khāshe go-yö' pe:* | Does he want some? |
| *Kho-la so ŝuk gyak-ghi-yö'-pai:* | Has he got toothache? |

*δ*. Quite a different method of expressing the interrogative is also to be met with. No syllable is appended to the verb; but, instead, a short abrupt interjectional particle sounded *eh* or *é*, is interposed before the utterance of the final verb:—

| | |
|---|---|
| *Yul-ngen é jhung ?* | Is a tempest arising? |
| *Di ḍong-pa la ná-ts'ang é yö' :* | Are there lodgings in this village? |
| *Dák-la l̂amkhen chi yö'pa é yö' :* | Am I to have a guide? |
| *Dhá-p'en é ma ts'ar :* | Is it not finished by now? |

ε. A curious expletive, sounded o-GO, is often heard added on to interrogative sentences, chiefly negative ones, evidently intended to impart a persuasive turn to the question. In common talk it may be said to answer to our "won't you," "will you," at the end of any hortative injunction:—

| | |
|---|---|
| *Mánḍro, o-go :* | Don't go, will you? |
| *Yong-gyu-yimpa, o-go :* | You will come, won't you? |
| *Khyi-la ma táng, o-go :* | Don't let go of the dog, will you? |
| *Ling-po jhe'-la chhing, o-go :* | You'll tie it up securely, won't you? |
| *Mángu, o-go :* | Don't cry, will you? |

*Remark*: The practice of re-iterating the verb in negative imperatives is common. Thus *ḍo mánḍro* is as frequent as *mánḍro*.

10. USE OF "NYONG."—The employment of this verb is peculiar. *Nyong-wa* means primarily "to taste" and hence comes to signify "to experience—undergo:" whence it seems to have been gradually utilised as an auxiliary in cases where a sense of perpetuity was to be imparted. Accordingly *nyong* is now used as a suffix when the general meaning of "never" or "ever" is to be indicated; but its use is confined to sentences employed in the past sense and more commonly in the negative:—

| | |
|---|---|
| *Ngárang dhéru song ma nyong :* | I have never been there. |
| *Ngen-la ngá pechha m̂ángpo ŷige ḍok ma nyong dhenḍai :* | I have never read so many books before. |
| *Ngạ́rang-ghī ñyá ŝá ma nyong :* | I never did eat fish. |

| | |
|---|---|
| *Khyö'kyī dzo chhempo dhenḍai s̃hik t'ong é ma nyong :* | Did you ever see so big a *dzo* (yak) as that? |
| *Khyö'kyī ts'ur-la nam-yáng yong ma nyong-ngá (m) :* | Have you ever been here before? |

11. Potential Mood.—The ability or possibility of carrying out an action, or of compassing anything, is expressed in literary Tibetan by adding the verb *Nus-pa*, "to be able," to the root of the active verb affected. The verb *Nus-pa* is thus added inflected in any required tense. In the colloquial this verb, sounded *nü-pa*, is still heard, but other potential auxiliaries are oftener resorted to; e. g. *Chok-pa*, and *T'ub-pa* (sounded *T'u-pa*). Anyone of these may be affixed either to the verbal root or (less commonly) to the gerund:—

| | |
|---|---|
| *Ngá tănda ḍo chok :* | I can go now. |
| *Khyö-kyī P'iling ké lap chok :* | You are able to speak English |
| *Ngá-rang dhü-gyün jhye' nü :* | I can always do it. |
| *Khorang khá-sang ñyo chok ma song :* | He could not buy it yesterday. |
| *Nge ṭák-la dzák t'u-ghi-me' :* | I cannot climb the rock. |
| *Khyö' nyin-sang laptse t'ong t'u yong :* | You will be able to see the pass-top to-morrow. |

*β*. When the potential assumes an interrogative form, the potential auxiliary nearly always takes the future tense:—

| | |
|---|---|
| *Khyö' p'á-ghi-ru gyukshá lö' t'u yong-nga :* | Can you run there? |

(*N. B.*—In Lhasa, *gyukshá lö'-pa* "to run" is often said instead of *gyuk-pa*.)

| | |
|---|---|
| *Ḍo chok yong-nga :* | Can you go? |
| *Dhe dzak t'u mi yong-nga :* | Cannot we climb up it? |
| *Su ang-ki dhangpo lep t'u yong :* | Who can get first? |

But the future is not used in such as these:—

| | |
|---|---|
| *Khyö'-rang-ghī Pö'-yi(k) lo t'u-ghi yö'dhang me' :* | Can you read Tibetan or not? (*lo-pa or lok-pa* "to read.") |
| *Kho khá-sang s̃á chok song-nga :* | Could he eat yesterday? |

γ. Such expressions as "what you can" and "as—as you are able," can be rendered by the form *ghang chok-pa* :—

| | |
|---|---|
| *Ghang chokpa nang ro dze :* | Give as much as you can. |
| *Ngá ghang chokpa gyokpo chhyin-pa-yin :* | I went as quickly as I could. |
| *Khyö' ghá-ru chokpa dzok s̄hi' :* | Climb up as far as you are able. |
| *Khyö'-rang ts'a-po ghang t'u-pa t'ung :* | Drink it as hot as you can. |
| *Ngá m̱angpo ghang chokpa t'op yong :* | I will get as many as I can. |
| *Khyö'-rang ghá-dhü chokpa ḍo ren du' :* | As soon as you can, it is time to go. |

Another verbal form equivalent to *chok-pa* is found in Ts'uk-pa, to be able :—

| | |
|---|---|
| Can he see us? | *Khorang-ghī ngá-chá-la t'ong ts'uk-ká ?* |

As the traveller journeys west of Shigatse, he will find both these potential auxiliaries entirely replaced by *T'ub-pa*, which word is also often heard at Lhásá.

12. THE POSSESSIVE VERB "TO HAVE."—As in most of the Oriental idioms, this form requires to be expressed by a circumlocution. The construction is either the common one of "To me, him, &c., there is;" or that in vogue in Hindustani: "Near me, him, &c., there is." With pronouns, the former is the ordinary usage :—I have a horse: *Ngárang-la tá chik yö'*. With a noun-substantive the latter construction is more general :—The child has a pretty face: *Di p'ugu-la dong ts'arpo yö'* or *Di p'ugu tsánai dong* &c. when *tsánai* is used, it would be more correct to place the preceding noun in the genitive: *Lámá-yi tsánai ngul ts'ongma du' :* "Near the Lama all the money is" = "The Lama has all the money."

The Past construction requires as auxiliary *jhung du'*, e. g. *ná-ning ngá-la s̄hámo sum jhung du'* : "Last year I had three hats." Again: "Because I had a little business, therefore I could not come: *ngá-la le-ka tiktse jhung-pe, dhe-ne yong t'ub ma song.*

13. OPTATIVE FORMS.—The sense of "must," "ought to," &c., is expressed in a manner akin to the French *il faut* with the dative of the agent. The verb used is *go-pa* "to be necessary" which is always employed in the impersonal form preceded by the root of the verb affected, the agent being placed in the dative; thus "I must go" is *ngárang-la ḍo go;* and "I must go home" would be *ngárang-la khyim-la ḍo go* (*lit:* "To me to home to go is necessary.") *Go-pa* also means "to wish," "to want;" and "I want," &c. must likewise be rendered with the dative as just stated. Thus "I want a guide" would be *ngárang-la lamkhen chik go;* "The merchandise he wants is apricots" = *khorang-la go-pai ts'ong-zok chu-li yö'* (*lit:* Merchandise to him which is necessary is apricots" *N. B. go-pai ts'ong-zok* is participial construction).

Another verb, not unlike *go-pa* in sound, namely *kho-wa* is frequently preferred in the above phrases. Often this word takes the expanded form *kho-jhe' yö'pa* "to be in want of" or "to want," or "to be needful to"; and still requiring the dative:—

| | |
|---|---|
| If you want the dog, please send 13 rupees: | *Nyi'-la khyi di kho-jhe' yö' na gyá-tam chusum tang ro ŝhu* (*or tang ro dze'*). |
| I don't want it: | *Ngárang-la kho-wa me'.* |
| The kinds which you wanted cannot be bought here: | *Khyö'la kho-jhe' yö'pai ṛik di dir ñyo ma chok.* |

Sometimes the future is heard:—

| | |
|---|---|
| I shall not want to travel at present: | *Ngá-la ting-sang ḍul kho-gyu me'* (or *goi-gyu-me'*). |

## CONSPECTUS OF PARTS OF ACTIVE VERB.

Nyo-wa : to buy.

### Indicative Mood.

| | | |
|---|---|---|
| Present Tenses : | *Nyo :* | (I, thou, he, we) buy. |
| | *Nyo-ghi-du' :* | am buying, is buying, &c. |
| | *Nyo-kap-du' :* | am, is, just buying. |
| Past Tenses : | *Nyo jhung :* | (I, thou, he, they) bought. |
| | *Nyo-pa yö' :* | has, have, bought—did buy. |
| Imperfect Tenses : | *Nyo-go-sam-jhung :* | was buying. |
| | *Nyo-ṭap-yin :* | was just buying, nearly buying. |
| Future Tenses : | *Nyo yong :* | (I, he, you) shall buy. |
| | *Nyo-gyu-yin :* | shall be buying, will buy. |
| | *Nyo-war du'* or *Nyo-wa-la du'* | shall probably buy. |

### Imperative Mood.

| | |
|---|---|
| *Nyoi shik !* | Buy ! |
| *Ma nyo !* | Don't buy ! |
| *Nyoi ro nang !* | Please to buy ! |
| *Nyo jhyi chik :* | Cause to be bought ! |
| *Nyo ro jhyi chik :* | Please cause to be bought ; or Please to buy. |
| *Nyo chuk :* | Let him buy. |

| | | |
|---|---|---|
| Potential form : | *Nyo-chok ;* or *Nyo-nü' :* | Can buy. |
| Optative form : | *Nyo goi :* | Ought to buy. |
| Participle Present : | *Nyo-wa* or *Nyo-khen :* | Buying. |
| Participle Past : | *Nyo-nai :* | Having bought. |
| Gerundial forms : | *Nyo-la :* | On buying. |
| | *Nyo-pai :* | By buying. |
| | *Nyo-ching :* | In buying. |
| | *Nyo-nyo-la :* | While buying. |
| Supine forms : | *Nyo-gyu :* | To buy, to be bought. |
| | *Nyo-wai dhöndhu :* (or *dhöndá-la)* | For buying: in order to buy. |

## SECTION C.—THE VERB PASSIVE.

1. In the Tibetan idiom little provision seems to have been made for expressing the verb in a distinctive Passive sense. Such grammatical niceties as occur in European languages——whereby, for example, we should be able to say "The corn has been eaten by the horse" as discriminated from "The horse has eaten the corn"——are not attended to in this Eastern speech. Nevertheless, as we have noticed, the whole Tibetan verbal scheme is moulded on what might be termed the Passive construction, and that even in sentences of most active transitive significance. Accordingly in the sentence just instanced, the form would be literally akin to our Passive phrasing, *i. e.*, "By the horse, as to corn, an eating was." But, for all practical purposes it is evident that—as already indicated—we should treat these forms as if they were pervaded by Active verbs.

2. In Tibetan, however, when neglect of a special distinguishing form for the Passive would allow the exact meaning to be conveyed to remain ambiguous, even then the Active construction is often resorted to. Thus the sentence, "The girl's heart is unpolluted with sin" is heard rendered *kyön-kyī menshar-kyi sem-la ma go* "Sin does not taint the girl's heart."

3. Nevertheless when no agent is introduced into a sentence, we cannot avoid making use of a Passive form in English. Thus we must say: "The corn has been eaten," no other turn being possible for such expressions. And so likewise in Tibetan. Whenever assertions of that class are required to be made, we shall find the Tibetan verb frequently assuming a particular shape by the annexation of the auxiliary *du'* both in present and perfect tenses. *Lā* (really *lags*), an elegant synonym for *du'*, is also employed. For the perfect tenses however *du'* is preceded by the root of

the verb *ts'ar wa* "to complete, finish" and sometimes the root of a synonymous verb *zin-pa*. Thus *Ḍu di ŝái ts'ar du'* = "the corn has been eaten," though we have heard it turned loosely *Ḍu di ŝa song*. To the use with the above auxiliaries we may, we think, apply the term Passive Voice.

The Present of this Voice is rarely required; but such phrases as "I am injured," "I am beaten," when used in the sense of "being injured," "being beaten," implying present time, can be best rendered by the gerund in *nai* with *du'* or *lā* appended. Thus "I am being beaten" would be *ngárang dung-nai du'*.

The Perfect tense of this Voice may be contrived in two ways.

(1) By annexing *ts'ar du'* or *ts'ár yö'* to the verbal root
(2) By adding *song* to the gerund in *nai* :—

| | |
|---|---|
| *Pé chhá di ts'ong ts'ar du'* : | The book has been sold. |
| *Khorang dung ts'ar du'* : | He has been beaten (struck). |

The gerund with *song* has more the pluperfect signification :—

| | |
|---|---|
| *Ngáts'o lepnai, ḍu di ŝá-nai song* : | When we arrived, the corn had been eaten. |

Frequently expressions passive in form in our language take the impersonal form in Tibetan. Here are a few phrases of the kind :—

| | |
|---|---|
| *Ngárang-la ḍhelwa yö'* : | I am busy. |
| *Nyï'rang-la ḍhelwa yö'pa yimpe* : | Have you been busy ? |
| *Ngá-la mákhá ŝhik jhung* : | I have been wounded (lit. "a wound has arisen to me"). |
| *Ngá-la ŝuk gyak-ghi re'* : | I am ill. |
| *Mar-la ser-ru gyak jhung* : | The butter has been turned rancid. |

A Future Passive occurs; and it generally seems to be

formed by adding the ordinary future tense of *yongwa* or *jhungwa* to the Infinitive present, or to the bare root, of the required verb :—

| | |
|---|---|
| *Ghur di ṭ'alḍik ŝhak yong-gyu-yin :* | The tent shall be placed ready |
| *Kásal di je' jhung-gyu-men :* | The order shall not be forgotten. |
| *Nyi'la sálchhá tanda ṭ'aldhu p'ul yong-gyu-yö' :* | Particulars shall be immediately sent to you. |

Another method of expressing this tense is met with; namely, by appending *yoṅg·lā* or *gyu-yin-lā* to the verbal root :—

| | |
|---|---|
| *Dhe'yi dhöndhu tanda ṭ'aldhu ts'ol yong lā :* | Search shall be immediately made for it. |
| *Dhe kor yik-len chi' p'ul-gyu-yin-lā :* | A reply about it shall be sent. |

*N. B.*—*Dhe* alone might be used instead of *dhe-yi dhöndhu* "for it," because the verbs *ts'ol-wa* itself means "to make search for."

## SECTION D.—IDIOMATIC AND COMPOUND VERBS.

In general, a compound form is preferred for verbal expressions. The mere bald root of a verb denoting any action is rarely used if the meaning can be more vigorously paraphrased. Thus a large number of compound verbs have been manufactured by annexing to the nouns of kindred signification certain favourite verbs of wide and general sense which in a measure may be regarded as auxiliaries.

*a.* A numerous class arises by the help of the ordinary causative verb JHYE'PA to do, make—as is the case in many languages.

Thus the simple form *gá-wa* "to rejoice," "be glad," is generally avoided; and, taking the substantive *gá-ts'or* "joyousness," "gladness," we find *ga-ts'or jhye'pa* "to be glad." Again, *gán-de jhye'pa* "to be kind."

Again, instead of the simple form *ku-wa* "to steal," we usually hear *kün-ma jhye'pa,* literally, "to do the thief;" instead of *gying-wa* "to despise," we hear *gying-pág jhye'-pa,* literally "to make disdain;" for *te'pa* "to believe in," the compound *te'pa jhye'pa* is preferred; and instead of *gyö'pa* "to repent," the compound *gyö'pa jhye'pa* "to make repentance." Many instances occur in our Vocabulary. We have seen that to emphasize the imperative form of verbs, *jhye'pa* is frequently added as an intensive, though quite pleonastic (ante V. B. 4).

Then, also, there is the idiomatic use in certain phrases. *Nang-dhák* = the inner Ego, the inner self; from which we draw the idiom *nang-dhák jhye'pa* "to perceive," "to take heed of." *Kham-chhu* = the lips; from which we draw the idiom *kham-chhu jhye'pa* "to bicker," "to quarrel." *Nyémo* = near; whence is derived the phrase *nyémo jhye'pa* "to love, be attached to." There are many similar forms.

### COMPOUNDS WITH JHYE'PA.

| | |
|---|---|
| *P'áknyen jhye'pa :* | to play the eaves-dropper. |
| *Düm-ma jhye'pa :* | to take counsel with. |
| *Káb-kyön jhye'pa :* | to upbraid. |
| *Yur-le jhye'pa :* | to thrash (corn, &c.) |
| *Zün jhye'pa :* | to tell a lie. |
| *Ke-chhá jhye'pa :* | to have a talk. |
| *Ná-len jhye'pa :* | to give shelter to, to lodge. |
| *Kurim jhye'pa :* | to worship, make "pujah." |
| *Le jhye'pa :* | to work, labour. |
| *Khá-yá jhye'pa :* | to co-operate with. |
| *Khákpo jhye'pa :* | to be in difficulties. |
| *Khok-t'uk jhye'pa :* | to be anxious. |

| | |
|---|---|
| *Chhák-chhák jhye'pa :* | to scatter. |
| *Dir-dir jhye'pa :* | to thunder. |
| *Soi jhye'pa :* | to cure. |
| *Nyam-len jhye'pa :* | to learn by heart. |
| *Sháp-shop jhye'pa :* | to trick, defraud. |
| *Shal-ŝhe jhye'pa :* | to promise. |
| *Káduk jhye'pa :* | to take pains. |
| *Gyáp-lok jhye'pa :* | to retreat. |
| *Gye-pa jhye'pa :* | to state fully. |
| *Ḍo-gyu jhye'pa :* | to prepare to start. |
| *Shu-long jhye'pa :* | to supplicate. |
| *Yom-yom jhye'pa :* | to oscilate, swing. |
| *Yapmo jhye'pa :* | to beckon, signal to. |
| *Shuk jhye'pa :* | to knock out of the way. |
| *Mi-pang jhye'pa :* | to argue in favour of (object placed in Gen.) |

*β*. A less extensive series of compounds depend upon another common verb Ḍo-wa to go.

Thus in preference to the primitive verb *p'ampa* "to be defeated," the modern custom makes use of *p'am ḍo-wa,* literally "to go to be defeated." Again, in lieu of *p'ung-wu* "to sink under" "to perish," we hear *p'ung ḍo-wa.*

This auxiliary joined to the gerund of another verb implies reason to expect that any action or event will come to pass. Thus in the example: "The Pass most likely is blocked," we add *ḍo* to the gerund of *kák-pa* "to be hindered," saying *Lá di kák-ne ḍo.* We even append it to itself in such a sentence as: "I think I shall go"—*Ngárang ḍo-ne ḍo.*

*γ*. Another auxiliary of this class is *chuk-pa,* which, however, partakes more of the nature of a causative. It is likewise heard in the sense of "to permit," "to let":—

| | |
|---|---|
| Boil the potatoes: (or: Get the potatoes boiled.) | *Sho-ko di khol chuk !* |
| Allow me to walk in front: | *Ngárang-la ngen-la ḍul chuk.* |

δ. A common appendix occurs in the use of *šir-wa* "to undergo," which is used in a variety of phrases indicating what is felt or passively experienced. Thus, instead of *na-wa* "to be ill," we generally hear *ne'kyī šir-wa* lit. "to suffer by sickness;" again, *ḍhang-ghī šir-wa* "to be cold."

ε. Perhaps the most characteristic of these formative verbs, and one of very varied application, is to be met with in the emphatic word GYA'KPA which when standing alone bears thẹ signification "to throw." In several districts of Tibet the word assumes the form GYABPA or *Gyáp-pa;* and west of *Ṭáshi-lhümpo* the latter form is the one most commonly heard. This auxiliary is conjoined to substantives only; and has so extensive a range that in combination it affords quite a remarkable series of expressive and vigorous compound verbs. In composition the verbal portion alone is inflected, the preceding noun to which it is attached remaining unaltered.

The following are the combinations more frequently occurring; *gyakpa* or *gyap-pa* being interchangeable according to the custom of any district:—

| | |
|---|---|
| *Lu gyakpa :* | to sing a song. |
| *Hái gyakpa :* | to exaggerate. |
| *Hára gyakpa :* | to throw dice. |
| *Ḍu-la ge' gyap-pa :* | to thrash corn. |
| *Híre gyakpa :* | to pile up a corn-stack. |
| *Mendá gyakpa :* | to fire a gun. |
| *Zong gyakpa :* | to traffic. |
| *Ḍoi gyakpa :* | to consider one's plans. |
| *Burko gyakpa :* | to sculpture or emboss or walls. |
| *Shop gyakpa :* | to singe (*e. g.*, a horse). |
| *Boira gyakpa :* | to shout. |
| *O-sho gyakpa :* | to jeer at. |
| *Um gyakpa :* | to kiss. |
| *Wur gyakpa :* | to make a noise. |

| | |
|---|---|
| *Lo gyakpa :* | to cough. |
| *Yikúk gyakpa :* | to hiccough. |
| *Par gyakpa :* | to print. |
| *Ḥlempa gyakpa :* | to sew a patch. |
| *Shū-ḍá gyakpa :* | to whistle. |
| *Arbá gyakpa :* | to cast lots. |
| *Sá-bön gyakpa :* | to sow seed. |
| *Dhákhá gyakpa :* | to shoe a horse. |
| *Suk gyakpa :* | to hurt, injure. |
| *Tsi gyakpa :* | to paint. |
| *Lap gyakpa :* | to chatter. |
| *Higká gyakpa :* | to sob. |
| *Yukpa gyakpa :* | to flog. |
| *Ghur gyakpa :* | to pitch a tent. |
| *Lá gyakpa :* | to surmount a pass. |
| *Nyi-chhol gyakpa :* | to walk in one's sleep. |
| *Ták gyakpa :* | to achieve fame. |
| *Ḍhángka gyakpa :* | to count. |
| *Lé'mo gyakpa :* | to imitate. |
| *Ding gyakpa :* | to suspect. |
| *Khá-kün gyakpa :* | to pretend to have lost. |
| *Pi-tsuk gyakpa :* | to kneel. |
| *Mönlam gyakpa :* | to pray. |
| *Zün gyakpa :* | to make pretence. |
| *Dhong gyá gyappa :* | to seal. |
| *Ṭá-shák gyakpa :* | to give a kick. |
| *Ják gyakpa :* | to rob (violently). |
| *Go-la s̃uk gyakpa :* | to have a headache. |
| *Salpo gyakpa :* | to make bright. |
| *Gomba shik gyakpa :* | to found a monastery. |

# CHAPTER VII.

## PRONOUNS.

### 1.—PERSONAL PRONOUNS.

*a.* We find a variety of personal pronouns of synonymous meaning in use in Tibet; some of these, however, being current in certain provinces only.

| Nominative. | Genitive or Possessive. | Accusative. | Agentive. |
|---|---|---|---|
| *Ngá* : | *Nge* or *Ngáchen* | *Ngá-la* | *Ngá-yī* or *Ngē* |
| *Ngárang* : | *Ngárang-ghi* | *Ngárang-la* | *Ngárang-ghī* |
| *Dák* : | *Dák-ki* | *Dák-la* | *Dák-kyī* |
| *Kho-wo* : | *Kho-woi* | ................ | |
| *Ngátşok* : | .................... | ................ | |
| *Ap'o-ngá* : | .................... | ................ | |
| I. | of me, mine. | me, to me. | by me. |
| *Khyö'* : | *Khyö' kyi* | *Khyö' la* | *Khyö'kyī* |
| *Khyö'rang* : | *Khyö'rang-ghi* | *Khyörang la* | *Khyörang-ghī* |
| *Khye'* : | *Khye' kyi* | *Khye' la* | *Khye' kyī* |
| *Nyi'rang* : | *Nyi'-rang-ghi* | | *Nyi'-rang-ghī* |
| *Nyi'chák* : | | | |
| You. | of you, your. | you. | by you. |
| *Kho* : | *Khoi & Khochen* | *Kho-la* | *Kho-yī* or *Khö* |
| *Khorang* : | *Khorang-ghi* | *Khorang la* | *Khorang-ghī* |
| *Khong* : | *Khong-ghi* | *Khong-la* | *Khong-ghī* |
| He. | of him, his. | him, to him. | by him. |

| Nominative. | Genitive or Possessive. | Accusative. | Agentive. |
|---|---|---|---|
| *Ngáchák :*<br>*Ngáts'o :*<br>*Khowo-chák :*<br>*Ngé'-ts'o :*<br>WE. | *Ngáchák-ki*<br>*Ngáts'o-i*<br>....................<br>....................<br>of us, our. | *Ngáchák-la*<br>*Ngáts'o-la*<br>..................<br>*Ngé' la*<br>us, to us. | *Ngáchak-kī*<br>*Ngáts'o-yī*<br><br>*Ngé'-kyī*<br>by us. |
| *Kho-wa :*<br>*Kho-pa :*<br>*Khochák :*<br>*Khong-ts'o :*<br>*Dhe-dak :*<br>THEY. | *Khowachen*<br>*Kho-pachen*<br>*Khochak-ki*<br>*Khong-ts'oi*<br>*Dhe-dag-ghi*<br>of them, their. | *Kho-wa la*<br>*Kho-pa la*<br>*Khochák-la*<br>*Khong-la*<br><br>them, to them. | *Kho-wá-yī*<br>*Kho-pa-yī*<br>*Khochak-kī*<br>*Khong-ts'ö*<br><br>by them. |

*β.* GENDER AND NUMBER. In the application of the foregoing pronouns there is not much attention paid to the gender of the persons or things represented. There is, nevertheless, a feminine form for *kho-wo* "I," where the speaker is of the female sex, namely *kho-mo.* There is usually no distinction made between "he" and "she;" but the latter pronoun occasionally is differentiated by substituting for the ordinary *kho*, the feminine monosyllable *mo* "she." The neuter "it" can be expressed by *dhe.*

The discrimination of number, moreover, is avoided except where any ambiguity would arise. It will be observed that *chák* and *ts'o* are the plural affixes, either of which may be added to the singular pronouns of the 1st and 3rd persons. Where feasible we find *ngá* or *ngárang* used equally to express "we" as well as "I"; and *kho, khong,* &c., frequently signify "they." However *ngachák, khochák,* &c., are in common use also, and must be chosen whenever stress is laid upon the number of persons indicated.

*γ.* FIRST PERSON. The most popular word for "I" is

*ngárang* which is used in common converse much more frequently than *ngá*. The possessive form "mine" is generally *ngáchen;* whilst "my" and "of me" are usually rendered by *ngárang-ghi* or *ngái* (*nge*). Jaeschke says that *kho-wo* is often used by a superior personage in easy conversation with his subordinates :—

| | |
|---|---|
| That meadow is mine : | *Ne-ma dhe ngáchen yö'.* |
| My fox-skin hat is new : | *Ngárang-ghi wá-shá di sarpa du'.* |
| Let us pitch our tent near the rock : | *Trák-ki ḍamdhu rang-ghi ghur gyak-yong.* |
| God will give us help : | *Konchhoa-kyī ngáchák la ram-da nang-gyu du.'* |
| I loved the child when I saw him on his birthday feast : | *Khoi ming-töm-mo la p'ugu t'ong-la ngárang-ghī kho dzá-wo jhá yö'.* |
| Give me a receipt . | *Dák-la ṭ'ö-ŝin chi' nang ro nang.* |

*Dák* means really "self" and is a common word for the first personal pronoun both in speaking and in letter-writing, being mostly employed in the objective case for "me." Another term for "me" used chiefly in correspondence but also in talk, is one of assumed humility. This is the term *ṭ'en* or *ṭ'en-rang* (ཕྲན *p'ran* or ཕྲན་རང་ *p'ran-rang*) meaning "insignificant one." Thus in a letter :

"I send you my good wishes" would be rendered *T'en-rang-ne rang-ghi semkarpo p'ul jhung,* i. e. "From your humble one his goodwishes are sent."

*T'en-chhung* and *t'em-bhu* are likewise in vogue.

2. As to the use of *rang-ghi* a word must be here interposed. It answers precisely to the *apna* of Hindustani speech and stands for "my" "your" "his" whenever these possessives refer to the nominative or acting subject of the sentence :—

| | |
|---|---|
| I will bring my gun : | *Ngárang rang-ghi mendá khyer yong.* |

| | |
|---|---|
| He will bring my gun: | *Khorang ngái mendá khyer yong.* |
| He will bring his gun: | *Khorang rang-ghi mendá khyer yong.* |
| He will bring the gun with him: | *Khorang mendá di rang dhang nyampo khyer yong.* |
| Begin your work at once: | *Rang-ghi le-ka tanda ṭ'eltu go dzuk:* |

δ. SECOND PERSON. The common word among equals for "you" is *khyö'rang*, which frequently sounds to the ear as if it were spelt *t'yö'rang* (Chap. I, page 13). In the dative, *khyö'-la* seems to be more usual than *khyö'rang-la*; thus:—

| | |
|---|---|
| *Ts'ong-wai dhön-dhu khyö'-la gong-gá yö'pe:* | Have you any eggs to sell? |

Possessively this term is the common word also:—

| | |
|---|---|
| *Khyö'rang-ghi m̃ing ghang ŝer-ghin-re':* | What is your name? |
| *Di p'ugu di khyö'-kyi yö' pe:* | Is this child yours? |

ε. However, in formal conversation with strangers, and in addressing anybody with politeness, the words *nyi'* and *nyi' rang* are generally employed:—

| | |
|---|---|
| *Nyi' gháne yong:* | Whence have you come? |
| *Nyi'-la dhön ŝhik yö'pe:* | What is your business with me? (Have you any business?) |
| *Nyi'rang-ghi khyim (or nang) ghá-re':* | Where is your house? |
| *Kusho, nyi'rang ngá-la sem-la nge pa':* | Sir, do you remember me? |

Another honorific term is said to be *khye'*. It is not so often heard as the plural form *khye'-ts'o*, used in addressing a deputation or company of people. Also *khye'chák*.

ε. THIRD PERSON. The usual term is *khorang*, and both

"he" and "she" are expressed by the word. In certain districts we have heard *mo* employed for "she," but never *kho-mo.* The possessive feminine is sometimes *moi,* whilst the masculine is rarely *khoi,* the form "his" being generally *kho-rang-ghi.* *Kho-wa* is said by Jaeschke to be a special term for "they;" though *kho ts'o* is the word brought to our notice as the usual plural: but we have also heard *kho-pa*:—

| | |
|---|---|
| *Kho-pa nyi p'irlok jhung du'*: | Both of them were outside. |
| *Kho-la song lap*: | I told him to go. (*Lit*: "I told him 'go'") |

The neuter "it" as a nominative is never expressed; and when occurring in the objective case, resort is made to the demonstrative pronouns, *e. g.* "He shot it" would be "shot this" or "shot that."

All the personal pronouns are frequently unexpressed when the sense is apparent, the verb alone being spoken.

## 2.—DEMONSTRATIVE PRONOUNS.

*a.* The simplest forms are *di* this, *dhe* that. When reference is made to anything just mentioned *dhe* is invariably used, never *di*; and so, likewise, when what is to follow is referred to without using a noun, *di* is always the pronoun selected. Thus a person, referring to what he has just said, would in Tibetan never say: "I mention this" but "I mention that." So, too, with respect to place, "this" and "that" are not used so loosely as they are in English speech. The demonstrative pronouns follow the noun they qualify, and are declinable. Thus:—

| | |
|---|---|
| Throw a stone at that tree: | *Shing dhe-la do gyop!* |

*β.* In the province of Tsang and in Sikkim, we have *wudi* or *audi* and *p'idi* in use for "this" and "that" respectively; moreover these pronouns then precede the noun:—

| | |
|---|---|
| Who is this girl? | *Audi pumo ghang yö'pe?* |

γ. When the pronouns stand unattached to nouns, they often take the affix *ka* or *ga: di-ka* = this, this one; *dhe-ga* that, that one. In Tsang the affix *ni* is added in the same way.

| | |
|---|---|
| Which do you want, this or that? | *Di-ka dhe-ga, nyi'la ghang goi gyu?* |

δ. Tibetans make use of forms of the demonstrative pronouns which enable them to discriminate with considerable nicety the exact position of any object they wish to indicate. Thus, *di* = this, close by; *há-gi* = that, just yonder; *p'á-gi* = that, much further off, that far away; *yá-gi* = that, up there; *má-gi* = this down below. When used with any nouns, these compounds generally precede it.

| | |
|---|---|
| That (over there) is mine: | *P'á-gi ngai yin.* |

Sometimes in these cases *di* or *dhe* is likewise used for perspicuity:—

| | |
|---|---|
| Run to that house (right over there): | *P'á-gi nang dhe-la gyukshá lö' tung (or lö' dhang).* |
| Turn down that path (just yonder): | *Há-gi lamkha di kyok song.* |

2. The plural affix is attached to the demonstrative pronoun and not to the substantive, *nam* and *ts'o* (sounded *ts'u*) being the common affixes; *chá(k)* is not often heard in Ui:—

| | |
|---|---|
| Take off those dogs: | *Khyi dhe-ts'o ṭ'i song!* |
| These men are a little late to-day. | *Dhe-ring mi di-nam tiktse gor song.* |

Where we have "these," "those," apart from any noun we hear *di-nam*, and *dhe-dák* or *dhe-ts'o*.

## 3.—INDEFINITE PRONOUNS.

These are used as adjectives and in the modern colloquial differ considerably from the older forms. Little more than enumeration is needed: *Ḍá:* "any;" *kh̆á-she* (ཁ་ཤས་): "some;" *ghangmo:* "the whole;" *t'amché* (never *kün*) or *ts'angma* "all:" *kün* "every;" *re* and *re-re* each; *ŝhü-ma:* others; *ŝhem-ma* another.

These can be employed alone or with nouns:—

| | |
|---|---|
| *Toktse-i tang-la ngai pe-chhá ḍa du'ka mindu':* | Are any of my books upon the table or not? |
| *Tanda ṭ'ëltu khá-she nang-la chhyin-pa-re'; ōn kyang t'amché tsa-ne nai-pa dhe sá-la de yö':* | Some had gone home at once; but all those living near sat on the ground. |

## 4.—INTERROGATIVE PRONOUNS.

(i) In asking questions, the interrogative pronoun must stand in the sentence immediately next before the verb, and therefore nearly at the end of such sentence. Those in common use are the following:—

*Ghang:* which, what; *Su:* who; *Kápá* or *Ghá-pá* and *Ghá-ru:* where; *Ghánḍe* (sounds *Kándé*)*:* how; *Ghá-dhui* (sounds *ká-tü*) when; *Ghá-ts'ö:* how much, how many?

All these are capable of declension, and thus we obtain the further forms:—

*Ghang-la:* why, for what; *Su-yi* (vulgarly *so-kyi*) whose; *Ghang-ne:* from what, from which; *Su-la:* to whom; *Ghá-ne:* whence; *Ghá-la:* whither; also a special form in *Ghá re':* where is?

*a*. In this connection, the difference between the use of *yin* and *yö'* may be illustrated *yin* being the more copualative auxiliary, such a phrase as *Su yin* could not be taken to mean "who is there," which requires the use of the verb *yö'-pa* meaning "to be present," "to exist," as well as "to be"-accordingly *Su yin* means "who is he" and *Su yö* means "who is there;" again, *Su re'pa yinna:* "whoever is it." *β*. The interrogative affix to the concluding verb is seldom necessary where the interrogative pronoun is used. When *yö'* concludes the sentence, the affix is often added, which is likewise the case with *yin*, the interrogative forms of which are *yö pe* and *yimpe.*

Sometimes a plural form of the pronoun *su* occurs, namely *su-su*, e. g. *Khye-pa di su-su yimpa:* Who are those traders?

ii. When the pronoun *gháng* has to be made use of in an adjectival sense, it stands in the sentence immediately after the noun and next before the verb, e.g. *ngá-chá ĺam gháng ḍo ghi-du'* "which way are we going?"

A variation of the position occurs in a few special instances, as in the phrases: *Kho ghang yul-pa leb-bhá:* From what district does he come? *Khyö ghang ts'e-la ḍo:* At what time do you go? *Gha-ts'ö* is used adjectivally in such sentences as: *Ṭashi-lhümpo-ne Lhásá la t'á ring t'ung gha-ts'o yö'dhá* what distance is it (how far is it) from Ṭashilhümpo to Lhásá?

## 5.—RELATIVE PRONOUNS.

i. The most common method of expressing relative clauses, namely by means of continuative and gerundial particles, has been already fully explained and illustrated (*ante* Chap. VI, B. 5, *γ*.)

ii. There remains to be indicated the rare form of construction where our European method is resorted to. Moreover, in many instances relative pronouns are used in combination with the gerundial construction. Lastly, there is a correlative use of the pronouns, of frequent occurrence.

*Ghang, su, nam,* are the relatives and correlatives in use.

iii. The ordinary relative construction may be chosen in such a sentence as the following :—

"Bring me the coolie who arrived just now."

Such a sentence may be expressed in two ways—First, with the relative pronoun, thus :—

| | |
|---|---|
| *Ngá-la khurpa ghang tanda rang lep-ne ṭ'i shok :* | "Which coolie arriving just now bring to me." |

Or else, we might hear the sentence turned somewhat in this style :—

| | |
|---|---|
| *Tanda rang lep-pai khurpa dhe ngá-la ṭ'i shok :* | The coolie arriving just now bring to me. |

Another sentence more precisely analogous in Tibetan dress to our relative construction would be this :—

"The dog, which shewed its teeth savagely, was fastened to the tent pole."

Here we might have the rendering :—

*Khyi ghang rang-ghi so ngárma ten-pa dhe ghur-ber la dam-ne yö'.*

It will be noted, however, that the relative clause is inserted between the antecedent to which it refers and the article of such antecedent, the verb of the clause occurring as a participle. Thus, save for this introduction of the relative pronoun *ghang,* the sentence resembles the participial forms already explained. Another example will suffice :—

| | |
|---|---|
| The guns which belonged to the men must be given up : | *Méndá ghang mi-ts'o la yö' pa di táng go-du'.* |

iv. Those sentences known as correlative rather than relative always require the introduction of the relative pronoun.

They will be best recognised by means of several examples:—

| | |
|---|---|
| *Potsoi ámá ghang yimpa dhe khá-sáng lep jhung:* | She who was the boy's mother arrived yesterday. |
| *Di ghang-ghī t'obpa ngá-la khur shok:* | Whoever gets it bring it me. |
| *Khyö' ghang ḍok-ghi-du' dhe há-go ghi-du':* | Do you understand what you are reading? (*Lit*: What you read, that do you understand?) |
| *Su-la pe-chhá di yö' pa di-la ḍok yong ná, ye-shei m̂angpo lop-yong:* | If anybody who has this book will read it, he will learn much wisdom. |
| *Khyö'rang-la t'song-wa ghang yö' pa dhe ngá-la ten-nang:* | Shew me what you have to sell. (*Lit*: What to sell there is to you, that shew to me.) |
| *Su yang ngá dhang nyampo yong-wa dhe-la ngul-p'ok ŷák-po ter yong:* | Whoever will come with me, shall be given good wages. (*Lit*: Whoever will come with me, to that one good wages will be given.) |
| *Khyö'rang-la to-chhá gháng ŷang gō-yö'-pa, dhe ger-ne yö':* | Whatever victuals you wanted have been provided. (*Lit*: To you whatever victuals were wanting, that has been provided.) |
| *Khorang ghang jhye'-kyi-yö'-na ŷang khye'mi du':* | Never mind what he is doing. |

*Jhye'-kyi-yö'* is the Narrative Present, *kyi* being used for *ghi* after the elided *d* of *jhye'*.)

*β*. Not only is the demonstrative pronoun inserted after the clause, but the article is also introduced after the relative pronoun in order to give a general or correlative sense to the latter. Thus *ghang di* "the what" signifies "whatever," and *su di* "the who" or "the whom" is equivalent to "whoever" or "whomever." This method is one of the commonest devices to express sentences of this kind in the colloquial; and we should recommend to the beginner recourse to it in the first place. Taking such a sentence as: "I shall wear whatever I like," we shall transmute it into the form: "To my thinking the what is, shall wear;" i. e., *Ngái šhempa-la ghang di ghön yong.*

γ. Lastly must be mentioned the usage where "as" occurs as a relative pronoun. We meet with the relative construction in a sentence of this kind: "Do as I tell you." In order to render this into Tibetan we must turn it "As I tell you, so do," or more literally, "According to what I tell, you according to that do!" *Ngárang ghá nangtar šer, khyö'-rang dhe nangtar jhyi' chik.* In Rudok and the West, *ghá-zuk* and *dhe-zuk* take the place of *ghá nangtar*, &c. In Central Tibet such a sentence is best rendered *Ngárang ghánḍe šer, khyö'rang dhenḍe jhyi' chik:* "Like what I say, you like that do!" In fact this latter phrasing is the more generally heard. The expression "So far as you can" is turned: until what ...... until that ...... e. g., *Khyö'-rang ghá-t'uk ḍo chok, dhe t'uk song.*

| | |
|---|---|
| *Kho-la ghánḍe go yö', dhende ter chik:* | Give him what he needs. |

# CHAPTER VIII.

## ADVERBS.

i. The Adverb can be formed from the Adjective by putting the latter in the Terminative Case. Very few Tibetans, however, make any distinction, in this class of Adverbs, between the Adverb and the Adjective. Thus we hear *gyo'po* in use for both "quick" and "quickly;" *gorpo* for "slow" and "slowly;" *süm-po* for "quiet" and "quietly." Properly the adverbial forms of these words should be *gyo'por* or *gyo'bar*, *gor-por*, and *süm-por.*

When the Adverb is formed from a Participle or from an Adjective of participial mould, the particle *ne* is employed, as in *tál-bu-chen-ne* "lingeringly."

ii. Custom has singled out certain words for adverbial use which are never employed as adjectives but which decidedly are not Primitive Adverbs. Thus *ghá-lü'* "gently," "softly" (Hind: *áhiste*)*; ták-nyomla* "evenly" "equally;" *ma-parpar-la:* "seldom."

iii. Adverbs from Nouns:—These are such as: *kang-t'ang* "on foot," *khá-ne* "orally" (*lit:* from mouth), *t'á-ma-la* "at the end," *dong-la* "in front," "first," *gyáp-la* "at the back," *ts'á-ḍhák* "hastily" "hurriedly," *ḍám-la* "close by, near" (*lit:* at the bank), *dhüi-gyün* (pr. *tü-gyün*) "always," *šhug-la* "behind" (from *šhug-gu* "the tail").

iv. Adverbs of Time.—Nearly all these are Primitive; but in some instances the original form has been augmented in the Colloquial by the addition of various syllables. The chief temporal adverbs are :—

| | |
|---|---|
| *Tănda* (or *tanta*) : | now. |
| *Tanda t'eltu* : | immediately. |
| *Tanda lamsang* : | at once. |
| *T'el t'el-la* : | without delay. |
| *Ting-sang* : | at present (Hind : *áj-kal*) |
| *Ngá-má* : | early. |
| *Chhyimo* (often *P'imo*) : | late. |
| *Ngen-chhe'* : | previously, formerly. |
| *Ting-la* : | later, hereafter. |
| *Dhé wona-le* : | since then. |
| *Le-ne* : } *Je-la* : } | afterwards. |
| *Angki jukma* : | last. |
| *Tákpa réshi* : | always. |
| *Kap-kap-su* : | sometimes. |
| *Re-shik* : | a little while. |
| *Chik-char-la* : } *Hlengyai-la* : } | all together, simultaneously. |
| *Dhá-chi* : | recently, lately. |
| *Dhá-rung* : | still, yet. |
| *Dhá-p'en* : } *Dhá-t'uk* : } | as yet, until now. |
| *Yang-kyar* : | again. |
| *Yang-kyar-ŷang* : | often. |

To these may be added a numerous list expressing specific times, but of which it will be sufficient to mention :—

| | | | |
|---|---|---|---|
| *Khó-sang* : | Yesterday. | *Shé-la* : | Three days hence. |
| *Dhé-ring* : | To-day. | *Gui* : | Four days hence. |
| *Dhá-rang* : | This morning. | *Chhui* : | Five days hence. |
| *Ts'en-la* : | To-night. | *Dhá-lo* : | This year. |
| *Sang-nyin* : | To-morrow. | *Khásang-lo* : | Last year. |
| *Năng* : | Day-after-to-morrow. | *Sangpö'* : | Next year. |

*N. B.*—The commoner term for "this morning" is *dhá-rang ŝho-ge*.

v. ADVERBS OF PLACE.—Some of these are Primitive roots :—

| | |
|---|---|
| *Di-pa :* / *Dei :* | here. |
| *Dhe-pa :* / *Dher :* | there. |
| *Ts'ur-la :* / *Diru :* | hither. |
| *P'áru :* | thither. |
| *P'á-gi-la :* | yonder. |
| *Há-gi-la :* | just there, over there. |
| *Yá-gi-la :* | up there. |
| *Má-gi-la :* | down thero. |
| *Kyen-la :* | upwards. |
| *Shö'la :* | downwards. |
| *Gong-la :* | above. |
| *Me'-la :* | below |
| *Di ŷen-la :* | at npper part. |
| *Di m̂en-la :* | at lower part. |
| *Yar :* | up. |
| *Mar :* | down. |
| *Gyap-la :* | behind. |
| *Dün-la :* | before. |
| *Kün-la :* | everywhere. |
| *P'ár-tsam :* | beyond. |
| *Shám-la :* | lower down, further ou. |
| *Gyang-la :* | afar off. |
| *Nang-na :* | within. |
| *Bug-la :* | inside. |
| *Kyiltu :* | in the middle. |
| *P'i-la :* | outside. |
| *Tung-tu :* / *Tsá-ne :* | near, close by. |
| *Rik-te :* | close together. |
| *Há-chhok :* | opposite. |
| *Di-ne :* | hence. |
| *Dhe-ne :* | thence. |
| *Lok-ne :* | back again. |
| *P'ár ts'ur la :* | to and fro. |
| *T'ól-le :* | past, on. |

vi. ADVERBS OF MANNER.—In addition to those directly derived from adjectives as shewn above, the following should be noted :—

| | |
|---|---|
| *Multar :* | accordingly. |
| *Chikpu :* | alone. |
| *Dhenḍa :* | like that ; a'piece. |
| *Mangpo :* | mnch, mostly. |
| *Dinḍa :* | thus, so. |
| *Rang-ŝhin :* | of its own accọrd. |
| *Chhá-lam :* | rather. |
| *Kyang-pa :* | only. |
| *Ye-ne :* | quite. |
| *Chhyi-l̂ok :* | backwards. |
| *Gyün-la :* | continually. |
| *Ts'angma domne :* | altogether. |
| *Rimŝhin :* | by turns. |
| *Shenma :* | otherwise, another way. |
| *Há-chang :* | too much, very. |
| *Tü-gyün dápu :* | as usnal. |
| *Nenten :* | certainly, really. |
| *Mu-ne :* | exactly, precisely. |
| *Holte :* | loose |

vii. NEGATIVE ADVERBS.—All negative particles used with verbs are naturally adverbs, and these have been already explained and illustrated (VI, B. 8, ii.) Two or three others require notice: *ŷema* (with verb) and *ĺa-re me'* "not at all," *re-ken* "by no means;" also *nyong* which, when preceded by *ma* and annexed to a verb in the past tense, has the force of "never,"—but see VI, B. 10. However, with the present and future tenses *nyong* seems to be inadmissable, the expression *tsá-wa-ne* followed by the verb in the negative being then resorted to:—

| | |
|---|---|
| I shall never go again: | *Ngá ŷang-kyar tsá-wa-ne ḍo gyu me'.* |
| He never comes to see me now: | *Tanda kho ngá-la tá-gyu-la tsá-wa-ne lep-kyi-min.* |
| I shall never be afraid again: | *Ngá ŷang-kyar tsá-wa-ne ŝhe'mi yong.* |

*Námáng* with a negative future or imperative also occurs:—

| | |
|---|---|
| The body of the abbott will never decay: | *Khempo-i p'ungpo námáng tor mi yong.* |
| When you come to a chhorten, never turn to the right: | *Chhörten-la lep-ne, yäi-ngöi-la ná-máng ma kyok.* |

viii. A number of characteristic adverbs in common use are formed, as in the case of many adjectives, by re-duplicated syllables. Sometimes in the second syllable a vowel is varied. Thus: *ts'er-ts'er:* often, time after time, *zol-zol* anyhow, *ŝop-ŝop:* topsy-turvy, *ráp-rip* awry; also "dimly," *tap-tip* upside down, *chhág-gha chhog-ghé* all in a heap, *tap-tap-te* or *tap-tap-por:* suddenly, *sam sum:* quietly, *hrik-hrik:* all around, *shrang-shrang:* alone.

ix. Certain adverbial expressions qualify with a sense of indefiniteness proposed actions or past sensations. These introduce in reality indefinite relative pronouns. We refer to phrases of this sort: "so far as I can," "so far as I know." One mode of expression is to couple *ghang* or *jhi* to the requisite verb, and to introduce this clause immediately preceding the subject of the sentence :—

| | |
|---|---|
| I will do the utmost (as much as possible) : | *Jhi nye' ngárang-ghī jhyá-gyu yin.* |
| So far as I know he set out yesterday : | *Ngárang ghang she-pa khorang khʻásang jhyön song.* |

But see under Relative Pronouns (iv, γ.)

Again *tsam-ŝhik-la* = "as soon as" :—

| | |
|---|---|
| As soon as the sun sets, blow up the fire : | *Nyima di gái tsam-ŝhik-la m̂é p'u dhang.* |

# CHAPTER IX.

## POSTPOSITIONS.

1. These, the Oriental substitutes for the prepositions of European languages, may in Tibetan as in other tongues be divided into two main classes, namely, Primitive Postpositions and Derivative Postpositions. The Primitives, which are all monosyllabic, comprise the case signs and a few others. The Derivatives, which are mostly words of two or three syllables, have been formed—often by an ingenious and interesting process of evolution—from adverbs, adjectives, substantives, and verbs. Many of the colloquial Derivatives are of modern development and are never to be seen in books.

2. The Primitive Postpositions are the following: *Kyi, ghi* "of;" *La* "to;" *Na* "in;" *Nai* or *ne*, "from;" *Lai* or *le* "from among;" *Kyī, ghī* "by" "by the agency of;" *Dhang* "with;" *Dhu, ru, tu,* or *su*, "into," "unto," "for."

The usage of these will require some illustration.

La, in the colloquial, is not only the sign of the accusative (contrary to the literary usage it is seldom the sign of the dative) but also possesses the locative significations of "at" and "on":—

| | |
|---|---|
| Look at him: | *Kho-la toi shik!* |
| I shall start at dawn: | *Ngáráng kyáreng-la gyu yong.* |
| Put wood on the fire: | *Me-la shing chuk!* |
| The bird is pale on the breast: | *Jhyá di ḍhang-la kyákoré yö'.* |
| Hide-boats float safely on the surface of the Yeru River: | *Ko-á Yai-ru Tsangpo-i khá-t'ok-la ling-ghyi ding du.'* |

Sometimes *la* carries the meaning of "in":—

| | |
|---|---|
| Throw the small fish into the water: | *Chhu-la nyá chhung gyop!* |
| I have headache (pain in the head): | *Ngá-la go-la ȋuk gyak.* |

In assessments of price, &c., *la* corresponds with our preposition "for":—

| | |
|---|---|
| The book has been sold for 15 Galden tangkas: | *Pe-chhá di genden tangka chongá la, ts'ong ts'ar du'.* |

Occasionally "from" and "by" require this postposition:—

| | |
|---|---|
| The finial fell from the chhorten: | *T'ok di chhorten-la bap song.* |
| Hold the bird firmly by the wings: | *Dap-shok-la jhyá di ling-ghyi dzin!* |

*La* used in the sense of "to" is confined almost to its use before pronouns and after verbs of giving, saying, and sending.

NA is rarely heard in Tibet Proper as a locative postposition; and when it correctly enters into the composition of certain compound postpositions, *la* is often substituted.

NAI or NE has usually the pure ablative sense of "from;" but likewise is found in the sense of "out of" and "through":—

| | |
|---|---|
| He sprang out of the lotos: | *Kho pema-nai jhung.* |
| From Darjiling to Pemiongchi: | *Dorjeling-ne Pema-yangtse t'uk-pa-la.* |
| It is eight years' ago: | *Di-ne lo gye' jhung.* |

This postposition is discriminated from LAI or LE, which besides the special meaning "than" (vide IV, 9, *a*,) conveys the sense of "from out" "from among":—

| | |
|---|---|
| Choose me two sheep from the flock: | *Khyu-le ȋuk nyi ngárang-la p'e jhyi!* |

| | |
|---|---|
| Out of nine only three were saved : | *Gu-le sum mempa* (or *ma-tok*) ཐར *dei min du'.* |
| Saved from the Queer-heads (robbers) : | *Go-lok-le t'ar-ne yö'.* |

DHANG is not ordinarily classed as a case sign, though it carries the meaning "with" in its most distinctive sense. It is attached in particular to certain verbs (such as *ḍhalwa* "to be separated" and *ḍelwa* "to meet") and is also joined with certain compound postpositions.

As a conjunction it has a distinctive use. (Vide: Ch. X, 1.)

3. *Derivative or Compound Postpositions:*—The first quality to be noted respecting these Postpositions is that the majority of them govern the Genitive case. Accordingly each of these must be linked to the noun, adjective, or participle, which it affects, by means of another postposition, to wit the Genitive case-sign. Much nicety is requisite in selecting the proper postposition to express the intended relationship with exactness and idiom. We have endeavoured in the lists which follow to give the precise shade of meaning attached to each in order to avoid, where possible, double significations; and, with this view we have sometimes omitted allowable renderings, assigning the sense more commonly understood in colloquial usage. Many of the postpositions are identical with, or have been derived from, the corresponding adverbs. Some of this class have been compounded by adding the simple case-sign to different adverbs. In ancient Tibetan such affixes would be those expressing the Terminative case; in modern times the Dative or Locative case-sign has replaced the Terminative; though some of the forms familiar to readers of classical Tibetan are still heard in modern conversation.

## POSTPOSITIONS GOVERNING GENITIVE CASE.

| | | | |
|---|---|---|---|
| *Khá-wok* : | beneath. | *Ting-la* : | after (time). |
| *Wok-la* : | below, under. | *Töndá-la* : | for (also *tön-la*). |
| *Khá-t'ok-la* : | on the top of. | *Nang-šhin* : | like, as. |
| *Tang-la* : | above. | *Nang-tar* : | according to. |
| *Kong-na* : | in the midst of. | *Gáng-la* : | on, upon. |
| *Sep-la* : } *Hrák-la* : } | between (*i. e.* two, &c.) | *Dhöndhu* : | in order to. |
| | | *Len-la* : | in return for, for. |
| *Nang-la* : | in, within. | *Dündhu* : | before, in the presence of. |
| *P'i-la* : | outside of. | | |
| *T'e kyá-la* : | towards. | *Ts'ap-la* : | instead of. |
| *Chhirtu* : | for, in behalf of. | *Kap-su* : | on the occasion of. |
| *T'e nyá* : | opposite to. | *Tsá-ne* : | at, near. |
| *Tsu-rol-na* : | on this side of. | *Tsar* : | to, towards. |
| *T'uk-pa* : | up to, unto. | *Ḍo-ru* : | beside, adjoining. |
| *Gám-la* : | close to, up to. | *Wángdhu-shor-na* : | concerning, as to. |
| *T'á-nyepo* : | near. | | |
| *Mempe* : | except. | *Gyap-la* : | at the back of. |
| *P'ár-la* : | away from. [of. | *Dong-la* : | in front of. |
| *P'árkhá* : | on the other side | *Der-la* : | on the side of, (or "face of.") |
| *Jei-la* : | after (place). | | |

## POSTPOSITIONS GOVERNING ACCUSATIVE CASE.

| | | | |
|---|---|---|---|
| *Shuk-la* : | behind. | *P'en-la* : | until. |
| *Yen-la* : | over. | *Ngo-la* : | towards. |
| *T'ö* : | above. | *Ten-ne* : | with respect to, as to. |
| *Kor* : | about, regarding. | *Ts'ün* : | within, by the time of (in the sense of "not later than.") |
| *Menchhe'* : | underneath, not so far as. | | |
| *P'enchhe'* : | beyond, further than. | *Sur-ne* : | along, beside. |
| | | *Chhok-la* : | in the direction of. |

## POSTPOSITIONS GOVERNING THE ABLATIVE IN DHANG.

| | | | |
|---|---|---|---|
| *Nyampo* : | with, together with. | *Ḍá-te* : | like, equal to. |
| *Chá-su* : | containing, belonging to. | *Mi ḍá-wa* . | unlike, different from. |

*N. B.*—In the colloquial *ḍa* or *ḍe* (really འདྲས་) has quite taken the place of the literary word ལྟར་ in the sense of "as," "like," &c., especially in compounds.

4. Use of Compound Postpositions.—These can govern either substantives or adjectives or verbs. When governing the latter, the postposition is placed at the end of the sentence, converting it into a gerundial clause. Subjoined are a sufficient series of examples illustrating both methods of employment:—

| | |
|---|---|
| You will find rain-shelter beneath that rock-boulder: | *Khyö'rang-ghī ḍhák bhong di-i khá-wok chhar-kyib nye-yong.* |
| The path passes between those chhortens up there: | *Yá-gi-la chhorten dhe-i sep-la lamkhá di t'ál ḍo.* |
| Let us go up to the monastery: | *Gompá-yi gam-la ḍo-gyu nang.* |
| Don't go beyond the tree down there: | *Má-gi-la shíng di p'enchhe' ma ḍo.* |
| The road runs along the river-bank: | *Lam di chhu-ḍám sur-ne gyu.* |
| Come after two days: | *Nyinmo nyí-kyi ting-la shok!* |
| This money is for your help: | *Di ngul di khyörang-ghi ro-rám kyi len-la du'.* |
| I shall arrive in three days: | *Nyin sum ts'ün lep yong.* |
| There is nothing but snow up there: | *Yá-gi-la ghang-ghí mempe chang min du'.* |
| All except two have been found: | *Nyí-ká-i mempe kün di nye' ma jhung.* |
| No one except you grumbles: | *Khyö-kyi mempe su yang ṭ'o-t'á ma jhye' kyi-du'.* |
| Go outside the tent at once: | *Di ghur-kyi p'i-lu gyuk tanda t'eltu!* |
| The shops are opposite the Cho-khang: | *Sok-khang di Cho-khang-ghi t'e-ñyá ndi song* ("are placed"). |
| I will go with you instead of him: | *Khoi ts'ap-la ngárang khyö dhang nyámpo ḍo-gyu-yin.* |

| | |
|---|---|
| It is different from that: | *Di-ka dhe dhang mi-ḍa-wa du'* |
| Come with me to Gyang-tse: | *Ngárang dhang nyampo Gyang-tse t'uk-pa shok!* |
| Hang it up above the window: | *Gi-khung-gi tang-la yar dak s̃hok!* |
| On the occasion of the lama coming, prepare pastry: | *Láma di yong-wái kap-su, khur-wa ṭ'ál-ḍhik jhyi chik.* |
| Instead of walking quickly home, you saunter along: | *Khyörang nyurdhu khyim-la ḍul-wá-yi ts'ap-la, kyáng-kyong jhye'.* |
| After he had gone, the ring was not to be found: | *Kho song-wai ting-la, sor-dub di nye'-chhok min du'.* |
| Down there is placed a chhorten containing many bones: | *Má-gi-la chhorten dung-rü m̃áng dhang chá-su chik s̃hak jhung* |
| The box containing books: | *Di ḍom pechhá dhang chá-su di* |
| Regarding that, I will send word to you to-morrow: | *Sang-nyin dhe kor khyörang-la lön p'ul yong.* |
| This is not for him: | *Di-ka kho-i tön-la ma re'.* |
| This is for your wife: | *Di-ka nyirang-ghi kyermen-kyi chhirtu yö'.* |
| Two rupees to buy the calf (for the purpose of buying): | *Gyá-tam nyi, pe-to ñyo-wái dhöndá-la.* |
| I will give this for that: | *Ngá di ni dhe-yi len-la p'ul yong.* |
| Prepare to set out: | *Ḍo-wai dhöndhu t'ál-dhik jhyi chik.* |
| What is he talking about: | *Khorang ghang kor-la she' kyin du'* or *s̃er-kyin-du'* or *ser-kyin-yö'pe?* |
| They went in that direction (towards that): | *Kho-ts'o dhe chhok-la song* or *dhe ñgo-la song.* |
| It came out of yonder cave: | *Há-gi p'uk p'i-ne jhung.* |
| He sold it for three sho: | *Khorang s̃ho sum la ts'ong-ne du'.* |
| Take aim among them: | *Dhe-yi ñang-na bem-la gyák.* |

# CHAPTER X.
## CONJUNCTIONS.

1. Those Conjunctions, which in English connect short clauses to each other and likewise link together longer sentences, are generally expressed in Tibetan by means of the gerundial and continuative particles elsewhere fully explained. (See: Chap. VI, B. 6, 8, ii, and Chap. XIII, 3.)

However, our common copulative "and" finds its counterpart in the Tibetan *dhang*, which literally signifies "with." Thus, such an enumeration as "horses and cows and sheep and goats" would in the Tibetan idiom be rendered: "with horses, with cows, with sheep, goats" *Tá-ts'o dhang, bhámo ts'o dhang, luk ts'o dhang, ráma-ts'o;* or, possibly, *Tá-ts'o dhang bhámo-ts'o, luk-ts'o dhang ráma-ts'o:* "cows with horses, goats with sheep."

Although *dhang* is usually translated "and," the point to keep clear in the mind is that it is really a postposition meaning "with," and therefore in such an example as the foregoing *dhang* belongs, not to *bhámo-ts'o* as if "and cows," but to *tá-ts'o* which precedes it.

2. In enumerations in the colloquial we mostly find this copulative omitted for the sake of terseness; and the sentence above would be spoken *tá-ts'o bhámo-ts'o luk-ts'o rá-má-ts'o*, or, more briefly still, *tá bhá-mo luk ráma-ts'o* or even *tá bhá luk rá-ts'o*, the one plural affix *ts'o* sufficing for the whole of the items:—

| | |
|---|---|
| Buy radishes, turnips and pepper: | *Lápuk ñyungma yerma ñyo shik!* |

| | |
|---|---|
| I have lost father and mother: | *Ngárang áp'á ámá ghü-la song.* (Lit: "I have gone in loss.") |
| Give me three mules and two jhomo: | *Ngárang-la ḍheu sum dhang jhomo nyi nang ro dze!* |
| I want to eat and drink: | *Ngá-la ŝá t'ung goi.* |
| I want both to eat and to drink: | *Ngá-la ŝa-gyu dhang t'ung-gyu goi.* |

When *dhang* is used in the copulative sense the accent is thrown on the preceding word and *dhang* spoken shortly and quickly.

Conversationally, where the conjunction needs to be expressed, the form *dhárung* is frequently substituted for *dhang*. *Dhárung*, signifying "more yet," is used precisely as *aur* is employed in Hindustani, both as "and" and as "more":—

| | |
|---|---|
| The man and his wife came: | *Mi-po di dhárung rang-ghi chhung-ro lep jhung.* |

Sometimes when "both"—"and" would be used by us, the Tibetan places the two nouns consecutively with *nyī-ka* "the two" appended, *e. g.* "The charges for both the men and the yaks" would be *mi yák-ts'o nyī-kai p'ok.*

3. The contrasting or disjunctive conjunction can be rendered by means of continuative particles. However two or three set terms are to be met with.

*a.* In short sentences where the sense of "although" is admissible the conjunction *rung* is employed. In such a sentence as: "I am permitted to eat mutton but not beef," we may turn it; "I am permitted to eat, though mutton, not beef," thus:—

| | |
|---|---|
| *Ngárang-la l̂ukshá rung bháshá ma ŝá chuk;* or *Ngárang-la l̂ukshá rung bháshá ŝa-wa ma chuk:* | (Lit: To me, though mutton, beef it is not permitted to eat). |

Another example elucidates the use more clearly —

| | |
|---|---|
| *Sampá gál rung gul ma jhyi' :* | Cross the bridge but don't shake it : |

(Lit : "Though crossing bridge, don't cause to shake.")

*Kyang* is equivalent to *rung*, and in Lhása more frequently heard.

These conjunctions may likewise be used to contrast two lengthy clauses :—

| | |
|---|---|
| *Khorang-ghī di ĩam-ŷik kur* (or *tang*) *gyu-la ŝhal-gyá jhe' rung, dhá-t'uk yok-po-yī khyer ma jhung :* | He promised to send the passport yesterday ; but the servant has not brought it yet : |

*β.* As *rung* means "although," if we require a more precise rendering of such conjunctions as "but," "notwithstanding," "however," we may resort to certain other forms which, instead of being annexed as *rung* to the preceding clauses, are placed as in English at the head of the clause to which they belong.

Two of these have come to our notice, *yin-kyang* and *áh-ma :—*

| | |
|---|---|
| *Khorang ŷang-kyar-ŷang ke tang rung, su ŷang lep ma jhung ; yin-kyang je-la drá ŝhik t'oi-jhung :* | He shouted again and again but nobody came ; however, at last a voice was heard. |

4. The alternative conjunctions "either"—"or" may be rendered by "yang-na"—"yangna," and even by "yang"—"yang" :—

| | |
|---|---|
| *Ká-nangwa ŷang má nang-wa ŷang lep-ne sang ngá-mo t'e-kang-la ḍo yong :* | Whether permission or no permission arrive, to-morrow morning I shall proceed straight ahead (shall advance on.) |

| | |
|---|---|
| *Yang-na ngai á-p'á ŷang-na ngai á-ma leb-yong:* | Either my father or my mother will come |

When the alternative conjunction lies between two sentences, the conjunction *won-te* or *ōnte* = "or else," may be employed :—

| | |
|---|---|
| *Khyörang lokne ḍo goi, won-te jong-pön kyī dak-la nye-pa tang yong:* | You must go back, or else the jong-pon will punish us (*dak* = self). |
| *Song ŷang-na lui ŝhik:* | Either go or stay! |

5. The conditional conjunction "if" is arrived at by attaching *na* to the root of the verb concluding the clause :—

| | |
|---|---|
| *Khyö'rang ĺamkhá di-la háchang gyōpo ḍul ná ŝák yong* (or *gyel yong*): | If you walk too quickly on the path, you will fall. |
| *Nuk-te ham-pa-chen ŝá-ne ťo-na, khyö'rang wolma dam yong:* | If you continue eating so greedily, you will choke. |
| *Nang-la do nang-na, ngá-la lön khur shok:* | Bring me word if I may go inside. |

Sometimes we hear "if" expressed more formally, by the use of *ke-si* (གལ་སྲིད) at the commencement, and *na* at the end of the clause :—

| | |
|---|---|
| *Ke-si pu ŝhik kye-na, dhe-yi míng-la Pün-ts'o ták ro nang:* | If a boy is born, please name him "Pünts'o." |

Such sentences as: "He asked if he might come" are transposed for translation into Tibetan, thus: "He asked, may I come," or "May I come, thus he asked," (*post:* XII, 7.)

6. The contrast between a positive and a negative assertion, which in English is made by the introduction of the

conjunction "or," is generally expressed in Tibetan without any formal link. Thus :—

| | |
|---|---|
| *Dhe-pa khyi ḍa du'ka mindu'* : | Are there any dogs there or not ? |
| *Dhe t'oktse wo'la du'ka mindu'* : | Is it under the table or not ? |

Sometimes *dhang* (pr. *tang*) is used : *e. g.* :—

| | |
|---|---|
| *Di Pö'kyi pe-chha re' dhang ma re'* : | Is this a Tibetan book or not ? |
| *Tá-di ngai re' dhang ma re'* : | Is this horse mine or not ? |

---

# CHAPTER XI.

## DERIVATIVES AND FORMATIVES.

1. FORMATION OF SUBSTANTIVES FROM ADJECTIVES.—Little change is usually necessary for the utilisation of any adjective as an abstract noun; but those heard are few in number. The servile particle belonging to the adjective, when it is *po* or *mo*, is generally altered into *pa* or *wa*. Thus *ts'ánmo* (pronounced *ts'em-mo*) "hot," becomes *ts'á-wa* "heat;" *münpo* "dark" becomes *mün-pa* darkness; *dhák-po* "pure," becomes *dhákpa* "purity;" &c.

Where we should add "ness" to an adjective, the Tibetan affix is *lū* or *tang*; e. g., *chhen-lū* "the greatness," *chhyuk-lū* "richness," *kön-tang* "scarceness, rarity," *ghóng-tang* "fulness."

In those cases where one idea is the direct converse of the other, the compound of the two words expressing these opposite ideas is used to specify the abstract quality of which their condition is an estimate. This is both curious and primitive. Thus, we have "the size" rendered *chhe-chhung* = "the great-small;" "the distance" is *ring-t'ung* = "the long-short;" "the temperature" *dhóng-ro* (གྲང་དྲོ་) = "the cold-warm;" "the weight" *ŷáng-chi* = "the light-heavy;" "the thickness" *bom-ṭ'á* = "the thick-thin;" "the height" *t'ön-mén* = "the high-low;" "one's means" *chhyuk-ül* = "the rich-poor;" and so forth.

Other similar substantives are derived from adjectives by the aid of the affix *khye* which itself signifies "difference."

These are akin to those just enumerated; *e. g.*, thickness" = *bom-khye*; a habit or custom (lit: "the accustomedness") = *ghom-khye*.

2. Verbal Substantives.—These may be formed by the addition of *lü* or *tang* to the verbal root; e. g., *ḍok-tang* the reading, *ŝa-tang* the eating, *t'unq-tang* the drinking, *do-lü* the going, the departure, *láng-lü* (*literally* "the being") the state, the condition, &c., &c.

3. The doer of an action is expressed by the syllable *khen* added on to the verbal root, and such forms are of very frequent occurrence. Thus: *sé'-khen* a slaughterer, murderer; *ḍok-khen* a reader, *jhyá-khen* the maker, *bák-khen* a carrier, coolie. Sometimes *po* is added instead of *khen*, but to the Infinitive, not the root.

This syllable may be also appended to noun substantives, when it serves to indicate one who has specially and habitually to do with the thing to which it is attached. So we have *shing-khen* the carpenter, *l̂am-khen* the guide, *ts'em-khen* a tailor, *tá-khen* groom, horse keeper, &c., &c.

4. Adjectives formed from Substantives and Verbs. *a.* In the colloquial of Tibet the derivation of adjectives from nouns is accomplished invariably by the use of the affix *chen*. The process is very regular and of extensive application, even the formation of ordinary possessives falling mostly under the same rule. Thus we have: *wang* power, *wangchen* powerful; *rák* fame, *rákchen* famous; *rin* the price, *rinchen* expensive, valuable; *sem* the mind, *semchen* intelligent; *n̂yák-ñyik* filth, *n̂yák-ñyik-chen* filthy; *lung* wind, *lungchen* windy.

In the case of possessives we find the genitive of the noun, where it expresses the quality or substance of another thing, rendered in the same way: *e. g.*, *dorjé serchen* a dorje of gold, or golden dorje; *khyim shingchen* a wooden house, or house of wood; but at times we might hear *ser dorje* and *shing-khyim* used for brevity with the same meaning.

The construction with *chen* is, however, frequently carried still further, being used for all manner of possession and even with the personal pronouns. So we occasionally hear *dukpo lámáchen* instead of *lámá-yi dukpo* for "the lama's coat," and *ŝhambu P'unts'o-chen* instead of *P'unts'o-i ŝhambu*, for "P'unts'o's cap." The pronouns "my," "his," &c., become *ngáchen, khochen*, &c., as indicated in the table of pronouns.

β. The affixes *chhok* and *nyen* are appended to verbal roots for the production of derivative adjectives, and indicate fitness, capability, &c. Thus from the verb *gál-wa* "to pass over," "cross," we obtain *gál-chhok* "passable" "fordable":

| | |
|---|---|
| *Dongtse-i wokné Nyang Chhu gál-chhok yö'*: | From below Dongtse the Nyang River is fordable. |
| *Yárka-la Ghang-lá-chhen Lá di jám-jám gál-chhok jhung*: | In summer the Kanglachhen Pass becomes smooth and passable. |
| *Di chhu di t'ung-nyen yimpe?* | Is this water drinkable? |

West of Shigátse *nyen* is more commonly heard than *chhok*; whilst further east *chhok* is always used and *nyen* quite disappears. Thus in Western Tibet we have *ŝa-nyen, khyer-nyen, gál-nyen*, &c.; whilst in the province of Ui are said *ŝa-chhok* eatable, *khur-chhok* portable, *do-chhok* capable of traverse, &c., *Rung* also occurs in the latter district as an affix of similar import: e. g., *ts'ong-rung* saleable.

The negative formative in these cases is usually *me'* subjoined in place of *chhok*, &c. Or else *mi* is placed first and *chhok* attached as before. *T'ung me', mi t'ung-chhok.*

γ. The negative substitute for *chen* is also *me'*. Thus we hear *shekchen* strong, *shekme'* weak (lit: "possessed of strength," "without strength;" *shek* or *she'* being a substantive = "strength"); *dhö'chen* tasty, *dhö'me'* tasteless. Also *go-me'* headless, and such like.

δ. The use with *chen* has already been shewn to be extensive. It is further available in more complex formations. Thus we find it combined with a double noun in such expressions as *jhyá-yib-chen* " having the shape of a bird " or " bird-shaped ; " *khyö'-rang-ghi yib-chen* " having your shape " = " like you."

Indeed *yib* itself is almost a formative and occurs frequently with *chen* :—

| | |
|---|---|
| That mountain is shaped like the head of a bull : | *P'á-gi ri dhe lang-ghi go yib chen du'.* |
| Yonder peak is like a Noi-jin king : | *P'á-gi ri-tse di Noi-jin gyalpo yib chen yö'.* |
| He resembles his sister : | *Khorang singmoi yib-chen yö'.* |
| It is like mine : | *Di ngái yib-chen du'* ; or *Di ngáchen yib-chen yong.* |

5. VERBAL EXPLETIVES.—The primary signification of the verb is capable of modification by means of certain syllables introduced or annexed. (i) *Bhag* is added to the verbal root and indicates inclination to do anything, disposition to feel anything. When used, the causative verb *jhe'pa* is generally employed in conjunction with it as an auxiliary to the primary verb ; a few examples will at once shew the occasions where *bhag* can be resorted to :—

| | |
|---|---|
| I am inclined to go on to another stage (of journey) : | *Ngárang-ghī ḍháng-sa šhem-ma t'uk ḍo-bhag jhe'.* |
| He is going to fall : | *Khorang gyel-bhag jhe'.* |
| If you don't tread carefully, I shall be disposed to beat you : | *Khyö tenpo mi kyö'-pai, khyö'rang la dung-bhag jhe'-gyu-yin.* |
| He is inclined to accompany you : | *Kho khyö'rang dhang nyampo gyu-bhag jhe'.* |

(ii) *Ḍhá-te* attached to the root of any verb acts as an augmentative, signifying that the action is carried on to an excess or at least in a degree greater than usual : *e. g.* :—

| | |
|---|---|
| He prays unremittingly : | *Kho kurim jhe'-ḍhá-te.* |

| | |
|---|---|
| The snow is falling abundantly : | *Khau-a di bhάp-ḍhά-te.* |
| Women chatter incessantly : | *Bhu'me' lάpchhά gyάk-ḍhά-te.* |
| Thank-you much, I have eaten abundantly : | *T'ukje-chhe, ngάrang to ŝά-ḍhά-te.* |
| Please drink plentifully : | *T'ung-ḍhά-te jhyi ro chi !* |

(iii) A kindred augmentative exists in the particle *ni*, which is used however in a different way. For the sake of emphasis the verbal root is repeated and *ni* is inserted between the repeated syllables. We may render the particle by such English expletives as "indeed," "assuredly," &c. :—

| | |
|---|---|
| They indeed said so : | *Dhenda ŝer ni ŝer-ne yö'.* |
| You shall assuredly go : | *Khyörang ḍo ni ḍo-gyu-yin.* |

It seems to be more frequently employed when some contrasting statement is about to be put forward :—

| | |
|---|---|
| Though he indeed went, he did no good : | *Khorang song ni song rung, demo chyö' ma jhung* or *Khorang song ni song-ne, ma le-mo chyö-ne yö'.* |

(iv) Leisure or time to do anything is very conveniently expressed by annexing the syllable *long* "vacant time" to the verbal root. Thus we obtain such a series as the following which might be indefinitely extended :—

| | | | |
|---|---|---|---|
| *Sά-long :* | time to eat. | *P'ep-long :* | time to come. |
| *Sim-long :* | leisure to sleep. | *Kyo-sang-la jhe'-long :* | time to take recreation. |
| *Ḍok-long :* | time to read. | *De'-long :* | time to stay. |

| | |
|---|---|
| *Ngάrang-la lap gyak-long me' :* | I have no time to chatter. |
| *Gompa dhe-la tok ŝhik-long re' :* | Is there time to look through that monastery ? |

(v) Opportunity in the sense of a chance or occasion offering may be expressed by adding *t'άp* as an affix to the verbal root; but though a favourite mode of speech with individuals, it is hardly a universal locution :—

| | |
|---|---|
| *Kyapgön dhang jál-kha nye't'áp yö'pe :* | Is there any chance of gaining audience of (or "access to") the Protector? |
| *P'ep-t'áp na, ngá-la lön nang ro chi :* | If there is an opportunity of going, please give me notice (send me word). |

# CHAPTER XII.

## IDIOMATIC PHRASES.

(1) A gerundial clause is grammatically speaking only an expanded adverb and an adverb is a contracted gerundial clause. Thus in Tibetan we often find the adverb expanded into a gerundial clause :—

| | |
|---|---|
| He was beating the horse very severely : | *Khorang ṭak-po jhye'-năi tá-ṛo dung-gin-duk.* |
| Pull the boat slowly to the shore : | *Kále jhye'-năi ḍam-tu ko-á di ḍong tang.* |

The literal translation of these sentences is :—

He, doing it severe, the horse was beating.
Doing it gently, unto the shore the boat pull.

(2) This mode of turning the phrase occurs also in such expressions as "in such a manner," "in the best way he could," "according to the king's command" :—

| | |
|---|---|
| The girl climbed up the ridge in the best way she could : | *Pumo-ī ghang ts'uk kyī jhye'-năi gang teng la dzek song.* |

*Note* :—GHANG TS'UK KYĪ is a phrase in itself, meaning "by what one is able" = "to the best of one's ability."

| | |
|---|---|
| The Regent is supposed to issue orders according to the Dalai Lama's wishes. | *De-sī di Gyá-wa Rimpo-chhe-ī gong-pai nang-s̆hin jhye' năi kăgyur nang-gyu nyam-pa-yin.* |

(3) Our very common expression "I think that" is rendered *Ngái sampa la* "to my thought ;" also "I know that"

can be phrased *Ngái shĕi-pa la* or when uttered in a warning manner *Ngái khyen la* :—

| | |
|---|---|
| I think that it will snow to-day: | *Ngái sampa la tering khau-a di bab-gyu-yîn.* |
| I think he will not stay here: | *Ngárang-ghi sampa-la kho dir dö̆gyu ma re'* (also *Kho-woi sampa la*, &c.) |
| I know you will not come back: | *Ngárang-ghi khyen-la khyörang lok yong-gyu-ma re'.* |
| I know that she went home: | *Ngái shéi-pa la mo-yī khyim la song.* |
| The hermit considered his place was lonely: | *Gomchhen-kyi sampa-la ngai sá-chha di empa du'.* |

Similar also is the construction in phrases beginning "I like" which are turned *ngá-i šhempa la* or *ngá-i ḍho-wa la* ("to my taste"); and again this is akin to the method of rendering "I want" by *goi* and *kho-wa.* (See Ch. VI, B. 13).

(4) When it is desired to express the arrival of the time at which anything should happen or has happened, &c., the verb *bábpa* ("to descend") is invariably made use of. Thus, for the phrase "It is time," a Tibetan will say "It has come down to the time of." So, for "It is time to start," he would turn the phrase "It has come down to the time of going:" *Gyu-pái dhui-la báb-jhung*; or, using another form of the participle: *Gyu-khen-kyi gang-la báb song* :—

| | |
|---|---|
| When the day for paying you arrives, I will remember this: | *Khyörang-la lá p'inpái nyin la báb-ne, kap-kyen di ḍhen-dhu šhuk yong* (སྐབས་རྐྱེན་འདི་དྲན་དུ་གཞུག་ཡོང་།) |

However, *ren du'* is a vulgarism for "It is time to."

(5) The verb "to be" and the pronoun in the dative is he mode of expressing "to have," "to possess," as already

indicated; but the construction with the dative occurs in other phrases also, such as :—

| | |
|---|---|
| *Dhá-ta ngárang-la ḍhelwa re'* : | I am busy now. ("There is business to me now.") |
| *Dhéring ngárang-la ne' yö'* : | I am unwell to-day. |
| *Pumo dhe-la shek-chhung yö'* : | That girl is weak. |
| *Dhe-la shek-kyī chhokpa yö'pe* : | Is that strong enough? |

(6) The *Verbum loquendi* takes the usual Oriental circumlocution. When a message is sent or any direction given what is to be said, the speaker projects himself into the position of his deputy, using in the direction the exact person in pronouns and verbs which he supposes will be spoken when his direction is carried out. Thus, "Tell him not to come" is in Tibetan phrased as "Tell him 'do not come;'" and "He told me he had seen you" would be turned "He told me 'I have seen him.'" These two sentences in Tibetan colloquial would be :—*Kho-la ma yong lap* and *Khorang ngárang dhe-la t'ong jhung lap song.* (*N. B.*—Probably in the last sentence *dhe-la* which we have used for "him"—really "that one"—would be expressed as *kusho-la* "the Saheb"). Sometimes, however, our European phrasing of such sentences is resorted to, and it is not unknown even in literary works where, *usually*, the expression of the *verbum loquendi* is still more formal.

(7) Not dissimilar is the usage where the solution of a doubtful state of things is requested, and where we should employ an interrogative "if" or "whether." Thus, "See if he is coming" becomes "See, is he coming?" Again "Try whether the bridge is firm" becomes "Try, is the bridge firm?" In Tibetan, therefore :—*Toi shik! khorang yong-ghi-yö'pe?* and *Ts'ö' toi shik! ŝampa tempo é yö'?* The last sentence might be varied into *ŝampai ts'ö' toi shik! tempo é yö'* : "Make trial of the bridge—is it firm?" Again :—

| | |
|---|---|
| *Khorang lep jhung-ngá shin-gi ma re'* : | "I do not know if he has come" |

However, both the positive and negative alternatives are often expressed in injunctions of this kind : *e. g.* :—

| | |
|---|---|
| Make strict enquiry whether the pass is blocked with snow, or not : | *Lá di khau-di chur-wa-i kar-ták jhyi-chik !—Yö'pa re' me' pa re' ?* |

(8) It will not be out of place once again to direct attention to the predilection of the Modern Colloquial for expanded forms, especially in the case of verbs. This usage is adopted in certain instances solely for perspicuity, as :—

| | | | |
|---|---|---|---|
| *m̂ik tá-wa ;* | instead of | *tá-wa :* | to see. |
| *to ŝi-wa ;* | „ „ | *ŝá-wa :* | to eat. |
| *ŷi-ge ḍok-pa ;* | „ „ | *ḍok-pa :* | to read. |
| *nyi' ñyal-wa ;* | „ „ | *ñyal-wa :* | to sleep. |

But in many cases, apparently from mere love of expansion :—

| | | |
|---|---|---|
| *ḍho-wa ta-wa ;* | for *ḍho-wa :* | to taste. |
| *sam-lo tang-wa ;* | for *sem-pa :* | to think. |
| *gyuk-shá lö'pa ;* | for *gyuk-pa :* | to run. |
| *ge'mo ghe'pa :* | for *gö'pa :* | to laugh. |
| *kü-ne khurwa :*<br>*ku-ma kü-pa ;* | } for *ku-wa :* | to steal. |

Similar expansions are noticeable in such phrases as *ká-le khákpo re' :* " it is difficult " now used for the old form *ká yö' ; dhárang sho-ge* " this morning " used for *dhárang ; ṭak-p'uk* " a cavern " for *p'ukpa ; chhu-t'o* " lips " for *chhu ;* &c. Again *be'pa :* " to try, endeavour " is never heard now, the present expression being *tsön-ḍü* (བརྩོན་འགྲུས) *jhye'pa ; kyong-wa* " to help " is supplanted by *ro-rám jhye'pa ;* whilst numerous other examples might be instanced.

---

## HONORIFICS.

(1) The custom of employing special words in lieu of the ordinary expressions when addressing persons of superior position remains to be briefly noticed. This usage, which in the Corean language has reached the extreme of elaboration, is likewise in the Tibetan tongue governed by systematic

principles. Not only are the names of things changed on these occasions but also the verbs and pronouns are affected, the adjectives alone retaining their common forms. Moreover, there are two departments of this respectful speech; first, the series of terms to be used in actually speaking to, or of, a person of rank or sanctity; secondly, a more limited set of words employed when talking of one self, or to others of ordinary position, *in the presence of* superiors. The first class are *Honorifics*, the second *Elegancies.*

(2) For practical purposes, a few of the more frequent terms will be sufficient to acquire. Especially should be noted the honorific forms of the pronouns; *khye'* and *nyi'rang* being used for *khyö'rang,* and *nge'* as an *Elegancy* should be employed instead of *ngárang.* However, in addressing superiors, the pronouns should not be used abruptly, but each sentence or question should commence with the word *kusho,* answering to our "Sir," or in the case of a great lama the better style is *Jetsün* or *Jetsün Rimpochhe.* When mentioning parts of the great man's body each term denoting these should have the syllable *ku* prefixed. The principle verbs to remember are the verbs *p'ep-pa* meaning both "to come" and "to go" and *p'ulwa* to express your "giving" to the superior while *nang-wa* denotes his "giving" to you. Also, instead of the common *jhye'pa,* we have *dze'pa* as the honorific and *gyi'pa* as the elegant synonym used in polite talk between equals. Other honorific verbs are the following, most of which in the original spelling have either ཟ་ or ཞ་ as the initial:—

| | | | |
|---|---|---|---|
| *ŝhu-wa:* | to address. | *she'-pa* / *sung-wa:* | to speak (of superior himself speaking). |
| *ŝhen-pa:* | to desire. | | |
| *ŝhe'-pa:* | to laugh. | *ši-wa:* | to see (superior seeing). |
| *shum-pa:* | to weep. | *sen-pa:* | to hear (ditto). |
| *šhū-pa:* | to sit, stay. | *šim-pa:* | to sleep (ditto). |
| *šheng-pa:* | to get up, rise. | *de-war sheg-pa:* | to die (ditto). |
| *šhe'-pa:* | to wish. | *sol-wa šhei-pa:* | to eat. |
| *šhei-pa:* | to receive, accept. | *sol-wa:* | to dress, put on. |

So, also, with the honorific names of things which chiefly, we find, commence with the letter *s* :—

| | | | |
|---|---|---|---|
| *ŝhák* : | day. | *u* : | the head. |
| *ŝháp* : | foot. | *shang* : | the nose. |
| *ŝhál* : | mouth, face. | *chhyák* : | hand. |
| *ŝhip* : | flour. | *pu* : | hair. |
| *šhok* : | the side. | *t'uk* : | heart, mind. |
| *sang-ma* : | food. | *sol-jhá* : | tea. |

One often hears *ku* prefixed in the sense of "your," e. g., *ku kham* : "your health," *ku sháp* : "your foot." Before utensils and eatables *sol* is put : *sol-shá* "meat," *sol-bing* "tea-pot." As an elegancy, *šhei* is prefixed to eatables and *ŝhal* to articles used in connection with the face ; thus :—

*šhei-pák* "bread," *šhei-kyem* "drink."
*ŝhál-ŝák* "a pipe," *ŝhál-gyen* "moustache."

When reference is made to personal articles belonging to the Grand Lama of Lhásá, or to his characteristics, the word *ser*, "golden," is prefixed. So his "tea" is styled *ser-jhá*, his "nose" *ser-shang*, &c. When he dies, moreover, they say *Ŝhing-la p'ep song* "he has gone to the field ;" while of a great man they would say *de-war sheg song*, and of any ordinary person *shi song* "he has died."

# CHAPTER XIII.
## COMPOSITION.

1. Order of Words.—The usual order of words in a simple sentence is Subject, Object, Predicate. Of the words attached to the chief substantive of the Subject, we note that any Possessive or Genitive is placed before the chief substantive, any ordinary adjectives immediately follow the substantive, any numeral follows the adjectives, any demonstrative pronouns, indefinite pronouns, or article follow the adjective or the numeral if there be one. The same order is observed in the component parts of the Object in any sentence. All extensions of the Predicate precede the main verb. In any sentence whatever, including gerundial and participial clauses, the verb stands last.

In any sentence where the verb takes an impersonal form, the dative connected therewith stands at the head of the sentence, *e. g. Woma-la serru gyak jhung :* "The milk has become bad;" or "To the milk badness has befallen."

The interrogative pronoun is placed immediately before the verb: *e. g., Luk-ghi kang pa chhak-paị shempa di ghána yö'pe :* "Where is the butcher who broke the sheep's leg?"

Any expansion of the substantive, of the nature of a relative clause, may either precede or follow the substantive upon which it is dependent. In the former case the participle of the clause is placed in the genitive; in the latter construction the participle remains in the case of the substantive which it follows, the article being placed after the clause. (See Ch. VI, 5, γ, N. B.)

2. Government by Verbs.—Many of the verbs in use of transitive sense take as Object an uninflected Accusative. There are, nevertheless, a certain number which require the Object to be inflected by the addition of the affix *la.* The case thus formed may be sometimes the Dative, sometimes the Accusative, and at times even the Locative which rarely in Central Tibetan assumes the ordinary Locative affix *na.* Other verbs, moreover, necessitate the assumption by the Object of the Ablative Case in *dhang.*

α. Verbs of giving, shewing, speaking, teaching, take the Dative in *la.*

β. The following verbs, with others, must be followed by the Locative in *la* :—*ŝhák-pa* to put, place, *tá-wa* to behold, look at, *duk-pa* to strike against, *ḍhe'pa* to dread, *gar-wa* to fasten.

γ. The Verbs requiring *dhang* are *ḍe-wa* to meddle with, *khá-ṭ'ál-wa* to separate from, *jalwa* to wait upon, pay one's respects to, *ṭ'e'-pa* to meet, with a few others.

3. Continuative Particles.—In Tibetan composition the finite verb occurs much less frequently than in European idiom. The main clause or sentence is almost undiscoverable in any long statement or paragraph. The whole style of composition is a chain of gerundial and participial clauses, depending only technically upon one another. The chain of clauses or sentences proceeds continuously, each successive clause in form, though not in sense, a sequence from the other, until at length a final verb—by no means the most important or main one in meaning—brings a break in the connexion. In written compositions this style is more observable than in lengthy spoken sentences, but the better-educated resort to the participial or gerundial construction even in speaking. All the affixes forming the different gerunds ennmerated in Chapter VI. Section B, might be denominated with equal accuracy Continuative Particles, for nearly any one from

among those may be added to the concluding verb of each successive clause to carry on the chain of connexion. Of course where the construction, in signification as well as in external form, is really gerundial, the choice of particle annexed should be differentiated in accordance with the distinction of kinds of gerunds already set forth, and the sense may in fact be affected by such choice. In addition to the affixes already given, *te* and *dhang* may be mentioned as Continuative Particles; *te* being added to the root of any verb and *dhang* being appended to the infinitive; or, in other words, *dhang* requires to be connected with the verb to which taste or random selection may have attached it by the insertion of *pa* or *wa* after the root of such verb.

Example of use of Continuative Particles :—

"The soldiers arrived at the city and remained standing outside the gates. They were clad in yellow coats and felt boots, and wore on their heads Lit'ang-shaped hats. By means of those hats we knew they did not belong to the Lhásá Government; and were afraid."

For translation, we arrange the wording thus :—

"The soldiers having arrived at the city, remained standing outside the gates. Being clad in yellow coats and felt boots, and wearing on their heads Lit'ang-shaped hats, because of those hats, we knew they did not belong to the Lhásá Government; and were afraid."

*Mákmi-ts'o ḍhong-khyer-la leb-nai gyalgo-i p'i-la lang-nai de'pa dhang chhupa serpo bhe-pák-la ghyön-la dhe-yi go-la Lit'ang-yibchen šhámo ghyön-pai šhámo dhe-yi chhyir-dhu kho-ts'o De-wa Jong-la ma t'i-wa ngo-shei-te ngáchák ts'er jhung.*

In the foregoing there is no finite verb, nor any but gerundial construction, observable until the concluding verb *ts'er jhung*. However, in the English sense of the term, that is not correct; *de'pa* and *ngo-shei-te* are in reality both of them finite verbs which, after the Tibetan style, are conjoined, each to the sentence following, by *dhắng* and *te*, respectively, which are thus Continuative Particles, pure and simple.

So seldom are these Particles needed in the Colloquial, that nothing further on the subject can be added here.

4. Letters and Correspondence. In modern letter-writing, especially in commercial and domestic correspondence, the Colloquial development of the language is clothed in the old literary style only so far as the spelling of the words is concerned. Thus if the rules for pronouncing the written forms are applied in inverse order to the details of grammar and vocabulary as given in this work, there can be no difficulty in epistolary correspondence, provided the characters, printed and cursive, are first mastered. The rules as to spelling and pronunciation are explained elsewhere, and if the printed characters, as there displayed, should be used by the traveller or student in letter-writing, any Tibetan will at least be able to read his effusions. To acquire the cursive alphabet may be taken as a work of supererogation for the majority of those interested in this tongue. However, in Csoma Korösi's Grammar the various types of handwriting are fully illustrated, and doubtless by practice fair proficiency in Tibetan calligraphy would be easily attainable.

As specimens of the modern epistolary style, we transcribe two letters received by the author, one from a Tibetan lama of moderate acquirements, the other from a man well-known as a Tibetan scholar. Naturally, we give these in the ordinary printed character, appending likewise a literal translation of each epistle.

### LETTER FROM TIBETAN LAMA—

བདག་གི་དྲིན་ཆེན་བླ་མ་པ་དེར་ས་ཧེབ་ལ།

སྙན་ནས་དང་འདུན་གྱི་ཞུ་གསོལ་ཉིད་སྐུ་གཟུགས་བདེ་མོར་བཞུགས་

པ་ལས་སྔོན་ནས་ཡི་གེ་ཅིག་འབྱོར་བ་མ་ཚད་ད་ལྟ་ཀྱང་ཡི་གེ་གཅིག་
གནང་འབྱོར་ཐུགས་རྗེ་ཤིན་ཏུ་ཆེ་ འདིར་བདག་ཀྱང་བླམ་དཀོན་མཆོག་གི་
བཀའ་དྲིན་ལས་བདེ་བར་ཡོད་ ཟླ་བ་བརྒྱད་དགུ་ཞིག་གི་སྔོན་ནས་འདི་ན་
མི་གཅིག་གི་ཙུར་རྗེ་བཙུན་མི་ལ་རས་པའི་དཔེ་ཆ་ཞིག་མཆིས་འདུག་ཀྱང་
མི་དེ་ནས་དཔེ་ཆ་རྒྱ་ཊཾ་བཅོ་ལྔ་ལ་ཚོང་ཚར་འདུག ད་རུང་ཉིད་ཀྱི་ཕྱིར་མི་
ལ་རས་པའི་དཔེ་ཆ་ཞིག་འཚོལ་སྐབས་ཡོད་ ཐོབ་ན་དེ་ཕྲལ་ཉིད་ལ་གསལ་
ཆ་ཕུལ་ཡོང་ལགས་ ད་རེས་འདིར་མི་གཅིག་ཙར་རྒྱ་ཊཾ་བཅུ་གསུམ་བྱེད་
དེ་སློབ་དཔོན་པདྨའི་རྣམ་ཐར་ཐང་ཡིག་གསེར་འཕྲེང་ཞིག་ཚོང་རྒྱུ་འདུག་
པའི་ ཉིད་ལ་མཁོ་བྱེད་ཡོད་ན་རྒྱ་ཊཾ་བཅུ་གསུམ་མ་ནི་ཨོར་གྲར་ལ་ཕྲལ་
ཏུ་བཏང་རོགས་ཞུ་ འདི་ནས་དཔེ་ཆ་དེ་ཉོས་ནས་ སྐུར་ཕྲལ་སྐུར་བཏང་
ཡོང་ ཕྲན་དབུ་རྒྱན་གྱི་མཚོ་ནས་ས་ལམ་མང་པོ་བཅས་ཕུལ།

(*Translation.*)

To his Graciousness the Padre Saheb Lama—

Faithful and earnest wishes are presented from your humble one that you are well in bodily health. Very, very great thanks not only for preparing your former letter but also for sending a letter just now. Here am I a lama well also by the favour of God. Some eight or nine months ago, a man here had a book by the Reverend Milaraspa; but the book was sold by that man for fifteen rupees (*gyá-tang*). I am looking out for Milaraspa's book for you once more. If it is obtained particulars shall be immediately transmitted to you. At present a man here will sell a copy of "The Skein of Golden Precepts and Biography of the Lotos Teacher" (*i. e.* The *Padma Tang-yig*), asking thirteen rupees. So if you require it, please to send at once in a Money Order (མ་ནི་ཨོར་ཌར་) thirteen rupees. When I have bought the book from him, it shall be sent as quickly as possible. Many salaams are offered from your humble Urgyan Gyá-ts'o.

[It should be noted that the Tibetan of the foregoing letter is not in places strictly accurate. Thus, several times the Ablative is used instead of the Instrumental Case. The use of གནང་ with འབྱོར་ should be remarked in both letters. "Salaam," too, is not a Tibetan greeting.]

## LETTER FROM A TIBETAN SCHOLAR—

དཔལ་ཡིས་སྲུས་ཁྲི་སྟུའི་རིང་ལུགས་དྲི་མ་མེད་པར་འཛིན་པའི་དགེ་བའི་བཤེས་གཉེན།

ཧཱུྃ་བཙུན་དགོར་ཧམ་སེཧྣ་བེར་གས་བླ་མ་རིན་པོ་ཆེའི་ཞབས་པར་དྲུང་དུ་གས་ཞུ། དེང་ཡང་ཟླ་བ་བཅུ་གཉིས་པའི་ཚེས་བརྒྱད་ལ་ཀ་ཊ་ཀ་ནས་ཕྱག་བྲིས་གནང་འབྱོར་བཀའ་དྲིན་ཆེ། འདིར་ཡང་འབྱུང་ཁམས་བདེ་བར་གནས་ཞིང་གཞུང་མཆོག་ཆེན་པོའི་ཞབས་འདེགས་ལ་བརྩོན་ཁྲལ་དུ་མཆིས། མཚམས་ཞུ། སྐུ་ཉིད་རང་དང་ལྷུམ་མེ་མེམ་ལྷ་མོ་ལྷན་ཀྱིས་སྐུ་གཟུགས་བདེ་ཞིང་བཞུགས་འཛུགས་པ་ནི་ཤིན་ཏུ་ལེགས། ཉིད་རང་གི་མཛོད་ཋ་འབྲས་ལྗོངས་སྐད་ཀྱི་དཔེ་ཆ་དེ་བཞིན་བདག་གིས་བརྟག་པ་དཔྱད་པའི་སྐབས་ཡིན་ལགས། སར་ཨོལ་ཕེ་རེཊ་ཀྲབཊ་ནས་འདིར་ཉིད་རང་གི་ཆོས་གསུམ་གྱི་ཕྱག་བྲིའི་དཔེ་གཅིག་ཀྱང་བཟུངས་འདུག་པས། སང་ནང་དེ་སློར་ཡིག་ལན་ཕྱུལ་གྱི་ཡིན་ལགས། སླར་ཡང་སྐུ་ཉིད་རང་ནས

བདག་ལ་བརྩེ་བའི་དགོངས་པ་མི་གཡེལ་ནས་ཕེབས་ཚོགས་ཀྱང་རིམ་བཞིན་སྟོལ་བ་མཁྱེན། ཞུ་འདིགས་སེམས་དཀར་མོ་བཅས་ཆོས་བཟང་ལ་དགེ་བར་སྤྲུལ།

(*Translation.*)

Down before the lotos-feet of the most precious lama the Reverend Gerham Sendbergas, the friend of virtue who lays hold on the 30,000 stainless observances of the chivalrous!

Respects be offered! Having to-day received your letter written from Katak, on the 8th day of the twelfth month—many thanks. Here am I continuing still well in health and profoundly anxious to render any services with the very utmost attention.[1] Please excuse what is omitted[2] (*i. e.*, what may be omitted in my proffers of service)! You yourself[3] and your wife, the partner of your seal, the goddess mem being well in bodily health and prosperously settled, it is indeed well. With regard to your work—the book of the Sikkim language, I have had occasion to examine it thoroughly. Your letter which you wrote on the 3rd instant has been sent here from Sir—————— To-morrow a reply to it

[NOTES ON THE ABOVE.—1 "With the very utmost attention;" གཞུང་མཆོག་ཆེན་པོའི་

2 Literally མཚམས = "Vacant or intermediate space," and hence "What is left out," and so is now always inserted after the polite expressions and proffers of service which form the preface to every Tibetan letter. It implies a request that what has been left unsaid through want of space or inadvertence should please (ཞུ) be taken as meant to be written down.

3 སྐུ signifies really "body," and is used as an honorific form for "yourself," *i. e.*, "Your own body." The ordinary word for "body" is ལུས *lüi*.

shall be despatched.[1] As to the kind expressions of thought which, unwavering, come yet again from you to me, pray accept my repeated thanks. Sincere[2] wishes and compliments for happiness on the good date (*i. e.*, Christmas)[3] are offered.

[1] Mark here the future passive tense ཕུལ་ཀྱི་ཡིན་ལགས་ "Shall have been sent," or "Shall be sent." ཕུལ་ is honorific for ཇིངས་ as ཕེབ་ is for ཡོང་བ་

[2] དཀར་མོ་ means, of course, "white," and hence, in this phrase, may be rendered "pure" or "sincere."

[3] The writer of the letter, though not a Christian, very appropriately and thoughtfully renders "Christmas Day," in this decorous expression.]

# PART II.

## CONVERSATIONAL EXERCISES

AND

## TECHNICAL LISTS.

# CONVERSATIONAL EXERCISES

AND

# TECHNICAL LISTS.

## NOTES ON CERTAIN LETTERS.

Wherever GH occurs in these pages it will be best understood (when spoken by Englishmen) if it is sounded merely as K. Thus *ghang* "what," may be conveniently pronounced *kanġ*; *ghá-pa*, "where," as *ká-pa*. So also DH, though correct, may be always sounded T, and indeed D is by natives frequently sounded as T. Thus *dhön-la* "for" (Hind: *ke-waste*) is heard often as *tönla*, *dhátá* "now" as *tátá*, (or vulgarly *tandá*) *ghánḍe* "*how*," may (though improperly) sound *kánṭe*; and the common word *dhang* should be pronounced *tãng*.

So, too, JH, though correct, had best be spoken as is CH. Thus *jhá* "tea," may be sounded *chá*; but where the *y* sound follows *jh* as in *jhyá* "a bird," either *jhyá* or *chyá* may be used. The common verb *jhye'pa* "to do," often sounds *chye'pa*, and even vulgarly as *chyi-pa*. We advise *chye'pa* here; imperative: *chyī* "do!" Again; we print in these pages BH in words spelt in Tibetan orthography with initial *B*; but we advise the invariable use of P for BH. Thus *Pö'pa* "a Tibetan," for the more correct *Bhö'pa*.

We have printed LH throughout, but as the letter is somewhat guttural, the *h* should be sounded before the *l*; so, we say for *Lhásá*, always *Hlásá*, and *lham* "a boot," is *Hlam*

As to UI, EI, and AI, by which we have generally represented the elided final *s* in *us, es,* and *as,* these are not diphthongal sounds; but though the *i* is sounded separately, it must follow the *u, e,* and *a* so quickly and lightly as to be hardly audible as a distinct letter. In the case of AI, the sound of our diphthong *ai* in "rain," "stain," is approached and for convenience we recommend that sound, or that of the open *e*. So *yö'pai* "is!" may be pronounced *yö'pe.*

Final O in short affixes sounds like *u*, as in *yákpo* "good," *tákpo* "hard," &c.

The vowel *e* in some words seems vulgarly to change to the vowel *i*. Thus *ngá she-ghi-du'* "I know," is heard as *ngá shin-ghi-du'* and *jhye'-kin-du'* "is doing," is vulgarly pronounced *chyin-kin-du'.*

In Colloquial Tibetan the final letter of a syllable is generally very indistinctly heard; and certain letters when occurring as finals are completely dropped. Final G takes the sound of *k*, and in many parts of Tibet is hardly audible, at least in most words. Thus *t'ukje* "thank-you," sounds *t'u-je*; *yákpo* generally *yá'po.* Final B is changed to *p*, as *leb-jhung* "arrived," which is pronounced *lep-chung*; but this final *p* is frequently unsounded, as in *t'u(p)ŷong* "shall be able," *pá(k)-lé(p)* "broad." Where D is the last letter it is always inaudible, save for an abrupt almost imperceptible breathing. Accordingly, we have invariably omitted final *d*, at the same time indicating the elision by an apostrophe; e. g., *jhye'pa* "to do," for *jhyed-pa.* Final L, though often heard in the province of Ui, is frequently dropped, especially in Tsang; *e. g., Pál-po,* "a Nipalese man," sounds *Pá'po,* or *Pe'bo.* After *u* it modifies that vowel into *ü*, as *yü'* for *yul* "*country.*"

In Jaeschke's and Csoma's works, no distinction as to sound is made between the letters *ch* and *cḥy, chh* and *chhy,* and *j* and *jy*. As in listening to natives we have clearly detected the *y* sound, we have generally in these pages indicated the *y*-letter words where they occur. Thus *jha* (or *cha*) is "tea," but *jhya* (or *chya*) is "a bird;" *chhe* = "great" and "very," and *chhye* = "flour," *chhung-wa* = "small," but *chhyung-wa*, "to take out" "remove;" *je' pa* = "to forget," but *jye'-pa* = "to open."

[Where any difficulty is experienced in sounding the cerebrals *ṭ*, *ṭ'*, *ḍ*, *ḍh*,—and one is very apt to sound the ordinary dentals instead—it will be best to use *tr*, *t'r*, *dr*, and *dhr*, in their place. According to Mr. Rockhill this latter pronunciation is the Lhásá method. Sarat Chandra Das and others, who have actually visited Lhásá, contradict this assertion; but, although we are decidedly opposed to Mr. Rockhill's phonetic system in general, we are bound to admit that we have frequently heard the *tr* and *dr* used. Thus *drá* may be said for *ḍá* "the voice, *wö-tro* for *wö'-ṭo* "light" *mándro* for *ma ḍo* don't go," *t'rák* for *ṭ'ák* "blood," &c., nevertheless, the other is deemed the proper pronunciation by the educated.]

## BRIEF ORDERS.

| | |
|---|---|
| Come here: | *Ts'ur shok* or *Diru shok!* |
| Come near: | *Ts'ánai shok!* |
| Come back: | *Lokne shok!* |
| Come inside (*or* Come into the house): | *Nang la shok!* |
| Come to me: | *Nge tsar shok!* |
| Come along with me: | *Ngárang nyampo shok!* |
| Don't come to-day: come to-morrow: | *Dhe-ring ma yong: sang-nyin shok!* |
| Don't come so close: | *Dinḍa ts'ánai ma yong!* |
| Go outside: | *Chhyi-lok song!* |
| Go away (Be off)! | *Ha-la gyuk!* |
| Go in front: | *Ngen-la gyu* (often *Hen-la gyu*)! |
| Go behind: | *Shuk-la gyu!* |
| Don't go so quickly: | *Dinḍa gyo-po mándro!* |
| Don't go far: | *P'ár-tsam mándro!* |
| Get up: | *Kyére lang chik!* or *Yar long!* |
| Keep straight (Hind: *Sidha karo*): | *Khaddu chyi* or *Khaddu gyu!* |
| Make haste: | *Ts'á-ḍhák jhyi ŝhik!* |
| Run quickly: | *Gyō-po gyuk!* |
| Listen here (Attend)! | *Tsur-la nyön ŝhik!* |
| Give your mind to it: | *Nang-dhák jhyi ŝhi'* (*jhyi* sounds *chyi*)! |
| Take care: | *Rikpa jhyi*; or *Rik ḍim!* |
| Don't trouble me (Hind: *Dik mat karo*): | *Ngá-la nyăp chü ma p'i!* |
| Catch hold of it: | *Di-la zim*; also *Di-la she'!* |
| Stop! Stop: | *Ghuk-ta: ghuk-ta!* |
| Remain here: | *Di-pa dö' shik!* or *Dipa gu!* |
| Stay waiting here (Hind: *Hazir raho*): | *Di-pa gu'ne dö'!* |
| Sit down: | *Sá-la dö'* or (politely, with gesture): *Shu!* |

| | |
|---|---|
| Is it there or not—See: | *Dhépa 'indu mindu—Tö shok!* |
| It is time to go now: | *Tanḍa do-ren du'!* |
| Send him here: | *Diru kho tong!* |
| Hold in your dog, please: | *Rang-ghi khyi-la zim roch* (for *ro chik*)! |
| Throw it away: | *Yuk ŝhok!* |
| Blow up the fire: | *Mé p'u!* |
| Set it down; put it up; lift it up: | *Sá-la ŝho'; ŷar ŝho'; ŷá-te t'o!* |
| Fetch the horse here: | *Ts'ur tá-po di ṭ'i!* |
| Bring me more water: | *Chhu dhárung khur shok!* |
| Bring the Sahib some tea: | *Kusho-la so'jhá khur shok!* |
| Take away these things: | *Chhá-khá di-ts'o khur song!* |
| See where he goes: | *Ghá-la ḍo-wai kho-la tö shok!* |
| Look over there—up there—down there: | *P'á-gi-la—ŷá gi-la—m̂á-gi-la tö dhang!* |
| Give me that, please: | *Ngá-la dhe-ga nang roch* (for *ro chik*)! |
| That's enough (Hind: *Bas*)! | *Shang yong*; or *yong nge!* |
| Take off your cap: | *Shámbhu t'u!* |
| Don't forget (Hind: *Mat bhulo*)! | *Mánjĕ!* (last syllable abrupt)! |
| Keep in the middle: | *Kiltu ŝhog!* or *kiltu chyī!* |
| Go inside the blankets: | *Másen bug-la gyu!* |
| Go and see: | *Tá-la song!* |
| Never mind what I said (Hind: *Kuchh parwa né*): | *Ke-chha di tönla mi ṭo'!* |
| It is time to wake up: | *Nyi' se'pai ren du'!* |
| Put it back again: | *Di lokne ŝho'!* |
| Throw this thing away: | *Chhá-khá di yuk tong!* |
| Don't make such a noise: | *Wur dhenḍa ma gyap!* |
| Go and see who it is: | *Su yö'pe tá-la song!* |
| Make ready to start: | *Ḍo-gyu t'ál-ḍik chyi!* |
| Never mind the rest (what remains): | *Ḷhák-lüi la mi to'!* |
| Don't let it fall: | *Di ŝák ma chuk!* |
| Now you may go: | *Khyö' tanda ḍo chok!* |

| | |
|---|---|
| Go and call him : | *Gyu-ne kho-la ke tang ŝho' !* |
| Tell him to come here : | *Diru shok kho-la lap !* |

## EVERY DAY QUESTIONS AND ANSWERS.

| | |
|---|---|
| Can you speak Hindustani : | *Khyö' Hindi ké lap t'up-ki-yö' pai ?* |
| Can you speak English : | *Khyö' P'iling-ghi ké lap chok-pai ?* |
| What is this called : | *Di-la ghang ŝer-yong ?* |
| Speak in the Tibetan language : | *Pö'-kyi ké-la lap.* |
| What is the name of that hill : | *Há-gi ri-yi ming-la ghang ŝer ?* |
| I don't know : | *Ngá shen-ghi me'* (often : *shin-ghi má re'*) ? |
| Do you know that man : | *Khyö' mi di ngo-she yö' pai ?* |
| Do you understand : | *Khyörang ko jhung-nga ?* |
| He has a bad character : | *Kho-la shi-gyü' n̂gempa re'.* |
| Who is this boy : | *P'ugu di su re' ?* |
| Do you know : | *Khyö' shin-ghi-re'ta ?* (*shin* is really *she'*). |
| It is not mine : | *Di ngá-chen ma re'.* |
| That is mine : | *P'ági ngái yin.* |
| Is that for me : | *Ngái chhyirtu dhe-ga re' ?* |
| Has he come yet : | *Tandá khorang lep jhung-nga ?* |
| Who knows : | *Su she ?* |
| Did you know : | *She' jhung-nga ?* |
| What are you doing : | *Khyö' ghang jhe'-kyi-yö'* (or *chyi-ki-yö'*) *?* |
| I know : | *Shin-ghi-re'.* |
| Nothing ; Sir : | *Kusho ; ghang mindu'.* |
| Why are you doing that : | *Khyö' dhenḍa ghang-la jhe'-kyi-yö' ?* |
| Why are you asking : | *Khyö' ghang-la ḍi-t'ok ḍi-ki-yö' ?* |
| I don't understand ; did not understand : | *Ngá ké-chhá shin-ghi me' ; ké-chha she ma jhung ?* |
| Don't forget : | *Ma jé-pa jhyi* (sounds *chyi*). |
| I will not forget : | *Ngárang jé mi yong.* |

| | |
|---|---|
| Don't chatter so: | *Dhenḍe ke-chhá ma gyap:* |
| Don't let him forget: | *Kho je ma chuk?* |
| Everything has been arranged: | *Ghang-ga gho-chö' jhung.* |
| How can we go? | *Ghanḍe ḍo t'up yong?* |
| How was that done? | *Le-ka di ghande jhung song-nga?* |
| I can't say: | *Ngárang she' ma chok.* |
| Look! do you see him? | *Mik tö-dhang! kho-la t'ong-ngá?* |
| Look there! what is that? | *Déyi tö dhang! Dhe-ga ghang yö'?* |
| When did you see him? | *Khyö'-kyī kho-la ghá-dhü t'ong jhung?* |
| Where have you been? | *Khyö'rang ghá-ru song?* |
| What do you say? | *Khyö' ghang lap-ki-du'?* |
| When did he bring it? | *Di-ka kho-i ghá-dhü khur lep song?* |
| Where did you put it? | *Di-ka ká-pa ŝhak-pa-yin?* |
| What do you want? | *Khyö' la ghá go yö'.* |
| It will not be wanted: | *Ghang mi go.* |
| Can you begin at once: | *Khyö' t'el-t'el-la go-dzuk chok-ka'.* |
| I shall begin the work now: | *Tanḍa l̂e-ka di go-dzuk yong.* |
| Call him to come here immediately: | *Kho-la ke tong dhang, diru tanda t'eltu shok!* |
| Oh, never mind! (Hind: *Kuchch parwa nahin*): | *Ke-chha te dhönla mito'!* |
| Tell him not to come: | *Kho-la lap, ma yong.* |
| Why did you not come yesterday? | *Dang-la ghang-la yong-pa-me'* (or *lep-ma-song*)! |
| I was ill yesterday: | *Ngá dang-la ná jhung.* |
| Where do you live? | *Khyö' nai-ts'ang ká-pa yö'* or *Khyö' ká-pa de-ghi yö'?* |
| I live in this place: | *Nge nai-ts'ang di chhyok-la yö'* ("my dwelling is in this place"). |

| | |
|---|---|
| Run for my letters to the Post Office: | *Yik-khyim-la nge ŷi-ge chhyirtu gyuksha lö'tang !* |
| What is your name? | *Khyö-kyi ming-la ghang ŝer ?* |
| From what country do you come? | *Khyörang yu(l) ghá-ne yin ?* |
| I am from Gal-rong: | *Ngá Ghal-rong-le yin* (or *lep jhung*). |
| You must really come with me: | *Khyö' nenten nge nyampo yong go yö'.* |
| Be it as you command, Sir: | *Kusho ; ká p'ep rang nang !* |
| Ask him if he got the letter: | *Kho-la lap dhang ; ŷige dhe t'op jhung-nga.* |
| He says he received it: | *Kho lap-ki-du' ; dhe-la t'op jhung.* |
| How much shall I give you? | *Khyö'-la ter-wa ghá ts'ö ?* |
| Give me what you think right: | *Nang ro nang ku-khyen kusho ; khyen khyen.* |
| You know best, Sir: | *Kusho ; khyen khyen !* |
| May leave-of-absence be granted me: | *Ngá-la gong-pa nang ro chi'* (stress on *ro*). |
| Never mind what you have to do, come: | *Khyörang ghang jhye' gyu na ŷang khye' mi du', shok !* |
| Have you a substitute (Hind: *badli*)? | *Khyörang-la ts'áp yö'pe ?* |
| Please, give me an advance: | *Ngá-la ngül ngá-chhyi nang ro nang.* |
| I dismiss you: | *Khyörang-la gong-p'ok nang chi'.* |
| Sahib, do not be angry with me: | *Kusho ; ngá-la gong-pa* (དགོངས་པ) *ma t'sum ;* (instead of *ngá-la* often *t'em-bhu-la* " with the little humble one "). |

## ASKING THE WAY.

| | |
|---|---|
| Whose house is that? | *Nang dhe so-kyi re'?* |
| What is the name of this village? | *Ḍong-pa di m̂ing-la ghang ŷö'-pe?* |
| It is a large town: it is called Tse-t'ang: | *Di ḍong-khyer chhe di; Tse-t'ang ŝer yin.* |
| Is there a lodging here or not? | *Di-pa nai-ts'ang ŷö'pa re' me'-pa re'?* |
| On the further side of the town, is there any road out or not: | *P'á-lok-la ḍong-khyer-ne l̂am chi ŷö' pa re' me' pa re'?* |
| See those men building the new wall; the road begins there: | *Mi-t'so tsik-pa sarpa gyap-khan dhe-la tö' tang! Lam di p'á-gi go-dzuk.* |
| What is yonder peak named? | *P'á-gi ri-tse-la m̂ing ghang ser-ki-yö'?* |
| Shew me the way to Gyamda: | *Gyamdá-i l̂am di ngá-la ten roch?* |
| Kindly shew me the way: | *Lam di ten roch!* |
| Where to?—To Ṭáshilhümpo: | *Ghá-la?—Ṭáshi-lhümpo la.* |
| Where is the bridge? | *Sampa di ghá re'?* |
| Where are you going to? | *Khyö' ghá-ru ḍo-ghi-ŷimpe?* |
| Is it an easy path? | *Lam-kha di jám-jám yö'dhá?* |
| It is only a foot-track: | *Kang-l̂am chi man-na mi yong.* |
| The path is steep and narrow: | *Lamkhá di ghyen-ghyen tokpo du'.* |
| Is it a broad path? | *Dhe l̂amkhá yang-po chi yö'-pe?* |
| It is a steep ascent to the Pass: | *Lá di-yi ghyen-la ŝarpo du'.* |
| Is the road to Samye level? | *Samye kyi l̂am nyom-nyom é du'.* |
| How far is it from here to Shá-lu? | *Di-ne Shá-lu-la t'á-ring-t'ung ghá ts'o?* |
| Where is the road? | *Lam ká-pa ŷö'?* |
| Don't go across that bridge: | *Há-gi ŝam-pai ṭ'e' l̂am-la man-dro!* |
| How far is it to the next halting stage? | *Nye-wai sim-dang-sá la t'á ghá ts'o?* |

| | |
|---|---|
| Is it a long way to Chhábdo? | *Chhámdo la t'a ring-po é yö'?* |
| Which is the way? | *Lam ghang-ghi yin?* |
| Do you see that tree on the other side of the river? | *Tsang-poi s̆hō s̆hen-ngoi-la, khyö' shing dhe mik t'ong-ngá?* |
| Say that again; I don't understand: | *Lok-ne lap nang; ngá há-gho mi yong.* |
| Ah! I understand: | *O-ho! ngá há gho jhung.* |
| How can I find a way across the river? | *Ngárang-ghī chhui t'e' l̂am di t'op t'u' yong-nga?* |
| Go the second path on the left side: | *Yön-ngoi-la angki nyi-pai l̂am-khá gyu.* |
| Come along! keep in the middle: | *Nyampo shok! kiltu shok:* |
| Go straight on; afterwards slant-off to the left (*lit:* "slanting, go"): | *Ḍong-po ḍong-po song: lar-ne yön-ngö'-la kyok-ne gyuk.* |
| Keep straight: | *Khădu chyi* (i. e., *jhyi'*). |
| The path turns to the right: | *Lam di yái-ngö'-la ḍo ghi-du'.* |
| The right-hand path; left-hand path; a short cut: | *Yái-lak l̂am; yön-lak l̂am; gyok-l̂am.* |

## THE WEATHER.

| | |
|---|---|
| The night is very dark: | *Ts'en di la mün-nak song.* |
| It is becoming almost dark: | *Nám-shrö' yol song.* |
| It is now dark: | *Tanda münpa nák-po re'.* |
| It is now light: | *Tanda t'ang karpo re'.* |
| Rain is going to fall: | *Chhárpa bap-yong.* |
| The snow will not cease to-day: | *Te-ring khau-a di chhé mi yong.* |
| The snow is melting quickly: | *Khau-a di gyokpo* (sounds *gyo'-po*) *s̆hu ghi-du'.* |
| The rain has ceased now: | *Chhárpa di tanḍa chhé song.* |
| I see the mist rising: | *Ngá mukpa* (often *mu'pa*) *lang-wa t'ong-ghi-yö'.* |
| A snow-storm is at hand: | *Khá-ts'up chi' t'a-nyesa-la yong-ghi-du'.* |

| | |
|---|---|
| Thick mists are on the mountain side: | *Mu'pa mongpo ri-lok-la du'.* |
| It will be fine to-day: | *Dhering nam t'ang yong.* |
| Can you run quickly? | *Khyö'rang gyokpo gyukshá lö'-t'up yong-nga* (*gyuk-shá lö'pa* "to run.") |
| Don't go there; there is no shelter there: | *Dhe-pa mándro dhe-pa chhár-yap me'* (or *chhár-kyip me'.*) |
| Pitch the tent at once: the rain will pour down this instant: | *Ghur di ma-t'okts'e* (or oftener *tanda t'eltu*) *sho' tang: tanda lamsang chhárpa gyap yong.* |
| Climb the rock: over there is rain-shelter—beneath that boulder: | *Ṭak-la zok; há-kiru chhár-yap du'—p'á-bong-ghi wokla* (or *p'ong-ghi, &c.*). |
| The Pass is filled with snow: | *La di khau-a-yī kák du'.* |
| The mists will pass away when the rain ceases: | *Chhárpa chhé-ne, mu'pa di yel ḍo yong.* |
| The sun is very hot: | *Nyi-ma há-chang ts'ápo du'.* |
| The sun will cause pain in your head: | *Nyi-ma-yī khyö' kyi go nai yong.* |
| It snows: it is freezing: | *Khau-a bap-ki-du': khyák-ghi-du'.* |
| Down there, there is rock-shelter; under that it will be warm: | *Mákiru ḍhák-kyip yö'; dhe-yi-wá'la ḍhömmo yong.* |
| The river is frozen hard: | *Chhu di takpo khyák jhung.* |
| When does the moon rise: | *Dáwa ghá-tui* (or *ká-tü*) *shar yong?* |
| There is no moon to-night: | *P'iro di dáwa mindu'.* |
| The wind is rising; it is very cold*: | *Lhákpa lang-ghi-re'; nam há-chang ḍhangmo du'.* |
| The air will be mild at Shi-kha: | *Shi-kha la ngá-rá di jámpo rak yong.* |
| Shake the cloak well: | *Chhár-bhí di sop-sop jhyi nang.* |

* In such phrases as "it is cold," "it is warm," "it is fine," Tibetans always say: "the sky is cold, warm, fine, &c. Thus *nam lŏmpa du'*: "it is wet;" but only, of course, when speaking of the weather or atmosphere.

| | |
|---|---|
| When the mists are thick in a valley, snow is falling heavily on the mountains close by : | *Lung-pe nang-na mü-pa di mong po yong-päi, nye-tsáne ri-la khau-a di tu'pa bap-kyi-re'.* |
| It is not freezing now : | *Ṭanda khyák-*(or *khyá-*) *ghi-min-du'.* |

## AT AN INN, &c.

| | |
|---|---|
| Where can we find lodgings ? | *Nái-ts'ang ghá-pá nye' chok-ka ?* |
| In this house: inside the monastery : | *Nang di-la : gom-bai bug-la.* |
| Knock at the door, please : | *Go-la ták-ták jhyi' nang*). |
| Where is the landlord ? | *Nái-bo ghá-pá yö'-pai ?* |
| I am the landlady ; salutation, Sir ! | *Ngárang nái-mo di yin : Ku-sho, chhá-pe'.* |
| I want lodgings this night, please : | *Ngárang-la nái-ts'ang p'iro di go nang ro nang.* |
| Sir ; you are welcome : | *Kusho : chhá-pe' zhu nang.* |
| I have two rooms above ; the horses will remain underneath. | *Ngárang-la yá-t'ok nang-mik nyi du' ; má-t'ok tá-ts'o di dö-tu nang yong.* |
| I am tired : where is the bed ? | *Ngárang-la dup-kyo yin : nyá ṭ'i é yö'.* |
| Sir ; climb up the ladder and see : | *Kusho ! ken-zá-la dzek-te t'ong nang !* |
| Here are bed and bedding : | *Di-lá sim-ṭ'i mál-ting jhung.* |
| What bedding have you ? | *Khyö-rang-la mál-ting ghang yim-pe'.* |
| Fox-skins and a coverlet ; they are dry : | *Wá-pák, khebma chi : de-dák kem du'.* |
| Thanks madam hostess, I do not require them : | *Ká-ḍhim, naimo jhomo, dák-la kho-jhe me'.* |
| I have a hair-blanket myself : | *Ngárang-la rang-ghi chhálu du'.* |
| All right, Sir : (Sir, it is) : | *Lá, lá yö* (or *Lá, lá-so*). |
| Saheb, do you desire food ? | *Kusho, nyi-la solwa she'-pa-re' ?* |
| I want a little washing-water ; nothing else : | *Ngárang-la ṭ'ü-khu goi-pa yö' dhárung chang ma re'.* |

| | |
|---|---|
| Have you a wash-bowl; also water-for-washing-the-feet? | *Khyö-rang-la ṭ'ū-shong chi é yö'? sháb-sil yang é yö'?* |
| I have no bowl: it is not necessary: | *Ngárang-la shong chi me'-pa: goi-gyu mén.* |
| We Tibetans do not bathe: | *Pö-p'o-pa ngá-zhá mi ṭ'ū-pa.* |
| Have you a large pot? | *Khyö-rang-la k'og-chhen chi é yö'* |
| Bring me warm water I beg: | *Chhu ts'em-mo cm khyer shok ro nang!* |
| Are there bugs in this room? | *Dé-shik-ts'o nang-mik di-la yö' dhá.* |
| Give me a light: | *Ngá-la óng-gu chi nang ro nang!* |
| What is the charge? | *Nái-ghong ghá ts'ö?* |
| Farewell! Many thanks: | *O-ná ghá-le p'ep! T'uk-je chhe!* |

## MOUNTAINEERING.

| | |
|---|---|
| The weather is misty: | *Nam di la ná-bün t'ib jhung.* |
| As the rain is falling, the mist will soon pass away: | *Chhárpa bhap-ne, ná-bün gyō-po p'u-gyu-yin.* |
| Yes! it will indeed pass away; but not until evening: | *Yá-ya! p'u ni p'u-gyu-yin; yin-kyáng nub-mo t'uk mang.* |
| It is time to strike camp: | *Ghur lok tang-wái ren du':* |
| Fold up the tent: | *Ghur di ril tong* |
| Put some snow in the pan: | *Dhok-le nang-la khau-á shok.* |
| Melt snow and make tea: | *Khau-á t'im-ne, soljha shom chi'.* |
| Place the saddle on the pony: | *Tá-la gá te' shak.* |
| Be careful to draw the strap tight enough: | *Ts'ö' toi dhang ko-t'ā dik tangpo chhing!* |
| Now we will start. | *Dhá-ta shek-gyu-yin.* |
| Be off! Tread firmly: | *Há-la gyuk! tempo jhön chi'* (or *tempo kyö' chi'.*) |
| To which side does the path turn off? | *Chhyok ghang-la lamkhá sék-ḍhe-la gyu-wa?* |
| Keep to the right; to the left: | *Yái-chhyok-la song! yön-la.* |
| Don't loiter on the way: | *Lam-la gor ma gor!* |

| | |
|---|---|
| Go straight ahead: | *T'e-kang-la gyu!* |
| Go obliquely by degrees: | *Rim-rim sek-ḍhe-la song!* |
| After we have crossed the bridge, we shall ascend the ridge: | *Sampa la gál-nai, gang-khá dzek-gyu-yin.* |
| On the other side the mountain-face is very steep and a mass of loose flints: | *P'ár-kha-la ri-ngoi di gyen-šarpo chhe shálma-chen du'.* |
| There is no bridge; how shall we cross? | *Sampa chi' me' ne, ghá-tsul-na gál-wa?* |
| Blowing air into this yak-skin, we shall have a hide-raft. | *Yák-ko-a di nang-la lung p'u-nai, ngá-la ko-ḍhu shi' yong.* |
| The current is too violent; it is not safe and is fearful: | *Chhu-gyün di háchang ḍhakpo gyuknái, mi tempo yong-nai, ḍhe-po du'.* |
| Let us go together: | *Ngáchák hlengyai-la ḍo-gyu-yin.* |
| We must climb up this torrent-bed: | *Ḍhok-šar di la shö'ne dzek-pa goi.* |
| Being very steep, climb firmly: | *Sar ḍhá-te, tempo shö'ne dzok.* |
| I am feeling dizzy: | *Ngá-la khyóm-khyom jhung.* |
| Shall we descend the khud-slope: | *Kad-šar shö'dhu bhap-gyu-yim-pe.* |
| There is a ravine below: | *Men-la ḍhokpo ŝhik yong.* |
| Walk gently along that ledge: | *Lam-ṭ'ang dhe la dzemte ḍul song!* |
| Be careful: don't fall: | *Riko dim: zák ma chuk!* |
| Don't go further that way: | *Ngö dhe la dhárung mán ḍo!* |
| That chasm is unfathomable: | *Gyá-ser-ka di ting me lon du'.* |
| The path is very precipitous: | *Lamkhá šar-šar chhe shö'dhu bhap.* |
| The snow-bridges over ravines are all melted now: | *Gháng-ŝam ḍhokpoi tengkha di lib tanda ŝhu jhung.* |
| We call snow-bridges "God's bridges:" | *Ghang-ŝam la ming dindra ŝer: könchhoa-ghi ŝam ŝer.* |
| The hill-side has become wholly melted ice: | *Ri-ngoi di ts'angma khyák-ŝhu kokó jhung.* |

| | |
|---|---|
| As the fog is thick, it is difficult to see the edge of the precipice : | *Mū-pa mongpo yö'-pe, kad-ŝur di mik tá-la ká-le khákpo re'.* |
| Do we continue on this side of the river : (Lit : "Do we go, continuing," &c.). | *Tsang-poi ts'urkha ţ'o-ne ḍo-wa ?* |
| No : the path climbs from below, and beyond that rock yonder there is another bridge of split-cane : | *Mindu'* : *l̂amkhá di shö'ne dzeknai, p'á-gi ḍhak di-yi p'ártsám ts'ár-ŝam ŝhem-ma yö'.* |
| Where is the bridge (split-cane bridge) : | *Ts'ár-ŝam di ghá-re ?* |
| You will see it just now : | *Dhá-dhe dhárung di-la t'ong yong* ; or *Dhátá rang di-la t'ong-gyu-yin.* |
| I am not equal to this task : | *Ngárang di le-ká-i ya mi chok.* |
| Shall we pass under that overhanging rock : | *Dhe ḍhak-kib-kyiwok-la gál-gyu-yimpa ?* |
| A little more : and we shall see straight on : | *Dhárung ts'abik-nai t'e-kang-la t'ong yong.* |
| The other side, remains of snow still continue : | *P'ár-khá khau-ái ţ'o lüi jhung.* |
| What is the name of that valley down there below : (*Má-gi-la lung-pa-i ming la ghang ŝer) ?* | *Há-gi lung-pa shö-la di-yi m̃ing la ghang ŝer* (N.B., *há-gi* signifies "yonder" but closer to the observer's feet than *p'ági*. Perhaps *há-gi shö-la* by which we have rendered "down there below" would be replaced by *má-gi-la*). |
| Pitch the camp here : | *Di-pa ghur lang chi'.* |
| How far is the Pass from here : | *Ts'urne lá di t'ukpa t'ák-ring-t'ung ghá dzö yö'pe ?* |
| How far is Pal-dhe from here : | *Ts'ur-ne Pal-dhe t'uk-pa t'ák-ring-t'ung ghá dzö' yö'pe ?* |

| | |
|---|---|
| How far is that peak from the Pass-top: | *Laptse-ne dhe zoktse t'ukpa t'ák-ring-t'ung ghá dzö' yö'pe?* (*dhe zoktse* instead of *zoktse dhe* "that peak"). |
| It is a long distance from here to the Pass-top: | *Ts'ur-ne laptse t'ukpa t'ák ring-mo du'.* |
| If you descend quickly you will soon fall on your face: | *Khyörang gyō-po shö-dhv bhab-pai, nyurdhu khá dap yong.* |
| The water trickles from the rock down along my back: | *Ḍhák-lai chhu dzak-nai, ngá-i gyap kyi tang-la bhap-ki-du'.* |
| Is this water good to drink: | *Di chhu di t'ung-wai dhöndhu, yakpo é yö'?* |
| All is drinking water up here: | *Yá-gi ts'ur chhu t'ungchok* (or *t'ungnyen*) *ts'angma du'.* |
| A snow-slip is descending: | *Khá-ru chi' bhap-ki-du'.* |
| Ice, snow, boulders all from above: | *Yá-t'ok-ne khyak, khau-a, shálma lib!* |
| Is there any cave near: | *Tsá-né ṭak-p'uk ŝhi é yö'?* |
| Yonder, yonder; below: | *P'á-gi, p'ági; má-gi-la!* |
| Run for your life (*i. e.*, "Running preserve your life.") | *Gyuk-ṇai sön-te shrung!* |
| There is only rock-shelter—yonder under that boulder-mass: | *Mempe ḍhák-kyib mi du'—p'ági p'ábong-ghi wok-la!* |
| Run into the cave over there: | *Hági ṭak-p'uk nang-la gyuk:* |
| This is not a cave; we call this "grotto-shelter:" | *Di-ka p'uk chi' ma re': ghyám-kyip dhenḍe ŝer.* |
| I am not at all hurt: | *Ngárang ye nyam-pa ma jhung.* |
| With spikes on your boots, you do not slip often: | *Rang-ghi lham-la kang-dzer dam-pe, m̂angpo shor-nai gyel-gyu-min.* |
| Fasten spikes on my boots please: | *Ngá-i lham-la kang-dzer dam ro jhyi!* |
| See the Pass-top now: | *Tandá laptse tö shok.* |
| Beware of the Pass-poison (poisonous air on passes). | *Lá-dhuk rikpa ḍim!* |

| | |
|---|---|
| Here we are! Hail, hail, to the mountain-gods! Victory, victory, to the gods! | *Ts'ur lep jhung! Lhá sollo, lhá sol-lo; Lhá gyal-lo, lhá gyal-lo!* |
| Beware the demons on the left side: | *Yön-lák-kyi ḍé-tso la rikpa ḍim!* |

## PAYING AND RECEIVING VISITS.

[On receiving a guest in your own house the orthodox greeting to be uttered to him is: *Chhák p'ep šhü' nang* or *Chhak p'ep nang chik!*—the meaning of the first form being "On arrival and departure salutation springeth forth," and of the second "On arriving let salutation be given thee!" The correct reply for the visitor to make to this welcome is *Lhá yö'* (or *lá yö'*) "Sir it is" or "Be it so, Sir."

To an inferior comer the salutation is *Tanda lep song*: "Now you have arrived;" (akin to our "Well, so you have come!") When the visit is a formal one, it is usual for the caller to present a visiting scarf styled *jáldar* or *khátá* (lit. *khá btags* "that which binds the mouth.") This may be either accepted if the visitor be of average means; or, if he be poor, though the scarves carry the most trifling pecuniary value save in rare instances, it may be returned to him by tieing it loosely about his neck; first, however, courteously and graciously receiving it]:—

| | |
|---|---|
| Is the master at home: | *Kusho di šhu-ki-yö'pe?* |
| He is at home—not at home: | *Khong šhu' yö'—šhu' me'.* |
| Will his Reverence give me an interview: | *Je-tsün-kyī dö'dhu chug-ghá?* |
| His Reverence does not receive to-day: | *Dhe-ring Je-ts'ün-kyī dö'-dhu mi chuk.* |
| Announce me! | *Lön kyur-pa nang!* |
| Pray sit down: | *Shū!* |
| Take a seat on the cushion: | *Shuten la šhū!* |
| Take some tea: | *Soljhá šhei nang.* |

| | |
|---|---|
| Thank you, Sir: | *Lhá t'ukje!* (often heard as *t'orje*). |
| Bring the tea-pot here: | *Ts'ur-la sö' bing di khur shok!* |
| Do you drink tea or beer: | *Chhang soljhá khyörang-ghī ghang t'ung-gyu-yimpe?* |
| Place the broth on the stove: | *T'ukpa di jhálang-la ŝhók.* |
| Is your sacredness quite well: | *Je-tsün Lhá-yi kham dé lā-sam?* |
| I am quite well, are you well: | *Dók yé-demo; nyi' demo é yö'?* |
| Sir, I am: | *Lhá, lā-so.* |
| Take tea, Sir: | *Kusho, soljha šhei!* |
| Many thanks, Sir: | *Lhá, t'uk-je chhé* (pr. *t'orje-chhe*). |
| Take more tea: | *Soljhá dhá-rung šhei ro.* |
| I have enough: | *Ngá-la tá-yong lā-so.* |
| Have you come alone: | *Nyi'rang shráng-shráng la é yong?* |
| From where have you come: | *Khyö' ghá-ne lep jhung!* |
| I must go now: | *Tanda ngárang ḍo-ren du'.* |
| Now pray dismiss me: | *Tanda gong-pa nang ro.* |
| Farewell (*lit.* "Be happy!") | *De-war ŝhu shik!* |
| Grant me your protection! | *Ku-yi kyab-tu ngembu-la nang ro!* (*ngembu* depreciative title for "me.") |
| Please come again soon: | *Yang gyō-po p'ep ro nang!* |
| Many thanks, Sir: | *Lhá, t'ukje chhe* ("*t'orje-chhe.*") |
| Accept this scarf: | *Khátak di šhei ro nang!* |
| Come again and again: | *Yang-kyár-yang p'ep!* |
| May we meet again next year: (on parting for indefinite period). | *Sáng-pö' jál-wa chhok!* |
| *Visitor:* I wish you farewell: | *Wona ghále ku šhu nang.* |
| *Host:* Well; go gently: | *Woná ghále p'ep!* |

*N.B.*—It is etiquette in Tibet, before leaving the room after a visit of ceremony, to empty any tea left in your tea-cup into the *shá-luk* or slop-basin standing on the low table.

## COOKING AND DOMESTIC UTENSILS.

*Sol-dong*: a churn of hollow bamboo used for compounding tea with soda and butter previous to boiling. Instead sometimes the butter is put direct into each tea-cup afterwards.

*Dong-mong* or *Do-mong*: a large tea-churn, made of two half-logs hollowed out and coopered into a barrel-form with willow twigs.

*Khok-chhen*; or *Sol-ŝang*: tea-kettle of copper, somewhat urn-shaped with handle on either side but no spout, in which the tea ingredients, after churning, are boiled.

*Jhámbing*, or *Sol-bing*: brass tea-pot with spout and lid, as with us, into which the tea is ladled from the urn for pouring into cups.

*Khok-t'il*: another name for a tea-pot.

*Sing-ts'ál*: tea-pot of another shape, in use in Tsang province; often made of red or black pottery.

*Tibril*: round tea-pot, as styled in Lahul and Ladak.

*Dzámbing*: earthenware tea-pot.

*Jhábtuk*: stirring-stick for tea while boiling in *ŝang-bhu*.

*Mé-kyok*: fire or charcoal shovel.

*Sol-t'um*: ladle for transferring tea from urn to tea-pot.

*Jhá-ts'ak*; or *ŝhi-ma*: tea-strainer made of very fine split bamboo or cane.

*P'orpa*: cups or bowls of various kinds of wood, box-tree and vine-root, (but maple-knot the most valuable), used for tea, soup, and all food, generally carried in coat-pocket (*p'orṣhuk*).

*Bü'pa*: bellows. (In Tsang: *Bi'pa.*)

*T'árbak*: iron plate for food.

*T'erter*: dish for meats.

*Rák-t'um*: large brass ladle.

*Dhok-le*: large open iron pot with handles, used for cooking victuals.

*Chák-mak*: tinder and steel.

*Sang-bhu*: general term for copper degchies, tinned inside.

*Már-páru*: round tin butter-box.

*Chhye-kyal*: flour-bag.

*Tsám-khuk*: tsamba-bag.

*Chhu-t'um* : large metal ladle for getting water at springs.

*Dzá-ma* : ghara, or clay vessel for holding meal, water, &c.

*Láng-gá* : iron pan in which to parch barley for tsámba.

*Sem* : wooden cask or barrel.

*Chhubšom* : wooden pail with lid for conveying water on back up hills.

---

## ARTICLES OF FOOD.

*Tsám-ba* : barley-meal, prepared by first parching the grain and then grinding it into flour more or less coarse.

*Pák* : porridge made by soaking tsamba in hot-tea, and often as thick as dough.

*Sen* : the meal soaked in beer or hot-water instead of in tea, kneaded into large tough balls and eaten warm or cold.

*Pá'-lep* : this mass made very thick and with the addition of ginger and aconite as yeast, baked into flat-cakes.

*Çhur-ra* : a sort of flat cheesy maccaroni, made by boiling down milk into a curdy mass and drying it; a little flour being often introduced. Often in granulated masses.

*Khur-wa* : cakes fried in fat, made of various meals.

*Gyá-khur* : Chinese cakes fried in oil.

*Bá-chi* : cake made of maize meal.

*Mo-mo* or *mok-mo* : pastry-puffs in which is enclosed minced meat and chopped vegetables, sometimes sugar also.

*Khabse* or *Shé-to* : flour and fat rolled into pastry of worm-like form, coiled into cakes of different shapes and baked.

*Tr'e-tse* : vermicelli made of millet.

*T'uk-pa* : general term for broth made either from meat or, like gruel, only from meal-stuffs.

*Gyá-t'uk* : "Chinese broth"—a more substantial soup, being *chur-ra* and onions cooked up in meat-broth.

*Pá't'uk* : broth thickened with barley.

*T'uk-t'ál* : barley-meal first boiled in meat-broth and, when strained out from the broth, then roasted on an iron-plate; hence styled "soup-dust."

*Sá-t'uk* : soup made from a pungent wild vegetable, nearly as hot as the chilli.

*Ḍái-t'uk* : rice and meat soup.

*Ḍai-tsám*: rice parched and ground.

*Yák-shá*: yak-beef (usually boiled).

*Luk-shá*: mutton (usually boiled).

*Rá-shá*: goat-mutton.

*P'ák-shá*: pork.

*Bo-ts'il*: bacon.

*Shá-chuk*: meat cut in strips and dried.

*Gyu-ma*, or *gyu-ma kárgyang*: sausages, or even the intestines cooked, as every part of an animal is consumed in Tibet.

*P'ákro* and *Lukro*: carcases of pigs and sheep roasted whole in their skins and sold thus for drying. The meat becomes hard and brittle and will keep for more than a year in the severe cold; the carcases being gradually eaten.

*P'ing-shá*: curried meat, sold dried on small skewers of wood.

*Kúm-chhin*: liver.

*Ts'ilku*: fat.

*Shá ts'ilme'*: lean meat.

*Dámchá*: duck.

*Khyimchá*: fowl.

*Wo-ma*: milk.

*Már*: butter. ("Some people have a supply of butter 50 years' old, laid by in their houses, sewn up in sacks and skins; this is produced with great pride on special occasions, as the oldest wine is brought out at European banquets:"—*Moravian Mission Report*).

*Chyema kára*: sugar (refined).

*Bhu-ram*: brown sugar sold in cakes.

*Gong-ngá*: eggs.

*Chu-li*: apricots dried and stoned; staple winter food in Western Tibet.

*Ngári kham-bhu*: name of these in East Tibet.

*Chu-li t'uk*: soup of dried apricots.

*Chu-li tághir*: boiled apricots mashed into pulp, made into cakes and then dried.

*Ḍai chu-li*: apricots with boiled rice.

*Wosé tághir*: mulberries, dried, pulverised, and made into cakes.

*Lá-pu'*: the white radish; a popular vegetable in Tibet—baked, or finely-grated in soup.

*Nyungma*: turnip (greatly prized).

*Sho-ko*: ordinary Tibetan potato.

*Ṭo-ma:* very small red sweet potato.

*P'iling kyiu:* English potato.

*Choma:* creeping fern-like plant with self-rooting runners and extensive system of roots underground bearing small tubercles. These are dug up and much prized as food. See Huc. *Potentilla anserina.*

*Tsŏng:* onions.

*Petse:* cabbage.

*Kung-lápuk:* carrot.

*Te-ma:* peas.

*Mamoipe Loto:* maize.

*Khálo:* spinnach.

*Tárgha:* walnuts.

*Debu:* apple.

*Kyerpa:* barbery.

---

## PREPARING AND EATING FOOD.

| | |
|---|---|
| Place the stove down here: | *Jhá-lang dhe di-pa p'áb ŝhik.* |
| Place the pot on the stove: | *Sáng di jhá-lang tang-la ŝhok.* |
| Make the fire burn brightly: | *Me di ṭ'ol-le ṭ'ol-le par chuk.* |
| Throw wood on the fire: | *Shing m̂e-la luk !* |
| What have we to eat: | *Ngá-la ŝá-wai chhir-tu ghang e yö' ?* |
| Go and buy some fish: | *Chhyïn-nai ñya ñyo shok.* |
| Here are minced-meat and bread: | *Tanda mo'mo' pá'lep du'.* |
| I have bought a whole dried carcase: | *Ngá shá-khak ghang-gá ñyo-pa-yin.* |
| You have bought too much meat: | *Khyö'-kyī shá háchang m̂angpo ñyo du'.* |
| Where is the saucepan: | *Sang-bu dhe ká-pa yö'.* |
| How many plates have we: | *Ngá-la derma ghá-ts'ö' yin ?* |
| The copper-pot has become dinted: | *Sang di dip song.* |
| Boil eight eggs: | *Gong-nga gye' kol shik !* |
| Is the tea-kettle full: | *Sol-ŝang tem-tem* (or *ghang*) *yö' pai ?* |
| Clean out the tea-pot and make fresh tea in the tea-kettle: | *Khok-t'il di ṭui-ne sol-ŝang-la jhá sarpa ŝö shi'.* |
| Blow up the fire again: | *Me dhe ŷáng-kyar p'u gyop !* |

| | |
|---|---|
| Fetch more fuel : | *Pü-shing ŷáng-kyar khur shok.* |
| I want milk and sugar : | *Ngárang-la ŵoma chyéma kára gö yö'.* |
| We Tibetans always mix butter in tea : | *Pö'pá ngá-ŝha dhui-gyün jhá-la m̂ar ṭe-ghi-yö'.* |
| Make the tea in the usual way : | *Dhüi-gyün nangtar jhá di jhyi* (*jhyi* is pr. *chi*). |
| Bring bowl and stirring-stick : | *P'orpa jháb-ṭuk khur shok.* |
| Pray don't let the water boil over on the hearth : | *T'áb-la chhu̇ di lü' ma chuk ro jhyi* (pr. *chi* or *chyi*). |
| The milk has boiled-over : | *Woma lü' song* |
| Then put butter on the hearth and say at once what I tell you : | *Dhe-ne t'ab-la kar-sur tong ; ngá khyö'-la ŝer-wa nangtar dhe tanda ṭ'eltu lap chi'* (*kar-sur = mar*). |
| Say like this : "O hearth-god, don't be angry ; I didn't know !" | *Dinde lap :* "*T'ab-lha, gong-pa ma t'um ; ngai ma she.*" |
| Give me Chinese broth : | *Gyá-t'uk nang chik.* |
| Remove the saucepan lid : | *Sang-bhu-i khep sang chik.* |
| Skim off the dirty grease on the surface : | *Kha-tok-la numtsi tsok yap chik.* |
| Throw salt in the broth : | *Ts'á t'ukpa-la táb* (or *luk*). |
| Is the barley-meal broth ready : | *Pá't'uk ṭ'al-ḍhik é jhung* (pr. often *t'alti é chung*). |
| It is spoiled : | *Dhe sáng jhung.* |
| Cut up the meat into bits : | *Shá di tsáp tsáp jhyi.* (*tsab-pa :* to mince). |
| Cut the mutton and put it in the pot : | *Luk-shá di t'upné, sang-na luk.* |
| Is it hot enough : | *Yong-su ts'á-po yö'pe ?* |
| There is not enough milk : | *Wo-ma ŝhang ma song.* |
| Is it sweet or not : | *Dhe ŝhimpo é-yö' m'é-yö'.* |
| Fill the tea-pot with water to the brim : | *Khok-t'i(l) nang-la chhu dhak-dhak ghang ghyong* (or *luk*). |
| What is there to eat : | *Ghang ŝá-wa ?* |

| | |
|---|---|
| Please give me some: | *Ngá-la ká-she nang roch.* |
| Is it good to eat: | *Di ŝá-na yá'po yö'-pai?* |
| The dried meat is old and brittle; I can powder it: | *Shá-chuk nying kok-chen re': nga ŝhibmo jhe' t'up.* |
| Powdering it, pour hot water on it: | *Dhe ŝhibmo ŝo-ne, chhu ts'ápo luk tang.* |
| This is old meat: it is not bad: | *Di-ni shá nying-pa du': ákpo mindu'.* |
| Tibetans do not eat ducks: | *Pö'pa yá-tse to ŝá-ghi me'.* |
| Englishmen are fond of fish-flesh and fowl-flesh: Tibetans not: | *P'iling-pa nyá-shá jhyá-shá la gá-ghi-du'; Pö'pa mindu'.* |
| Soak the liver in water: | *Chhinpa pang-ne ŝho'* (ཞོག་) |
| This hard dry liver is very bitter: | *Chhinpa kyong kem di khá-po re'.* |
| No matter! no matter! | (In Tsang) *mi-to', mi-to'!* (In Lhasa) *khye'mi yö', khye' mi yö'!* |
| I can't eat it: | *Ngá di-la ŝá ma chok.* |
| Are you hungry: I am not hungry: | *Khyö' tok-ghi re'-ta? Dák-la ṭo-pa tok-ghi mindu'.* |
| Eat more butter: it has not become rancid: | *Dharung m̂ár ŝo: di-la hamdi gyap ma jhung.* |
| In taste this is sweet: | *Di ḍho-wa-la* (བྲོ་བ་ལ་) *ngar-mo du'.* |
| Boil the fish and put salt with it into the water: | *Nyá kol* (or *kü*)*; chhu-i nang-na di nyampo ts'á luk-ne.* |
| Always fry the eggs in good butter: | *Gong-nga m̂ár sáng-la dhui-gyün sek jhyi.* |
| We have no salt: | *Ngá-la ts'á me'.* |
| Fill the *pak* into that skin: | *Gyu-má-i bug-la pák gyang ŝhik.* |
| The pak is like dough: | *Pák di kyoma dhang ḍa-te re'.* |
| Is the Chinese broth savoury: | *Gyá-t'uk dhe ḍho-wa ŝhimpo yö'pai?* |

| | |
|---|---|
| Peel the potatoes: | *Sho-ko di pákpa shu ŝhi'.* |
| Parch the barley-grain and then grind into flour and make tsampa: | *Nai lam-ne ehhyé-mar t'ak dhang tsamba ger chik.* |
| I want fresh milk: | *Ngá-la ŵomá sarpa goi yö'.* |
| What is the price of milk: | *Womá-i rin ghá ts'ö ?* |
| The soup is very weak: | *T'ukpa háchang lá-po du'.* |
| Put a piece of that butter in the leaf with a spoon: | *Shompa-la m̂ár di-yi dhumbu chi' t'urma-ne ŝho'.* |

## OVER THE KANGLACHHEN PASS BETWEEN WALLUNG AND TIBET.

[The Kanglachhen and the Tipta Passes are the two principal mountainous gateways out of Eastern Nipal into Tibet. The former is much used by the colony of Tibetans and Limbus settled in the Wallung Valley; and it was over this Pass, which is 17,000 feet at its apex, that Sarat Chandra Dás gained access to Tibet in 1882. Sir J. D. Hooker approached but did not ascend the Pass] :—

| | |
|---|---|
| The weather is clear: we will go up quickly toward the Pass: | *Nam dhángpo du' : ngá-ts'ó La di t'e-kyá la gyokpo ḍo-gyu yin.* |
| Where are my snow-shoes: | *Ngárang-ghi kang-hlam di ghápa yö' ?* |
| Help me to descend this declivity: | *Ṭak-šarpo di t'engla ḍo-gyu roram nang.* |
| Take care! It is very slippery: | *Rik-pa ḍim! Ḍe'ták shor-ghi re'.* |
| Don't fall! | *Gyel ma chuk!* |
| I was very nearly falling: | *Ngá tiktse min-na gyel-ṭap-yin.* |
| That gorge must be 2,000 or 3,000 *ṭ'uma* deep: (1 *ṭ'uma* = 18 inches): | *Gyá-ser di kyi ting ts'e la ṭ'uma tong nyi tong sum jál-gyu yin.* |
| This path runs along the face of the cliff; you will not fall: | *Lamkhá di ḍhák-šar kyi dong dong la gyu-kin-du' ; khyö' ŝák mi yong.* |

| | |
|---|---|
| There! you can see the corner of the rock: | *Há-gi! ḍhak-ghi khuk di t'ong chok.* |
| At that corner the path turns to the right and ascends: | *Khuk dhe la l̂amkhá di yái-na kor-ne dzek yin.* |
| Where is the bridge across this ravine: I don't see it: | *Ḍhok-po-i bhar-nangla ŝampa di ghá re'? ngarang m̂ik tá-wa mi chok.* |
| The bridge has broken: | *Sampa dhe chhák song.* |
| If you collect twigs and dung, we can light a fire: | *Khyö' kam-shing báng-kam du yong ná, m̂e dhū-pa chok yong.* |
| Look at that long plain of snow: | *Khau-á-i t'áng ring-po dhe la toi shok!* |
| It must be a glacier: | *Ghángchen chi' jhung goi.* |
| What is the name of that river yonder? Do you know? | *P'á-gi chhu-wo dhe kyi m̂ing ghá ŝer? Khyö shé-sám?* |
| It is the Yungma; the great river of the Wallung Valley: | *Yungma m̂ing di ŝer yö'; chhu chhempo di Wálung-ghi lung-pá-yi du'.* |
| The upper part of the valley is full of snow: | *Di p'u di khau-a tem-tem jhung.* |
| Don't tread there; the snow is quite soft: | *Te-la ma ḍul; khau-a di bol-bol du'.* |
| Ah, to be sure! It is a deep crevasse full of snow: | *Kye, te-ka yö'! Khau-á-ne tem-tem-khen ser-kha tang-ring chi' du'.* |
| Fresh snow has not fallen on the pass: | *Lá-i tang-la khau-á sarpa bap ma jhung.* |
| This long ridge of snow is called Chang Chhup Gya-lam: | *Kang-ŝam ring-po di Chang Chhup Gya-lam ŝer jhung.* |
| There is no path across the ridge: | *Kang-ŝam kyi bhar-nang-la lam-kha min du'.* |
| Never mind; mount on my back: | *Mitok! Nge gyap-la dzok.* |
| Can you bear my weight? | *Khyö' nge jig-ts'e khyer chok-ka.* |
| Be careful! Don't slip: | *Rik ṭim! Shor ma gyap!* |

| | |
|---|---|
| Hark! what is that noise? | *Nyen chi! ŵur-ḍa di kang du'.* |
| An avalanche is rolling down into the gorge below: | *Kha-ru chi má-ki-ru gya-ser kyi t'eng-la bap-ki du'.* |
| We have now left Chang Ch-hup Gya-lam. This rock is named Dzáma Nákmo: | *Tanda ngá-cha' Chang Chhup Gya-lạm nái gyu song* (or *tang ghye song*). *Ṭak di la m̃ing di Dzáma Nákmo šer yö'* |
| How far is it from here to P'ug-pa Karmo? | *Di-ne P'ukpa Karmo-la t'ák ring-t'ung ghá ts'o du'?* |
| Are you tired? | *Khyö' țang-chhe song-nga?* |
| We can take shelter there: | *P'á-gi-la kyib nye' chok.* |
| I am very tired: | *Ngárang háchang t'ang-chhe-so.* |
| You proceed to Kanglachhen from P'uk-pa Karmo in a due east direction: | *P'ukpa Karmo-ne Kangla-chhen t'uk chhyō-shar-la ḍang ḍo.* |
| It is two miles to the head of the pass from P'ug-pa Karmo. | *P'ukpa Karmo-ne lap-tse la nye-ring di pákts'e' nyi jál.* |
| That is of no importance: | *Di dho-kal min du'.* |

## TIME—AGE—SEASONS.

It is necessary to set forth briefly the Tibetan method of reckoning time; though in all estimates of time past, age, and the date of events, the whole race shew the same inaptitude for which the natives of India are remarkable. There seem to be systems of counting the years from particular eras in the history of the country; but, for the purpose of distinguishing the years within the memory of those living, what is termed a *ráb jhung*, or cycle, has been invented, which affords distinct denominations for each year in a period of 60 years. As each cycle of 60 years elapses the same series of names are run through again. When, however, a Tibetan informs you such and such an event happened in such a year, naming the year, you can only judge from the context of his speech, or other auxiliary circumstances, whether—for example—he means you to understand a date which is 30, or one which is 90, years ago. The sexagenery cycle has been formed in imitation of the Chinese mode of reckoning; but the Chinese cycle does not exactly correspond with the Tibetan cycle, the latter being said to be 4 years in arrears of the former. In order to form distinctive titles for every year of the sixty composing the cycle, there has been first arranged a set of twelve names to represent a lesser cycle of 12 years, called *lo-kor*. These which always recur in the same order are the names of 12 different animals or, rather, creatures:—

| | | | | | |
|---|---|---|---|---|---|
| 1. *Jhi:* | Mouse. | 5. *Ḍuk:* | Dragon. | 9. *Spre-u:* | Ape. |
| 2. *Lang:* | Bull. | 6. *Ḍul:* | Snake. | 10. *Jhá:* | Fowl. |
| 3. *Tak:* | Tiger. | 7. *Tá:* | Horse. | 11. *Khyi:* | Dog. |
| 4. *Yos:* | Hare. | 8. *Luk:* | Sheep. | 12. *P'ák:* | Pig. |

As soon as the 12 years, each named after an animal in the above order, have elapsed, the series re-commences, following the same names, and so on, *ad infinitum*. However, in order to vary the names so as to produce 60 different titles, another cycle of 10 years is made to run concurrently with the duodenary series. The 10-year cycle is composed of the names of five elements, each repeated twice, once with the masculine affix *po*, and once with the feminine *mo*:—

| | | | |
|---|---|---|---|
| 1. *Shing-po:* | Wood. | 6. *Sá-mo:* | Earth. |
| 2. *Shing-mo:* | Wood. | 7. *Chák-po:* | Iron. |
| 3. *Me-po:* | Fire. | 8. *Chák-mo:* | Iron. |
| 4. *Me-mo:* | Fire. | 9. *Chhu-po:* | Water. |
| 5. *Sá-po:* | Earth. | 10. *Chhu-mo:* | Water. |

The *po* or *mo* is generally dropped; and these names are combined in the following manner with the duodenary series. The two cycles begin simultaneously, the first-named element being conjoined with the first-named animal to denominate the first year; the second element in the list (which, however, is the same as the first-named) being next conjoined with the second-named, a different, animal; and so on. Thus we have :—1. Wood-mouse year; 2. Wood-bull year; 3. Fire-tiger year; 4. Fire-hare year: and so forth.

It is obvious that the 10-name series will be exhausted before the 12-name series. It is, however, at once re-commenced, the first element being conjoined to the 11th animal, the same being also conjoined to the 12th animal, which as both series run on concurrently causes fresh combinations. Variations for 60 years are thus produced, when, the 10-year scale having run exactly six times, and the 12-year scale exactly five times, they both once again commence together, forming the same sets of combinations as in the sixty years just concluded. The *ráb-jhung,* or sexagenary cycle, now in progress in Tibet commenced in the year 1863; in which year the 10-year and 12-year series began together. Accordingly we have for the approaching years the following titles whereby they may be discriminated :—

| | | |
|---|---|---|
| 1893: | Shing Tá Lo: | Wood-Horse Year. |
| 1894: | Shing Luk Lo: | Wood-Sheep Year. |
| 1895: | Me Ṭéu Lo: | Fire-Monkey Year. |
| 1896: | Me Jhyá Lo: | Fire-Fowl Year. |
| 1897: | Sá Khyi Lo: | Earth-Dog Year. |
| 1898: | Sá P'ák Lo: | Earth-Pig Year. |
| 1899: | Chák Jhi-wa Lo: | Iron-Mouse Year. |
| 1900: | Chák Lang Lo: | Iron-Bull Year. |
| 1901: | Chhu Ták Lo: | Water-Tiger Year. |
| 1902: | Chhu Yos Lo: | Water-Hare Year. |
| 1903: | Shing Ḍuk Lo: | Wood-Dragon Year. |
| 1904: | Shing Ḍul Lo: | Wood-Snake Year. |
| 1905: | Me Tá Lo: | Fire-Horse Year. |
| 1906: | Me Luk Lo: | Fire-Sheep Year. |

Another system of nomenclature, slightly different from the foregoing, is occasionally employed, wherein the 10-year cycle is composed not of the elements twice repeated, but of the five primary colours: *karpo* (white), *nákpo* (black), *marpo* (red) *serpo* (yellow), and *ngömpo* (blue), together with the names of five secondary colours which are considered shades of the first. These are combined in the same way with the twelve names of animals to form as in the other case a 60-year's cycle. Mention is also sometimes heard of a lengthy cycle of 252 years, supposed to be used in the chief monasteries for chronological records. The *Lo-t'o*, or kalendar, is a very abstruse affair in Tibet, little understood even by men of ordinary learning.

Tibetans apportion the year into lunar months (*dá-wa*), corresponding with the re-appearances of the moon, and reckoning ordinarily only twelve months to the year. This system would cause the commencement of each new year to occur some ten or eleven days earlier than its predecessor. However, in order to obviate the continuous travelling back of the opening day of the year, every third year an intercalery month, styled *dá-t'eb*, is inserted, which serves to bring the lunar year into some settled correspondence with the solar year. New Year's Day, or the first day of the first month, is made to occur some time in our month of February according to the date when the new moon is first *visible* to the naked eye. In 1891, the Tibetan New Year opened on February 11th, which was the first day of the first month and the beginning of the Great Festival of *Logzo*. Taking the kalendar for 1891, therefore, the months of the Tibetan year may be thus set forth, with the customary names and day of commencement of each month during 1891–92 :—

1891 :

| | | | |
|---|---|---|---|
| (1) | Feb. 11th | *Dá-wa dhangpo ;* | First Month. |
| | | *Tá-pa dá-wa :* | Horseman Month. |
| (2) | March 12th | *Dá-wa nyī-pa ;* | Second Month. |
| | | *Bo dá-wa :* | Blossoming Month. |
| (3) | April 10th | *Dá-wa sumpa ;* | Third Month. |
| | | *Nák dá-wa :* | Black Month. |
| (4) | May 10th | *Dá-wa šhipa ;* | Fourth Month. |
| | | *Sá-ga dá-wa :* | Ocean Month. |
| (5) | June 8th | *Dá-wa ngápa ;* | Fifth Month. |
| | | *Nrön dá-wa :* | Snake Month. |

1891:

| | | | | |
|---|---|---|---|---|
| (6) | July | 8th | *Dá-wa ḍhukpa;* | Sixth Month. |
| | | | *Chhu-nö' dá-wa:* | Waterpot Month. |
| (7) | August | 6th | *Dá-wa dünpa;* | Seventh Month. |
| | | | *Ḍho-šhin dá-wa:* | Wheat-faced Month. |
| (8) | Sept. | 5th | *Dá-wa gyepa;* | Eighth Month. |
| | | | *Ṭ'um-ṭ'um dá-wa:* | Threshing Month. |
| (9) | Oct. | 4th | *Dá-wa gu-pa;* | Ninth Month. |
| | | | *T'á-kár dá-wa:* | Zenith-Star Month. |
| (10) | Nov. | 3rd | *Dá-wa chu-pa;* | Tenth Month. |
| | | | *Min-ḍhuk dá-wa:* | Pleiades Month. |
| (11) | Dec. | 3rd | *Dá-wa chu-chikpa;* | Eleventh Month. |
| | | | *Go dá-wa:* | Month of Heads. |

1892:

| | | | | |
|---|---|---|---|---|
| (12) | Jan. | 2nd | *Dá-wa chu-nyi-pa;* | Twelfth Month. |
| | | | *Gyál dá-wa:* | Month of Victory. |

---

VOCABULARY.

Time, space of time: *Dhü-ts'ö.*
Year: *Lo;* Month: *Dá; dáwa.*
Week: *Gungdün.*
Day: *Nyinmo.*
Two hours: *Khyim.*
24 mins: *Chhuts'ö.*
This year: *Dhá-lo.*
Last year: *Ná-ning.*
Next year: *Sang-lo.*
To-day: *Dhering.*
Yesterday: *Khásang.*
Day before yesterday: *Khé-nyin.*
Two days before yesterday: *Mái nyin.*
Three days before yesterday: *Yan ngün-nyin.*
To-morrow: *Sang-nyin.*
Day after to-morrow: *Nang-par.*
Spring: *Chyi'ka.*
Summer: *Yárka.*
Autumn: *Tönka.*
Winter: *Günka.*
Last night: *Dáng-gong.*
Evening: *Kong-ta.*
All day: *Nyim-gáng.*
Yesterday morning: *Khánang.*
To-morrow morning: *Ngámo.*
This morning: *Dhárang.*
This evening: *To-nup.*
Day of the month: *Ts'ei* (Hind: *tarikh.*)
3rd day of month: *Ts'ei sum.*
10th day of month: *Ts'ei chu tampa.*

| | | | |
|---|---|---|---|
| 15th day of month : | *Nya.* | Two a.m. : | *Namchhyé' yol.* |
| Sunday : | *Sá-nyima.* | Three a.m. (or "To-morrow's head past") : | *T'orgo ŝin.* |
| Monday : | *Sá-dáwa.* | | |
| Tuesday : | *Sá-mikmár.* | | |
| Wednesday : | *Sá-hlakbo.* | Six a.m. ("rising of the night") : | *Nám-lang.* |
| Thursday : | *Sá-p'urbo.* | | |
| Friday : | *Sá-pásang.* | Eight a.m. (or "sun-risen") : | *Nyi-shár.* |
| Saturday : | *Sá-pembo.* | | |
| Midnight : | *Namchhye'.* | Ten a.m. ("sun-a'walk") : | *Nyi-ḍul.* |
| First Cock-crow (about 3 a.m.) : | *Jhápodang-po.* | Noon : | *Nyi-chhye'.* |
| Second Cock-crow : | *Jhá-po nyī-pa.* | 4 p.m. : | *Nyur-me' (myur-smad).* |
| | | Sunset : | *Nyi-gái.* |
| Third Cock-crow (about 5 a.m.) : | *Jhá-po sum-pa.* | 8 p.m. : | *Sa rup.* |
| | | 10 p.m. : | *Shrö'chhol.* |

---

| | |
|---|---|
| It is time to go to sleep : | *Nyi' nya'-la ḍo-ren du'.* |
| We must set off now : | *Tănda ngá-ts'o gyuk gö.* |
| The night has nearly gone : | *Nám lang-la khe' du'.* |
| The day has nearly gone : | *Nyima di yol-la khe'.* |
| The sun has set : | *Nyima di gái song.* |
| What time is it : | *Chhuts'ö' ghá ts'o re' ?* |
| About 3 A.M. : | *T'or-go-ŝin tsam-la.* |
| The "second-crowing" is near (2 A.M.) : | *Jhá-ke nyī-pa gyap-la ḳhe' du'.* |
| How long have you been waiting here ? | *Khyö' di-pa gu'ne yün ghá ts'o song ?* |
| I arrived at about dusk : | *Sap-sip tsam-la lep-pa-yö'.* |
| We must start at day-break : | *Nam lang-ne ngáts' o ḍo gö yö'.* |
| It is time to go indoors : | *Tanda nang-la pep-ren du'.* |
| Wake me early in the morning : | *Ngámo ngárang-la nyi' sö' rō chyi.* |
| How old are you : | *Khyö' lo ghá ts'o re' ?* or : *Khyö'-la lo ghátsam lönnam ?* |
| I am 18 years' old : | *Ngárang lo chobgye'ṛa yin.* |

| | |
|---|---|
| I am a "serpent-year" person: | *Ngárang ḍül-lo-pa yin.* |
| I was born in the water-tiger year: | *Ngárang lo chhu-ták la kye pa re'.* |
| How many years have you spent here: | *Khyö'-kyī lo ghátsam ne di-pa šhū-pa yin?* |
| Twenty-three years: | *Lo nyi-shu tsák-sum.* |
| The man who was here yesterday has come again: | *Khá-sang-ghi mi di lokne lep jhung.* (Lit: *The man of yesterday, &c.*) |
| Four months ago my brother died: | *Nge pün shi-ne dáwa šhi song.* |
| I think the gun will be brought to-morrow: | *Ngé sampa-la mendá di sang-nyin kyál jhá-gyu.* |
| What day will the Grand Lama give audience: | *Kyapgön chhempo di ŝhák ghang jál-khá nang-wa?* |
| You are very late: | *Khyö' yün ring-po gor song.* |
| What day of the month is to-day: | *Dhéring ts'ĕi-tang ghang re'?* |
| It is the eighth: | *Ts'ĕi-tang gye re'.* |
| Come to my lodgings in two hours: | *Nge nā-ts'ang la dhá-tá chhyi khyim chik shok.* |
| I want my dinner exactly at sun-down: | *Nyi-gái-kyi kap-la, ngá-la to-chhé' kho-wa.* |
| The reckoning of time at Lhása goes according to the Chinese method: | *Gyá-nak-kyi ts'ul nangŝhin Lhásá-la dhu'-ts'ö' tsi-wa di ḍo.* |
| In general the lunar month is used: | *T'un-mong-la dá-kyi dá-wa nangŝhin tsi-ghi re'.* |
| Two days' ago the tea was all done: | *Shak nyi ngün-la soljha di lib ts'ar song.* |
| From the 4th to the 15th day of the month the snow fell: | *Di khau-a di tséi ŝhi-ne šungte ts'ei nyá t'uk-la bap-kin jhung.* |
| The snow was falling all night long: | *Di khau-a di nám tang bap-kin-jhung.* |

| | |
|---|---|
| I arrived three months' ago (*lit:* From I arriving, three months have arisen). | *Ngárang p'epne dá sum jhung.* |
| I was delayed a long while—quite a week: | *Ngá-la yün ringpo gyang jhung —dün-ŝhak tang chi'.* |
| You are three days late: | *Khyö'rang ŝhak sum t'ep yö'.* |
| I have been calling you a whole chhuts'o: | *Dák-ghī khyö'la ke gyák-nai chhu-ts'ö kang-ga song* (or *chhu-ts'ö tang song*). |
| I have been ill for more than a week: | *Dün-t'rak p'ar-la dák ná-ts'a-yī ŝir jhung.* |
| I have dwelt at Lhásá three years: | *Lo sum t'uk Lhásá-la dö' nai yö'.* |
| Ever since last month until now have I been ill: | *Khásang-dá-wa-ne ŝungte dhátá-p'en ngá ne' kyī ŝir jhung.* |
| I will return in nine days: | *Ngá ŝhak gu ŝhuk-la lokne lep yong.* |
| This lama is 63 years old. | *Lámá di lo re-sum du'.* |

## PLANTS AND TREES OF TIBET PROPER.

*Sholpo:* poplar.

*Yarpa:* poplar (another species).

*Mal-chang:* large willow (Salix viminalis).

*Rong-chang:* cliff willow (Salix tetra-sperma).

*Yáli:* maple.

*Tákpa:* white-flowered rhododendron.

*Tákma:* red-flowered rhododendron.

*Se-shing:* spruce (Abies Smithiana).

*Dün-shing:* silver-fir (Abies Webbiana).

*Som-shing:* (Pinus Gerardiana) (?)

*Séma-dong:* (Abies Brunoniana).

*Sá-dong:* larch (Larix Griffithii).

*Ti-dong:* (Pinus longifolia).

*Tong-shing:* (Pinus excelsa).

*Ridp'ang:* Neosa pine.

*Tsenden:* cypress (Cupressus funebris).

*Ting-shing:* yew (Taxus baccata).

*Shuk-po:* (Juniperus pseudo-sabina).

*Páma:* (Juniperus squamosa)

*De-shuk*: (Juniperus recurva).

*Targa*: walnut.

*Gom-rok*: holly.

*Champaka*: magnolia (Michelia Champaka).

*Luduma*: (Decaisnea insignis).

*Shá'máli-shing*: a huge Bombax loaded with lovely scarlet blossom, producing pods bursting with long silky wool.

*Ku-shu*: Tibetan apple.

*Nyo-ti*: Yarlung pear.

*Sendu*: pomegranate.

*Choli*: apricot.

*Wosé-shing*: mulberry.

*Kye-dum*: plantain (in Zayul).

*Dhá-li*: dwarf rhododendron.

*Manupatra*: (Bryonia dioeca).

*Tu-nak*: (Helleborus niger).

*Li-tsi*: (Pyrus baccata). See Huc. vol. I, 24.

*Wamp'u-shing*: (Pyrus ursina,) stunted-shrub akin to rowan.

*Ser-lum*: wild yellow raspberry.

*Kyu-dema*: current bearing edible large red sour berries.

*Bhi-li-tsi*: wild gooseberry.

*Alhirso*: cranberry.

*Kunda kári*: cloudberry.

*Kyerpa*: barberry (Berberis Tibetanus).

*Nyang-ka*: wild current (Ribes petræum).

*Se-wa*: yellow rose.

*Ts'er-tar-kár*: Sallow-thorn (Hippophaë rhamnoides).

*Taru*, or *Kharmu*: (Nitraria Schoberi) "camel's thorn."

*Umbhu*: tamarisk.

*Burtse*: Eurotia.

*Dháma*: Tibetan furze.

*Brita*: (Cuscuta epilinum).

*Ts'e-pe'*: (Ephedra saxatilis).

*Chiṭáka*: (Anemone rivularis).

*Bhong-mar*: red aconite (Aconitum luridum).

*Bhong-nák*: (Aconitum napellus).

*Tong*: gigantic arum (Arisœma).

*Lá-chhu*: rhubarb.

*Ruta*: elecampane.

*Jhyá-kang*: (Orobanche cœrulia).

*Jhyá-po tsi-tsi*: (Impatiens Roylei).

*Jhang-chhup shing*: white narcissus.

*Yá-kyima*: (Saussurea gossypina).

*Kurkum*: marigold (Caltha scaposa).

*Khur-ts'ö'*: dandelion.

*Tikta*: chiretta.

*Dheima*: poa grass.

*Lu-dü'*: plant with edible tubers (Codonopsis ovata).

*Cho-ma*: (Potentilla anserina) having edible roots which are highly-prized in Tibet

(See Huc. II. 86, and Rockhill 180).

*Zá-tsa*: large nettle (Urtica heterophylla).

*De*: (Daphne papyraceæ).

*Ṭang-goi*: (Arenaria rupifraga).

*A-ṭ'ong*: (Arenaria Roylea).

*Sira karpo*: (Cuminum cyminum).

*Serchhe*: (Saxifraga flagellaris).

*Ladára*: (Delphinium glaciale).

*Ngömbhu*: Delphinium Brunonianum).

*Látsi-metok*: Musky Pedicularis.

---

## FAUNA AND AVI-FAUNA OF TIBET.

### Mammalia.

*Ḍong* འབྲོང་ Wild yak (Poëphagus grunniens).

*Ḍong-ḍi*: Wild yak-cow.

*Ḍong-ṭ'uk*: Wild calf.

*Yák* གཡག་ Tame yak (general term).

*Ḍimo* འབྲི་མོ་ Domestic female yak.

*Ḍimdzo*: cross between yellow ox and *ḍimo*.

*Dzo* མཛོ་ (often *Jo*) cross between yak-bull and common Indian cow.

*Dzo-mo*: female of this breed; the most common domestic animal in Tibet.

*Garpo—Garmo*: male and female resulting from further crossing of *dzo-po* or *dzo-mo* with common Indian cattle.

*Tolmo*: further cross, back towards yak by interbreeding *garmo* with yak-bull.

*Langto*: Common humped-ox (Taurus Indicus).

*Bhá-chu*: Humped cow.

*Ngá-gö'* རྔ་རྒོད་ Wild camel (Camelus Bactrianus).

*Ngá-mong* རྔ་མོང་ Domestic Bactrian camel.

*Gung* གུང་ Mongol Tiger: thick-furred and broad-headed species found on Chinese frontier (Mongol: *Kharakula*).

*Ták* སྟག་ Common Tiger (Felis tigris); variety of, found in Záyul and Pemakoichhen, S. E. Tibet.

*Sik* གཟིག་ Tibetan leopard (Felis irbis) akin to the Ounce.

*Sá* གསའ་ Snow leopard (Felis macrocelis); named *shan* in Ladak.

*Sá-chuk* གསའ་ལྕུགས་ Clouded leopard (Felis macroceloides) akin to the Rimau Dahan of Sumatra.

*Pungmar* དཔུང་དམར་ (also *Sik jug-kar*): Red-shouldered tiger-cat (Felis nigrescens: *Hodgs*).

*Sikmár*: Marbled tiger-cat (Felis dosal).

*Yi* དབྱི་ Tibetan Lynx (Felis isabellina) paler than Felis lynchus (in Ladak *i*).

*Tsokde* or *yi-chhung*: Pallas's Lynx (Felis manul).

*Sik-chhum*: Spotted Civet-cat (Prionodon pardicolor: *Hodgs*).

*Sá-chhyong* གསའ་འཕྱོང་ Common Civet-cat. (Viverra melanurus: *Hodgs.*)

*Chyá-sik*: Paradoxurus laniger: *Hodgson.*

*Shul-jhi*: Tibetan Pole-cat (Putorius Tibetanus).

*Tou-p'i*: Tibetan tree-marten (Martes toufæus: *Blyth.*)

*Tou-lo*: Indian Marten (Martes flavigula).

*Kálön-shrám*: Black Sable (Putorius zibellina).

*Bulákha*: Golden Sable of Tsang (Putorius auriventer); a rare and beautiful species found in Tsang, Lhobrak, and Jhya-yul.

*Kangshram*: Ermine (Mustela erminea).

*Ṭé-mong*: Pale Weasel (Mustela temon).

*Lá-kyimo*: White-nosed Weasel (Mustela canigula).

*Stré-mong*: general term for species of Weasel found in East Tibet, *e. g.*, Mustela Moupinensis, Mustela astutus, and Mustela Davidianus.

*Wok-kar* སྲོག་དཀར་ White-throated Ferret-Badger (Helictis monticola).

*Dhumpa* གྲུམ་པ་ Tibetan Badger (Meles leucura); found in Tsang.

*Dhum-pu-se*: Tibetan Shrew-Badger (Arctonyx albogularis).

*Ṭuk-shram*: Hill Otter (Lutra aureobrunnea).

*Chhu-shram*: Clawless Otter (Aonyx leptonyx).

*Wák-dongkha* འོག་སྡོང་ཁ་ Tibetan Racoon or Red Cat-bear (Ailurus ochraceus).

*Dhom* དོམ་ Tawny Bear (Ursus pruinosus: *Blyth*).

*Dhom-khdina:* Snow Bear (Ursus isabellinus).

*Ḍhe'mong* དྲེད་མོང་ Kö-kö-nur Bear (Ursus lagomyarius).

*Tik-dhompa:* Spectacled white Bear (Aeluropus melanoleucus) found in Moupin and probably north of Namts'o Chhyidmo.

*Chyang-ku* སྤྱང་ཀུ་ Golden Wolf of Tibet (Lupus Tibetanus). Called *shangku* in Ladak.

*Chyang-rok:* Black Wolf of Tibet (Lupus lycaon).

*P'archyang:* Wild Dog (Cuon alpinus: *Pallas*).

*P'ar-wa:* Lesser Wild Dog (Cuon primævus).

*Wá-mo:* Himalayan Fox (Vulpes montana).

*Wá-do-do* ཝ་གོ་གོ་ Yellow Tibetan Fox (Vulpes flavescens); found all over Tibet.

*Yi-gur* or *Wátse:* Rusty Fox (Vulpes ferrilatus).

*Wá-nák:* a black Fox.

*Gomkhyi:* Larger Tibetan Mastiff.

*Shang:khyi:* Small Mongol sledge dogs.

*Lingkhyi:* Greyhound.

*Chhi-wa;* or *Chhi-p'i:* the Tibetan Marmot; of which several species exist in Tibet, swarming everywhere.

*Kyang* རྐྱང་ Wild Ass of Tibet (Equus kyang).

*Bong-bhu:* Domestic Ass.

*Tá:* Horse.

*Wal-wa:* small black horse of Gyangtse.

*Dhe-po:* mule.

*Shá-u* or *Shá-wa:* large deer sometimes known in books as the Barasingh (Cervus Wallichii).

*Khá-shá:* Spotted deer.

*Séru* བསེ་རུ་ the Serow (Nemorrhœdus bubalinus).

*Tsö'* or *Tseu* གཙོད་ the so-called Hodgson's antelope; the *cho* of provincial Tibetans and *stsot* of the Ladaki.

*Go-a* དགོ་བ་ Ravine deer or Tibetan chamois (Procapra picticaudata).

*Lá-wa* གླ་བ་ Musk deer (Moschus moschiferus), of which there are 3 species.

*Kyin* སྐྱིན་ Tibetan Ibex (Capra sakeen).

*Danmo* ལྡན་མོ་ Female Ibex.

*Ná* གནའ་ or *Nápu* : the great Burrhel wild sheep (Ovis Nahur).

*Nyen* གཉན་ the Argali wild sheep (Ovis Ammon).

*Shapo* : Another wild sheep (Ovis Vignei).

*Jhang-luk* : the large load-carrying domestic sheep of N.-W. Tibet.

*Rá-wo* : Common goat.

*Rá-po-chhe* : Wild goat.

*Jagma* : Red Squirrel of Sikkim.

*T'ályi* : Squirrel; steel grey with jet-black tail.

*Ri-gong* : Hare. 4 species.

*Abrá* ; and *Zábrá* : Several varieties of Lagomys or tail-less rats are included under these names.

*Ting-Jing* དིང་སྦྱིང་ Brown-toothed shrew (Sorex Sikkimensis).

*Tak-lungchen* བྲག་ལྷུང་ཅན་ Spider shrew (Sorex myoides: *Blanford*).

*Shing-ting-jing* : Tree shrew of Khams (Tupaia Chinesis).

*Chhu-jhi-tse* : Tibetan water shrew (Nectogale elegans).

*P'u-se* or *Prá-li* : Tail-less shrew (Anurosorex squamipes).



*Tsi-p'u-tse* : Uropsilus soricipes.

*Pi-chhung* : Musk-rat (Sorex murinus).

*Suráman* : Brown mole of Kökö Nur (Scaptonyx fusicaudatus: *Milne Edwards*).

*Byu-long* : Short-tailed mole (Talpa micrura).

*Lá-tsi-byu-long* : Musk mole (Scaptocheiros moschatus): in N. E. Tibet.

*Jhi-tsi* : Common rat.

*Tsi-tsi* : Common mouse.

*Zikmong* : Porcupine (in Zayul, &c.)

*Gang-šerma* : Hedgehog: term for both the Erinaceus auritus and Erinaceus Amurensis (of Kökö Nur).

*Teu* སྤྲེའུ་ Greyish-yellow langur monkey with long tail (Semnopithecus schistaceus).

*Shtré-khö* : Larger Tibetan Macaque monkey found in Khams, &c. (Macacus Tibetanus).

*Mánu* : A brown monkey.

*A-nwo* : Szechuen monkey—Macacus cyclopis.

*Trá*, or *Shra* : སྤྲ White langur monkey.

*P'a-wang* : *Jhyá-soma* : *Gá-wang-Ṭe'kyi* : *Gá-p'ong* : } Names used with little discrimination for various species of Bats. The following kinds frequent different regions of Tibet :—

Plecotus auritus (Long-eared Bat).

Synotus Tibetanus (var. of Barbastelle).

Vesperugo noctula.

Vesperugo serotinus.

Vesperugo discolor.

Vesperugo Leslieri.

Vesperugo Maurus (in Dokde and Derge).

Vesperugo borealis (in Khams and Amdo).

Hipposiderus Prattii (Darchendo and Lit'ang).

Scoptophilus ornatus (Yunnan frontier).

Vespertilio mystacinus (East Tibet).

Vespertilio dasyeneme (Tsaidam).

Harpiocephalus herpia (Sikkim, Zayul).

BIRDS.

*Jhyá-lák* : Eagle.

*Jhángö'* or *Gho-wo* : Lammergayer.

*Kyák-lák* : White Scavenger Vulture.

*Gho-ser* : Himalayan Vulture.

*Nyá-lák* : Osprey.

*Ping-kyu-ma* : Kite.

*Né-lé* : Great Buzzard.

*Bhong-ṭ'a* : Tibetan Falcon.

*Ṭ'á* : Hawk (two or three species of).

*Ukpa* ; also *Singjhya Ukpa* : Owl, the many species of which are hardly discriminated by Tibetans.

*P'orok* ; also *Chhoi-kyong* : Raven (Pyrrhocorax graculus).

*Khá-ta* : Crow (Corvus pastinator).

*Kyungka* : Jackdaw.

*Ṭe-ka* : Magpie (Pica pica).

*Gomchhen kyá-khá* : Large-headed Magpie.

*Sa-sháka* : Jay.

*Jol-nák* : A species of Blackbird (Merula ruficollis) : the འཇོལ་མོ་ of Tibetan literature.

*Jol-ṭ'á* : A large piebald Merula, described as white in color with yellow markings, and red behind the ears.

*T'ung-t'ung* : Crane.

*Kangka* : Heron (Ardea prasinosceles).

*Kyarmo* : Bittern.
*Khamchhu Ringmo* : Snipe (Scolopax solitaria).
*Mábjhya* : Peacock.
*P'urgön* : Wood Pigeon.
*Ang-gu* : Dove.
*Shing-gön* ; Woodpecker.
*Lhájhyá Ghongmo* : Crossoptilon Tibetanum.
*Ri-kyek* : Lophophorus l'Huysii
*Ghong-yak* : Ithaginis Geoffryoi.
*Horpa-karpo* : Thaumalea Amherstiæ.
*Horpa* : Thaumalea picta.
*Juk-deb* : Wagtail.
*Ghong-sek* : Phasianus decollatus.
*Sekpa* : Partridge.
*Ong-lok* : Tragopon (Ceriornis Temmincki).
*Ou-nétso* : Parrot.
*Pupu-kushu* : Hoopoe.
*Kángbo* : Swallow.
*Chhilpik* : Sparrow.
*Ngangpa karpo* : White Goose.
*Ngangpa serpo* : Yellow Goose.
*Hwang-ya* : Sheldrake.
*Ngurpa* : Wild Duck.
*Ngur-ru* : Teal.
*Yá-tsé* : Common Duck.
*Kházhur* : Water-hen.

---

## SPORTING IN TIBET.

rifle : *me-dá*.
double-barrel rifle.
Turkish musket : *chák-ṭ'á*.
pistol : *rangbár*.
gunpowder : *medzé*.
bullet : *dik-ril*.
cartridge : *medzé-shup*.
small-shot : *ts'igu*.
gun-stock : *gumdá*.
gun-barrel : *dá-chák*.
powder-flask : *dze-khug*.
gun-cap : *me-do*.
(really "flint.")
trigger : *másha*.
gun-cock : *me-kám*.
hunting-knife : *rá-kyi*.
spear : *dung; dung-t'ung*.
saddle-cloth : *gá-khep*.
knap-sack : *khábtáka*.
to fire : *gyap-pa* (*me-dá*).
to shoot : *p'áng-pa*.
to aim at : *dik-pa*.
to hit : *khéi-pa*.
to wound : *má-chung-wa*.
to kill : *se-pa ; sok chö-pa*.
to lie in wait : *kok-jáb-pa*.
to creep : *p'e-wa*.
to stab : *sok-khung gyap-pa*
horns : *rácha*.
skin : *pák-pa*.
tail : *šhu-gu*.
bones : *rü-pa*.
feathers : *puḍo*.
claws : *der-kyu*.

[When the native explorer A—. K—. visited, in the year 1880–81, the northern parts of Tibet, he brought back word of the marvellous profusion of game of the larger kinds to be found roaming over the steppes of the Jáng-t'ang. Mr. Hennessey in the official report thus summarises the explorer's information:—"The Jángt'ang is a vast and marvellous expanse of high undulating land ...... only some 100 miles broad to the west near Skardo; it is widest on the meridian of 86° where it is some 500 miles across, and to the east it ends in an inclined width of some 350 miles, from whence it slopes further eastwards, rapidly losing its characteristics and merging into the cultivated lands of China. Its length is about 1,500 miles, and in area it is some 480,000 sq. miles ...... This enormous tract of high table-land is believed to be generally some 15 or 16 thousand feet above sea-level..... The whole Jángt'ang is coated by a short succulent grass, which from May to August, covers the undulations with the softest of green carpets, extending far away and visible for even 50 or 60 miles in the clear crisp atmosphere prevailing. But beyond the abundant grass, *nothing* else will grow on this high land; there is no wood or scrub of any kind for fuel; and, in a word, the products of the earth are solely suited for graminivorous animals, which run wild in enormous numbers, as the yák, goat, sheep, deer, &c.; and the weaker of these provide food for the wolf, jackal, and *yi* (lynx). It is said the grass does seed, and most probably is propagated chiefly by that means; but other seeds, as of wheat or barley, though they germinate and produce fodder for cattle, yield mainly seedless ears, and hence no food for man ...... The vast number of wild animals of the Jángt'ang sufferer diminution from one cause only—the occasional extreme severity of winter, when, deprived of grass, they die by thousands, as their skeletons testify."]

| | |
|---|---|
| The gun is not loaded: | *Me-dá di dze-me re'.* |
| Give me another gun: | *Ngá-la me-dá šhemma kur chik.* |
| When I have fired, hand me the other gun at once: | *Gyap song-ne, tanda t'eltu ngá-la me-dá ŝhemma kur chik.* |
| As soon as you see it, call out: | *Di-la t'ong ṭ'al, ke gyak!* (or *khá tang*). |
| I saw the antelope near the river down there: | *Má-gi-la chhu-i ḍo-ru tseu di mik t'ong jhung.* |
| Climb up that tree yonder and look round: | *Há-gi shing dhe dzek-la khor tö shok.* |
| Do you see anything: | *Khyörang-ghī ghang-yang ŝhik t'ongpe?* |
| I see nothing: | *Ngárang-ghī ghang-yang t'ong ghi ma re'.* |
| Follow me quickly: go carefully: | *Nyurdhu nge shug-la shok; chá-ghá song.* |
| That is the dung of what animal? Do you know: | *Dhü'ḍo gháng-la chi-wa di yimpe? Khyörang she-sám?* |
| Lukpa! where are you: | *Wá Lukpa! Khyörang ghá re'?* |
| Here? what is it, Sir: | *Diru! lá lá-sám?* |

| | |
|---|---|
| Be ready with the cartridges: | *Médzé shup dhe ṭ'álti ŝhák?* |
| If I miss it, there will be a struggle for life: | *Ngárang-ghī di-la mi khéi-ná* ("if I don't hit it"), *sok dhang tondá jhung gyu re'.* |
| Sir; I hold my life cheap (*lit*: "do not see my life"): | *Kusho; nge sok-la mik tá-ghi-me'.* |
| Bears live on that slope: | *Dhe-mo-ts'o dher gang-khá-la dö-ghi yö'.* |
| What is the name of that bird? | *Jhyá di-la m̂ing ghang ŝer?* |
| I don't know; I forget: | *Shen-ghi ma re'; ngárang je'-ghi re'.* |
| Pick that up; I want it: | *Dhe ruk chik! ngá-la kho-jhe yö'.* |
| We must climb up the torrent-bed: | *Ngácha ḍhokšar-la shö'ne dzek go.* |
| Hold on to the tree! take care: | *Shing di dzin: rikpa ḍim?* |
| I am slipping down: | *Shö'dhu ḍe'ták shor-ghi-yö'.* |
| Throw down the powder-flask: | *Dze-khu' dhe t'engla yuk chik.* |
| Let it fall gently: | *Di jám-jám gyer nang.* |
| I want help: give me your hand: | *Roram goi-pa: ngá-la lák sing tong.* |
| There is no grass: the plain is quite bare: | *Tsá me': t'áng di t'er t'er du'.* |
| Do you ever see wild yák on this plain: | *T'áng di la dü re shi' dong ḍa t'ong ki du' ka?* |
| I have never seen yáks here: | *Ngáráng-gī di-ru dong t'ong ma nyong.* |
| Many wild yáks are found beyond that lake yonder: | *P'á-gi ts'o dhe p'en-chhe dong m̂áng-po nye chung.* |
| Do you see those trees on the opposite side of the valley: | *Khyö' shing-ts'o dhe lung-pá-i p'ar-khá t'ong-ká?* |
| Look further on: you will see three go-wa deer: | *P'ar-tsam toi shok: khyö-kyi go-wa sum t'ong yong.* |
| Beyond the three go-wa are six nyen: | *Go-wa sum di p'enchhe nyen ṭuk yö'.* |
| I see them: until now I did not notice them. | *Ngá dhe-la mik t'ong: dhá-ta p'en dhe-la jhá-ra ma jhe'.* |

| | |
|---|---|
| Look again: take heed: | *Lok-te tö̩ shok: nyön chik!* |
| Look out! where are you going: | *Rik ḍim! kápa ḍo-ghi yin?* |
| Drag the body to the river-side: | *Chhu-yi ḍám-tu ɼo di t'en song.* |
| Can you skin it: | *Pakpa di shu ts'uk-ká?* |
| Work carefully: | *Chágha láika jhyi' chik!* |
| Collect dry dung and burtse, and light a fire: | *Bang-kám burtse t'u-ne m̂e ḍhuk ŝhi'.* |
| Where is the tinder-case. | *Mé-chák-khuk di ghá ɼe'?* |

---

## SHOPPING IN LHA'SA'.

| | |
|---|---|
| Where can I buy books: | *Pe-chhá-ts'o ghá-pa nyo t'up yong-ngá?* |
| Book-vendors remain standing near the western gate of Cho-khang: | *Pe-chhá-ts'ongpa Cho-kẖang-ghi nup-gyá-go tsá-nái táng-te de'.* |
| Do they sell printed books: | *Pár-ma ts'ong-ghi-re'?* |
| They sell both printed books and Manuscripts: | *Pár-ma yik-chha nyí-pa ts'ong-ghi re'.* |
| I want to buy the Pe'ma Tang Yik of Pe'ma Jungnái and the Pönpo book Lu Bum Karpo: | *Pe'ma Jungnái-kyi Pe'ma Tang Yik di dhang Pön-kyi pe-chhá Lu Bum Karpo nyo kho wa yö'.* |
| I have the first book; the second is not sold publicly in Lhásá: | *Ngá-la pe-chhá dhangpo di yö'; nyí-pa di Lhásá-la á-sál-la ts'ong ghi ma re'.* |
| What price do you ask for Gyal-rabs Sal-wai Me-long: | *Gyá-ráp Salwe Mélong-ghi rin ghá ts'ö' lap-ki yö'.* |
| I want twenty Gáldan ţangka: | *Ngárang-la Gänden ţangka nyi-shu göi-pa.* |
| Will you please abate the price: | *Khyö'rang khe-ru song ɼo dze'.* |
| Sir, I have fixed (*lit*: "cut") the price; I cannot abate: | *Kusho; rin di chö' pa yin; khe-ru ḍo mi ts'uk.* |
| You are outwitting me: | *Khyö'rang-ghi ngá-la ḍok long.* |

| | |
|---|---|
| I never cheat; we do not throw abuse like that in Lhásá: | *Ngárang lui ma nyong; Lhásá-la khá-ts'ok dhenḍe ma gyák.* |
| You fix the price too high: | *Di gong háchangne chö'-ki-yö'.* |
| I will lessen the price one ṭangka: | *Ngárang ṭangka chi' khe-ru ḍo-gyu re'.* |
| Taking the price, give me the book, please: | *Gong dhe len-te, ngárang-lá pe-chha nang ro nang.* |
| Where are the tea-shops; kindly show me: | *Jhá-i ts'ong-khang ghá re'; ten ro nang.* |
| Tea is sold in the market: | *T'om-la jhá ts'ong-wa.* |
| What kinds of tea have you: | *Jhái rik ghang yö'pe?* |
| Various kinds; all that are necessary: | *Ná-so-so; t'ámche kho-jhe yö'.* |
| What sort is this tea: | *Jhá di rik ghang é yö'?* |
| What is the weight of the brick: | *Párká-yi dek-khá ghá ts'ö'?* |
| The full weight of this kind: | *Di rik-kyi dek-khá ts'angma yö'.* |
| What do you call that tea: | *Dhe sol-jhá-i m̂ing-la ghang ŝer?* |
| This tea, Sir, is the best; it is named Ḍu-t'ang No. 1: | *Kusho, soljha dhe anjki t'eb-bo yö'* (lit: "that tea, it is the thumb," *i.e.*, best); *m̂ing di Ḍu-t'ang angki dhangpo ŝer jhung.* |
| The price is one shrang and two tangka each brick: | *Párka re-re-lá shrang chi' dha-rung ṭangka nyí di rin di re'.* |
| That other tea is Ḍu-t'ang No. 2; that is the second class: | *Jhá ŝhemma Ḍu-t'ang angki nyí-pa re'; dhe rik nyí-pa re'.* |
| The third kind is called Gyepa; and the worst is Goka: | *Rik sumpa di Gye'pa ŝer yö'; dhang t'á-ma di Goka re'.* |
| Show me, please, the way to the Nipalese merchants: | *Pá'po-i ts'ong-mi-la lam ten ro nang.* |
| They live in T'om-si-ghang near Wangdu chhörten: | *Dhe-ts'o T'om-si-ghang-la 'vang dhu chhörten tsánai dö'-ki-re'.* |
| What merchandize do they sell: | *Dhe-ts'o ts'ong-zok ghang ts'ong wa?* |
| They sell vases, ornaments and bells; they are the gold- | *Kho-ts'o-yí bhumpa, gyenchhá, ḍhilbhu; kho-ts'o Lhásáchen* |

| | |
|---|---|
| smiths and iron mongers of Lhásá; they are skilled artificers and make the large gilt-copper domes and gyap'ik for temples: | *sérgár chákgár yö'; kho-ts'o dzo-pa kyen-po yin-nai kambung gyáp'ik ser-śangchen chhempo dzo-ki-re' gompe tönla.* |
| Turn to the left; now see the Palpo workshops! | *Yön ngö-la* or *chhok-la ḍo goi; tandá Pá'pochen zo-khang la toi śhok!* |
| Over each door is a round red mark and under the red circle is a white crescent: you enter thus—beneath those low narrow door-ways, down three or four steps: | *Go-t'ö'la re-re ták mar-po ril-ril yö'te gormo marpo-yi wok-la dá-wa chhye'chok yö'pe: dhe go't'em-kyi wokla—men ṭ'ámo—t'emso sum śhi shö'dhu—dhenḍe nang-la p'ep ro.* |
| Some of these Nipalese are chemists and some are dyers: | *P'á'po khá-she mén-ts'ongkhen khá-she ts'oi-gyák-khen re'.* |
| This is a gold-worker's shop; enter and see what he sells: | *Di-ká ser-zo-pa-yi khang-pa re'; p'ep-la ghang ts'ongpa di tö ro chik.* |
| Sir, salaam; what can this humble one do for your worship: | *Kusho, chhá'p'ep; ṭ'embhu di nyí-rang-ghi dhöndhu ghang dze'cho-gha?* |
| I want a golden charm-box with turquoise and pearls: | *Ngá-la ser-gyi sung-gá-wo dhang yu-chá mutik dhang kho-jhe' yö'.* |
| Here is what you want: See upon it what kind of turquoises there are! six "yup'uk" the most precious sort, and many of the good kinds of turquoise "t'ukmar" and "t'uk-kar." Here also are coral beads. All those are the thumb. No bad ones at all: | *Ngi'rang-la ghang kho-wai dhe di-ka yö'. Dhe-la yu-kyi rik ghang toi ro nang shik! yup'uk ḍhuk chik rik rim pochhe t'ukmár t'uk-kar mangpo yukyi rik le-mo dhe-la yö'. Dir kyang jhu-ru-i ali yö'. Dheyi ts'angma angki t'eb-bo yö'nai; la-re rik akpo me'.* |

| | |
|---|---|
| I want a silver clasp and a kabzoma of gold with jasper and amber beads on it: | *Ngárang-la ngul-kyi chhabtse dhang ser-kyi kabzoma ŝhik dhang dhe-la yangti-i ali, poshel-kyi ali kyang kho-jhe' yö'.* |
| We sell silver things by weight: (*lit:* "Like what (*ghanḍe*) the weight of silver shall come, like that those things are sold.") | *Ngul-kyi karka ghánde yö'pa, dhenḍe ts'ong-wa yin.* |
| All is settled (*i. e.*, The business is concluded). | *T'ámche gho-chö' jhung* (or *chö' ts'ar*). |
| Weigh these ear-rings and buckles on the steel yards: What weight? | *Ai-kor chhabma di-ts'o gyáma-la tek ro chik: Karka ghá ts'ö'?* |
| Excellency: fourteen sho: | *Kusho; ŝho chubŝhi.* |
| Will you dye this pulo red: | *Kyö'kyí t'erma di marpo ts'oi gyak-gyu-re'.* |
| Only Tibetan cloth is legally permitted to be dyed: | *Ṭ'im-la Pö'kyi t'ruk kar-kyang ts'oi gyak chhok.* |
| Where do the Kashmiri merchants live? | *Khá-chhe ts'ong-pa di ghára de' pa?* |
| Their shops are very fine; there is nothing that is not collected together there: | *Dhe-yi ts'ong-khang dze-bo chhe re'; dher dzompa me'pa chik kyang me'.* |
| You can buy poultry, eggs, fruit, and tsampa at the Wangdu-siga market: | *Ṭ'om Wang-dhu-siga la khyim-jhya gong-do, shing-t'ok, tsam-pa, nyo ts'uk.* |
| This sheep is plump: | *Luk di ts'ömpo re'.* |
| Your servant will buy mutton at the Gya-gyo-wak-sha market: | *Nyi'kyi yokpo Gya-gyo-wak-shá ṭ'om-la lukshá nyo yong.* |
| Meat is very cheap in Lhásá: | *Lhásá-la shá kye-po re'.* |
| The sinful butchers are Mussalmans who kill all meat outside Lhásá at Chiri: | *Dikchen shempa Chiri-la Lhásá-i chhyi-lo' la shá kün-kyi shrok se' pa-yi Khá-chhe-pa yö'.* |

Buy some curry-powder for two khá-ghang; it is dear in Lhásá. — *Khá-ghang nyi-la p'ing-ship nyo chi'; Lhásá la dhe kyong-po re'.*

Weigh this carefully on the steel yard and reckon the price by your su-an-pan. — *Di-ka gya-ma-la nya-ra-kyí tek-nai nyi'rang-ghi su-an-pan nang s̆hin rin di tsi-nai gyak ro chi'.*

Measure the length of that: — *Dhe-kyi ring t'ung ts'e' jal chi'.*

---

## VISIT TO KIN-KHOR-DING.

[This is one of the appellations of the principal temple in Lhásá; but the place is also known familiarly as *Cho-khang* or the "Lord's House." Sarat Chandra Dás describes it fully under this name in his secret Report (unpublished as yet); whilst the Survey explorer A. K. alludes to it thus: "In the centre of the city stands a very high square temple called Jhio, the roof of which is covered with golden plates. The images in it are numerous, but the most important of these are of Jhio Sákia Muni and of Palden Lhámo. The idols are richly inlaid with gold and precious stones, and have various ornaments round their necks"]:—

To-day the Nirvana month begins: — *Dhe-ring Ságá-dáwa di jhung ("arises").*

To-day the Lord Buddha became Bhagawan: — *Dhe-ring-la Jho-wo Sáng-gyai di Chomdendai ḍub jhung.*

All persons will go to the Cho-khang to do homage to the precious lord: — *Kye-wo kün Cho-khang-la ḍo-nai, Jho-wo Rimpochhe-yi ŝháb-la ku-rim dze-yong.* Or: *Kün Jho-wo Rimpochhe-yi ŝháb-la ku-rim dze'pai dhön-dhu Cho-khang-la ḍo-gu-yin.*

Let us go early: — *Ngá-sar ḍo-gyu-yin.*

There will be a great crowd: — *T'om chhempo chi' ts'o yong.*

What shall we take with us: — *Ngáchá-la chhá ghang k̃hyer-wá;*

Everybody is taking incense-sticks: — *Kün-kyi poi-rengbhu len-ghi-du'.*

Anything else: — *Dhárung yö'dham?*

They are carrying bowls of butter for the sacred lamps; also scarves of various kinds: — *Már-me-yi dhön-dhu márchen-kyi p'orpa dhárung khá-tá ná-ts'o-ts'o khyer-ghi re'.*

| | |
|---|---|
| We will withdraw from the throng and go up this lane: | *Mi-ts'ok dhang ghye-nai l̂am-shrang di ghyen-la ḍo-gyu-yin.* |
| Now we are near the Cho-khang: | *Dháta Chokhang-ghi tsánai lep-song.* |
| Do you see yon tall poplar: | *Há-gi sho'po ringpo di t'ong chog-ghá?* |
| Well! what is it: | *Yákpo! Ghang é du'?* |
| That poplar grows up from the sacred hair of Buddha lying beneath it: | *Dhe wok-la Jho-woi ṭá-dho-ker kur tang šhu-pai, sho'po di ṭ'ung jhung.* |
| And do you see that column there: | *Pá-gi do-ring dhe-la t'ong-ghá?* |
| Tell me what it means: | *Dhe ghaṇg yin ngá-la she'.* |
| That column is a memorial of the victory by Tibetans over the Chinese: | *Pö'pa-yī Gyá-nák-pa la jóm-pa-i wang-dhu shor-na je-do ŝhik doring dhe lang-nai de'.* |
| Behold the portico of the Cho-khang! We will enter: | *Cho-khang-ghi ka-chen-kyi gyá-go di toi-shik! Nang-la ḍo-gyu-yin.* |
| First, we enter the Ṭi-tsang-khang: | *Ngün-la Ṭi-tsang-khang-ghi nang-la ŝhug-ghin-du'.* |
| Now the image-keeper comes; he will explain everything: | *Dhá-tá ku-nyer di yong-ghi-re'; khorang kün she'-yong.* |
| This one is the famous image of the most precious lord (Buddha): | *Di-ká Jho-wo Rimpochhe-yi ku-ten rák-chen di yö'.* |
| This image here is not the representation of him as Buddha: in this figure he is only 12 years old; and therefore you see a young prince but not the Victorious One Perfected: | *Di ku-ten di Sang-gye-kyi yib ma re': di yib-la khong* (for *khorang*) *lo chu-nyi ting-la mempe mi yong; dhenḍe gyál-shrái šhön-nu ŝhik t'ong rung, Chomdendai di t'ong-ghi-me'.* |
| See you; the face is remark-ably beautiful: | *Nyi-rang šī shik! Ser-ŝhál* ("the golden face," honorific for *ŝhál*) *di nyam-ts'árwa re'.* |

| | |
|---|---|
| Yonder stands the image of Tsong-khápa. Beside him has been placed the fossil rock named Amolonkha: | *Há-gi-la Tsong-khápa-yi ku-ten di ḍeng-te dö'. Dhe-tsá-né ḍhak kampo Amolonkhá dhen-ḍe jhá-wa di ŝhák-ne du'.* |
| Why is that piece of rock t̲here; and what is that bell upon it: | *Há-gi p'á-wong dhe ghang-la ten-nai, di ḍhilbu di yang dhe-i tengkha ghang du' ka?* |
| Tsongkhápa discovered that rock himself in a cavern; and that bell is the bell which was used by Mongal-puttra: | *P'uk-pa nangla Tsongkhápa nyi-rang-ghī p'á-wong dhe nye jhung; di ḍhilbu di Mongal-puttra-yī pempā jhye'ne yö'.* |
| Over there in that chapel you see the blessed eleven-faced Chenresi: | *P'á-ki lháten-la Chenresi chuchi-shálchen kálden di tá chok.* |
| That figure was made at the command of King Srong-tsan-gampo; and then the king and his four wives having died, their spirits were absorbed into that image: | *Song-tsen-gámpo Gyálpo-i ká solnái di kuten di ŝo jhung-te, dhe-nái gyálpo dne dhe-yi tsün-mo s̆hi ḍub ŝhing la p'ep-ne di p'ungpoi nangla khong-ghi sem-ts'o ts'uk jhung re'.* |
| It is a marvellous image: | *Ten ngo-ts'archen chi' lá so.* |
| Pass into the outer courtyard: | *P'i-yi khyam-rá-la ḍul nang.* |
| In the courtyard stands the effigy of Tho-wo-me-tsikpa: further on have been placed Tang-tong Gyal-po, and the lo-tsá-wa Marpa: | *Khyamrá-la T'o-wo-me-tsikpá-i kunḍá di ŝhák-nái-du': dhe pen-chhe' Tang-tong-Gyalpo dhang Marpa lo-tsáwa s̆hu-nái-re'.* |
| Tang-tong Gyalpo lived 60 years in his mother's womb before birth: | *Kye-wái ngen-la Tang-tong Gyal-po yum-kyi lhum-kyi bug-la lo ḍhuk chu s̆hu-ghi re'.* |
| But look! what numbers of mice are running about: | *Yinna-yang toi tang! tsiki du-du kor-kor gyuk.* |
| Monks have transmigrated into those mice: | *Khor-la ge-long-ts'o ni tsi-ki teru gyur-song.* |

| | |
|---|---|
| Upstairs there are other Tsang-khang and other shrines : | *Yá-t'ok la Tsáng-khang šhen tang kuten šhen šhú yö'.* |
| What gods shall we see upstairs : | *Yá-t'ok la lhá ghang ŝi-gyu ?* |
| In the Bar-khang are Lha-mo Mák-jorma and the god Tamdin : | *Bár-khang ki nang-la Mákjorma Lhámo Tamdin Lhá šhu-so.* |
| Greatest of all, the image of Paldan Lha-mo is above : | *Teng-la, ts'angma nangne chhem-po, Pánden Lhá-mo šhū-so.* |
| Well, well ; we must perform full homage another day : | *Yák-po, yák-po ; ŝhák šhen la ngá-chák chhŏi-jál yong-su ts'al gŏi.* |
| Yes, Sir : | *Lhá, lá-so.* |
| We cannot make the circuit of all at one time : | *Ngāī tsar-chik la kang-gha-ì chhŏí-khor gyu chok-pa me'.* |
| Give some bakshish to the idol-keeper : | *Ku-nyer la solrá* (or *chá-gá*) *ter nang.* |

---

## THE SCAVENGER BEGGARS.

| | |
|---|---|
| There are some scavengers hastening after me: | *Tá-tá ro-gya-wa ŝhik ngai je-la nyek-ki duk.* |
| I will not listen to them : | *Ngá dhe-tak la t'ŏi gyu min.* |
| I shall treat them with contempt : | *Ngá kho-chák la ngen-chhen ten-gyu-yin-no.* |
| An alms, an alms ; give, give ! | *Dom-bu, dombu ; ter-nang, ter-nang.* |
| I have nothing to give you : | *Ngá khyŏ'la ter gyu chang me'.* |
| We are very poor men : | *Ngáchá wūl-p'ongpa re.'* |
| You shall bestow some present : | *Khyŏ' la chá-gá ŝhik chin gŏi.* |
| Get away, you rogues, you vultures : | *Há-la gyuk ! ngempa-po khyŏ' ! chá-lák khyŏ' !* |
| Give, give ! you are rich : | *Jhin ! Jhin ! Khyŏ' chhuk-po duk.* |
| I shall call the watchmen : | *Ngái korchakpa la ke tang-gyu-yin.* |

| | |
|---|---|
| Call, call! you must give one ţanka: | *Rák! Rák! Khyö' la ţanka chik ter gŏi.* |
| One ţanka! not even a khá-gang: | *Ţangka chi'! Khá-kang chi' lá-re me.'* |
| You have been a month in Lhásá, yet there is nothing at all for us: | *Dá-wá chi' nai khyö'rang Lhásá-la p'ep rung ngá-ts'o-la chang me'.* |
| Who cares! Who cares! I shall not give you anything: | *Á-u-se! á-u-se! Ngárang-ghi ye ma ter-gyu-re'* (or *ye ter-gyu ma re'*). |
| Ah then! wait until we get you (*lit*: come to us): | *Jhyá-ra! ngá-ts'o-la leb-pa t'uk-guk-te dö'chik.* |
| Don't bawl like that, filthy Rogya-pa: | *Rogyá-pa ts'ichen! Dhende chá-cho ma gyap.* |
| All right; listen here! when you are a corpse, tying a rope to your neck we will drag you like a dog outside the gates of the city. | *T'ik-t'ik; di-la nyön shik! Khyörang ro-ne p'o-wa-la, rang-ghi ke-la t'ákpa chhing-nai, khyi dhang ḍa-ts khyörang ḍhong-khyer-kyi go-mo p'en-chhe' drü' yong.* |
| We will tear you to pieces: | *Chhák-ţum-la khyö'rang shral-gyu-re'.* |
| Come along: these scavengers are indeed the pests of Lhásá: | *Nyampo shok: ro-gya-wa di Lhásá-i ngen-rim mö'do.* |
| They have been bawling away at me: | *Khongts'o ngárang-la m̃angpo bár ghi-yö'.* |
| Where do they live: | *Ghá-pa de'-ki-du'?* |
| They live on the eastern side, beyond Bhanakshol, in houses built of bone: | *Shar-chhyok-la, Bhana-sho' p'en-chhe'-la, rui-pá-chen khyim-la nai-ghi-re'.* |
| Though they dress in rags, they are very rich: | *Shrulpo ghyön rung, kho-la ñor m̃angpo re'.* |
| Remember it is thus said of them:—"Though outside their houses bristle with | *Sem-la ngei chi'—"P'i-lok-la di khyim di rá-cho-ne tsup-tsup jhung rung; nang-lok-la* |

| | |
|---|---|
| horns, inside indeed they sparkle with coins." | *dhekho-na nak-kyang-ne sák sák ts'er" dhenḍe sung-ghi-yö'.* |
| Many persons are afraid of the scavengers who are very ferocious: | *Ngar-po-chen yö'pai rogyá-wa di gháchhen-kyī jik jhung.* |

---

## LAKES: RIVERS: BOATING.

Lake: *ts'o.*
Salt-lake: *ts'ákha.*
Mere: *ts'e-u.*
River: *tsáng-po; chhu-wo.*
Brook: *bap-chhu.*
Torrents: *rišárchhu.*
Streamlet: *chhu-ṭ'en.*
Spring: *chhu-mik.*
River's-source: *chhu-go.*
Bank: *ḍám.*
Reeds: *nyuk-ma.*
Running-water: *gyuk-chhu.*
Current: *gyün.*
Boat: *ḍhu* (in Khams: *dru*).
Small-boat: *nyen.*
Boat of hide: *ko-á.*
Ferry: *ḍhu-khá.*
Boatman: *ḍhu-pa, ko-khen.*
Boat-hire: *ḍhu-lá.*
Sail: *Darchhen.*
Oar: *kyá.*
Rudder: *kyá-júk.*
Bridge: *šampa*:
Rope: *ṭ'ákpa*: (of goats' hair).
Ford: *gál-ku; ráp.*
Storm: *ts'úbma.*
Row, to: *kyá gyap-pa.*
Swim, to: *kyálwa.*
Ford, to: *gálwa* (cross over).
Fasten, to: *chhing-wa.*
Bale, to: *chhu-wa.*
Pull, to: *den-pa.*
Bathe, to: *ṭ'u-wa.*
Bathed: *ṭ'üi song.*
Steer, to: *khá-lo gyurwa.*
Swamp, to: *nup chukpa.*
Sink, to: *jing-wa* (neuter verb).
Leaky: *chhe'po.*
Back water, to: *len-la sho-mo kempa.*
Landing-place: *tang-sa.*
Starting-place: *Sháng-khá.*

---

| | |
|---|---|
| This lake is 32 lé-bors round: | *Ts'o-i kor-lam di le-bor so-nyi yö'.* |
| There are many lakes in Rutok: | *Ru-t'ok nangna ts'o m̂ángpo šhū jung.* |
| The water looks smooth: | *Chhu dhe jam-jam nang-ki duk.* |
| The wind is rising: | *Lung lang-ki-duk.* |
| The water appears rough: | *Chhu dhe tsub-tsub nang-ki-duk.* |

| | |
|---|---|
| Are there any dangerous rocks in this lake: | *Ts'o-i nang-na nyén-chén-kyi ṭak dá šhak-pa?* |
| Is the current swift: | *Chhu-gyün ṭak-po yinna?* |
| Tie the boat fast: | *Ṭru di tsán chhing.* |
| The oar is broken: | *Kyá di chhak pa yin* (or *chhak song*). |
| Don't push with the oar: | *Kyá ché' năi, ma p'ul ts'ăk.* |
| Turn the boat to the right: | *Ṭru yăi-su gyur shok.* |
| The boat is not steady: | *Ko-á di dŏ'-ts'uk me'.* |
| Which way does the river flow: (*lit:* "The flow of the river is to where?)" | *Tsang-poi gyuk-chhu di ká-la yŏ'pai?* |
| Lower down, the current becomes more strong: | *Men-la, gyün di lhak ṭak jhung.* |
| The river is very full: | *Chhu t'ön chhe tám song;* or *Chhu há-changne t'ön song.* |
| Is there a bridge across the river: | *Chhu-wo'i kong-la šam-pa du'-ka?* |
| Is the river-water fit to drink: | *Tsángpo di-i chhu kyem yŏ' pai?* |
| We must not go too near to the cataract: | *Ri-šar-chhu-i ḍam-tu yong gyu mi rung.* |
| Where do the rivers meet: | *Chhu-do di kala yim-pa?* |
| Take care: the boat will upset: | *Nyön chik! Ḍhu di gyel yong.* |
| Row hard to the shore: | *Ḍam-tu rém-rém gyák.* |
| Look out! Take care: | *Tŏi shok! Nyön chik!* |
| Can you swim: | *Khyŏ' kyál chok-gá?* |
| Does the river pass through that narrow gorge: | *Di chhu-wo di p'áḍhi ḍak tok-po sep-la bab-kin du'-ka?* |
| Keep the coats dry, if possible: | *Tuk-po-nam di kem-kem shrung ro tong.* |
| There is a hole in the boat: | *Khún šhik ḍhu bug-la chung.* |
| Push the boat to the further shore: | *P'á-chhyok tuk ḍhu-la p'ul.* |
| North of Lhasa is a vast lake called Namts'o Chhid-mo: | *Lhásá-i jhangla ts'o chhempo chi' dŏ-ne dhe-i m̃ing-la nam-ts'o chhyi'mo dhenḍai šer yŏ'.* |

The Mongolian name of that lake is Tengri Nur: *Ts'o di-i khá sok-po di Tengri Nur ŝer duk.*

There are a few lakes in Tibet larger than Namts'o Chhidmo: *Pö'-yul kyi ts'o-nam khá-chik Nám-ts'o Chhuk-mo lăi chhé duk.*

The Yamdok lake is famous for the large island in the midst of it. The name of this island is To-náng: *Ts'o Yamdok di shung-ma la ling-ka chhempo tang den-pa rakchen jhung. Ling-ka-yi m̂ing di Tonáng ŝer yö'?*

What is the name of that flower: *Me-tok dhe-i m̂ing kang duk-ka?*

That one on the bank: *Dhe ḍam teng-ki m̂e-tok dhe yö'.*

Tie the boat-rope to that tree: *Ḍhu-rō di shing dhe tengla tak.*

---

## EXCLAMATORY PHRASES.

*Ṭá-shi shik:* Good luck to you!

*Toi shok:* Look out!

*Nyön shik:* Listen! Look here!

*Mi-kyön, mi-kyön:* No harm done!

*Mitok, mitok:* No matter, no matter!

*Kham-lok jhe':* It is sickening!

*Khü' ze' jhyi':* Hold your skirt out! (as receptacle for alms)

*Há-la khur song:* Be off with it!

*Khye' khye':* Quite enough!

*Dhe ghá-la p'en:* What's the use of that!

*T'ik-t'ik:* All right!

*Ala-lá:* Capital; excellent!

*Yá'-po, yá'-po:* Certainly; Good, good!

*Dhe-gá yö':* So it is! To be sure!

*Yá-ya:* Yes!

*Min:* No!

*A-tsáma:* Ah me! Alas! Oh dear!

*Oji; Oji:* Salaam (in Khams)

*Ghále ŝhu:* Stay in peace!

*Nyar goi:* We must take care!

*Chághá jhe:* Be careful with it!

*Rikpa gyim:* Take care!

*Ghang-la ŝhu:* Well then?

*Lá lá-so:* Aye, aye, Sir!

*Káso kái:* As you will, Sir!

*Chhák p'ep:* Welcome (salaam)!

*Ghá-le p'ep:* Farewell!

*Nyampo shok:* Come along!

*Tsá-ḍhak jhyi':* Make haste!

*P'imo ma yong:* Don't be late.

*Gyang ma jhyi':* *Gor ma gör:* Don't delay.

*Chang-rik jhyi' shik:* Really attend!

*Har-sé jhy'i:* Rouse up!

*Rem-rem jhy'i shik:* Exert yourself.

*Shu-le, kusho:* Good-day, Sir!

*Ah chhu chhu:* It *is* cold!

*Ká-dhi-chhé:* Many thanks!

*Tánpo kyot:* Tread firmly (form of farewell in Ladak).

---

## MEDICAL TERMS.

*amchhi*: a physician.

*so-t'ab*: his mode of treatment.

*men*: physic—drugs.

*ril-bhu*: a pill.

*chhyemái men*: a powder.

*t'ung*: a draught.

*de-ku*: a syrop.

*kyuk-men*: an emetic.

*shál-men*: purgative.

*ši-men*: an opiate.

*men-khang*: drug-shop.

*jor-men*: a plaister.

*num-šem*: a poultice.

*nyá-gyur*: cholera.

*lhen-ḍum*: small-pox.

*ts'e'pai-né*: ague.

*rong-ts'e'*: valley fever.

*ná-ts'a*: ordinary fever.

*mik-ser*: jaundice.

*ṭ'u-jong*: diarrhœa.

*lo-khok*: a cough.

*láng-t'áb*: griping of bowels.

*jhang-khok-la šuk*: intestinal pain.

*so-še*: tooth-ache.

*kyukpa*: vomiting.

*burpo*: a small boil.

*shu-wa*: an ulcer.

*boi*: lump from a blow; bump.

*shu-nák*: inflamed sore.

*wu-sákpa*: difficult breathing.

*wolma*: larynx, windpipe.

*nang-rol*: the bowels themselves.

*ṭen-khok*: chest and heart-region.

*ḍhö'pa*: stomach.

*lo*: side of the body.

*bho-longwa*: ankle.

*lü'-pa*: phlegm, mucus.

*ṭ'ák* (ཁྲག): blood.

*ngul-chhu*: perspiration.

*chhu-nák*: pus; matter.

*má*: a wound.

*chin*: urine (the vulgar word).

*ri-chhu* or *ṭi-chhu*: urine (medical term).

*kyák*: excrement.

*tukpa*: wind, flatulence.

*tsá-u tsukpa*: to lance.

*tsá gyakpa*: to bleed (surgically).

*tsá tángwa*: to go to stool.

*tsá tokpa*: to feel the pulse (which in Tibet is done three times successively with different fingers).

## MONIES, WEIGHTS, AND MEASURES.

### Money Table.

| | | |
|---|---|---|
| 1 *karma* | = ⅛ anna. | |
| 2½ *karma* | = 1 *khághang.* | |
| 4 *khá-ghang* | = 1 *ŝho-ghang.* | |
| 10 *ŝho-ghang* | = 1 *shrang.* | |
| 50 *shrang* | = 1 *do-ts'e* or *yámbhu.* | |

———

### Gold Pieces.

*Ser-ŝho* = Rupees 9½.
*Ser-sáng* = Rupees 60.
(Both coins rarely seen).

### Silver Coins and Ingots.

| | |
|---|---|
| *Khá-ghang* | = 1¼ anna. |
| *Kár-ngá* | = 2½ annas. |
| *Chip-chhye'* | = 3¾ annas. |
| *Sho-ghang* or *Miskal* | = 5 annas. |
| *Genden Ṭangka* | = 7½ annas. |
| *Gyá Ṭangka* is the Indian rupee. | |
| *Nák-sáng* | = 3¼ rupee. |
| *Luk-mi'-ma*: silver ingot, size and shape of a sheep's hoof | = R15 annas 10. |
| *Yák-mi'-ma*: "yak's hoof" | = R31 annas 4. |
| *Tá-mi'-ma*; or *Do-tse'*: ingot, shape and size of horse's hoof | = R156¼. |

*N.B.*—The common silver *ṭangka* coined in Tibet, and known variously as *nák-ṭang*, *chö'ṭang*, and *Genden ṭangka*, is about the size of an English half penny but thinner. The legend on this coin is རྣམ་རྒྱལ་དགའ་ལྡན་ཕོ་བྲང་ཕྱོད་ལས It is marked so as to be cut into various pieces; and the *khá-ghang*, *kar-ngá*, (i.e., 5 *karma*), *chipchhye'* and *ŝho-ghang*, are merely the *ṭangka* cut or broken into ⅙, ⅓, ½, and ⅔ parts respectively. In Khams, the Indian rupee, which is current all over Tibet, is preferred to the *ṭangka*, and is styled *P'iling gormo.* In Sikkim the rupee is termed *tiruk*, in Ladak *girmo*, in Central Tibet *gyá-ṭam* and *chhi-gor.* The large silver ingot, styled in Tibet *do-ts'e* or *tá-mi'ma*, circulates in Tibet, Turkistan, and Mongolia, *yámbhu* being the Turki name and *kurs* the Mongol term. Its value varies, being sometimes as low in Indian currency as Rs. 125.

| MEAT MEASURE. | CORN AND LIQUIDS. | TEA WEIGHTS. |
|---|---|---|
| 1 *gyári* = 1 lb. | 1 *chámka* = ¾ lb or 1 pint. | 1 *parkhá* = 4 to 5lbs. |
| 2 *gyári* = 1 *dum*. | 2 *chámka* = 1 *bre* or *ḍhe*. | 4 *parkhá* = 1 *ko-toi*. |
| 2 *dum* = 1 *lhu*. | 5 *bre* = 1 *bo*. | 3 *ko-toi* = 1 *gám*. |
| 3 *lhu* = 1 *zuk*. | 4 *bo* = 1 *khal*. | 2 *gám* = 1 *gál* or *gyáp*. |
| | 25 *khal* = 1 *bhor-ra*. | |

LINEAL MEASUREMENTS.

*Pi-t'o:* span between thumb and forefinger stretched without straining.

*T'o-ghang:* span between thumb and little finger.

*Kang-ghang:* length from elbow to knuckles.

*T'u-ghang:* distance from elbow to tip of middle finger.

*Domba:* distance from finger-tip to finger-tip, both arms outstretched.

(*N.B.*—A "piece" of *Nambhu* cloth at Gyantse measures 9 *domba* or 54 feet).

*Gyang-t'ák:* distance to which the voice will reach (about 300 yards).

*Ts'á-lam:* distance traversable before breakfast (about 5 miles).

*Nyin-lam:* a day's journey; differentiated also into *luk-pe nyinlam* "a sheep-driver's march" (6 miles); *kang-t'ang-ghi nyin-lam:* "foot-march;" and *tá-pe nyin-lam:* "a horseman's march" (22 miles).

The Chinese *Li* of 486⅛ yards is frequently used in Eastern Tibet.

---

## TITLES, &C., IN TIBET.

*Gyálwá Rimpochhe:* the Dalai Lama or Grand Lama of Lhásá.

*Kyáp-gön:* "Protector"—familiar designation when speaking of the Grand Lama.

*Dési* or *Sákyong:* the Regent or Temporal Ruler of Tibet, who is, however, always an ecclesiastic.

*Gyálts'ap Rimpochhe* and *Gyálpo:* popular titles of the Regent, especially in use in the provinces.

*Ká-lön:* official title of each of the five members of the Privy Council, or *káshák*, which advises the Regent in state affairs.

*Shá-pé* (ཞབས་པད་ "lotos-foot"): other and more popular title of a *kálön.*

*De-wa Jong:* popular designation for "the Tibetan Government" or "Grand Lama's jurisdiction."

*Kálön-shák Lhen-gyai* (བཀའ་བློན་ཀ་ཤགས་ལྷན་རྒྱས་): the full designation of the Regent's Council, supreme in Judicial, Legislative and Executive Administration.

*Kálön-Ṭ'i-pa:* the Speaker or Chairman of the Council.

*Chyi-khyáb Khempo* (སྤྱི་ཁྱབ་མཁན་པོ་): the sole ecclesiastical member of the Council (the other four being laymen) who is now the brother of the former Dalai Lama and known as the Lha-lu Tá Lama at Lhásá and also by the Chinese name of Tá Lama.

*Ampán* ཨམ་བན་: title of the two representatives of Chinese interests at the Court of Lhásá and whose "advice" is of paramount influence at the present day in Tibet.

*Panchhen Rimpochhe:* the Head Lama of Ṭáshi-lhümpo Monastery and titular temporal ruler of the province of Tsang. He is held to be the incarnation of the 4th Dhyani Buddha, Wö' pákme' (འོད་དཔག་མེད་)

*Génden De-pa Lama:* the Head of the Gálden Monastery, said to rank in Ui ecclesiastically next after the *Gyalwa Rimpochhe.* He is not an incarnate lama, but is nominated, under Chinese influence, ostensibly on the choice of the Kálöns.

*Kusho P'ákpa Ḍo-gön:* the Head of the Sá-kya Monastery.

*Möd-pa Lama:* the Head of the Sera Monastery, near Lhásá.

*Dong-pa Lama:* the lay co-ruler of Mindol Ling (སྨིན་གྲོལ་གླིང་) the principal Nyingma monastery in Tibet.

*Má Rimpochhe:* title borne by the Head of the great Jhang Táklung Monastery, 40 miles north of Lhásá.

*Chásák:* the Regent's secretary or deputy. The Grand Lama has also a Chásák.

*Dá lo-ye:* ampans' aide-de-camps (two in number).

*Ká-ḍhung* (བཀའ་དྲུང་): secretaries of the Ká-löns.

*T'im-pön-chyi:* the Chief Judge of Lhásá from whom appeal lies sometimes direct to the Ká-löns.

*Shál-chhe-pa:* literally "the Big-faced One;" another Judge.

*Chhák-dzö'-pa:* government Treasurers at Lhásá, five in number to whom the Jongpöns pay in the revenue they collect in the provinces.

*Jong-pön:* officials, mainly civil but with a limited military control, who govern the various Jongs (རྫོང་) or petty districts into which all Tibet (save in the Jhang-t'ang) is portioned out, collecting revenue, &c.; answering to our "Collectors" in India. Of these there are 53.

*Chyi-khyab* of Nyá-grong in Khams is the Dalai Lama's Commissioner for the administration of this special portion of the kingdom. He ranks above the 53 ordinary Jong-pöns.

*Garpön* of Rudok: a special governor of the western districts of Gart'ok and Rudok conjointly.

*Ḍhung-khor-pa:* civilian officers; working in Lhásá as subordinates to the *Ká-ḍhung* or Ka-löns' secretaries, but in the provinces under the Jong-pön, to the office of which they aspire to attain.

*Tse-rung-pa:* ecclesiastical office-clerks ranking with the foregoing and managing the financial business of very large monasteries

*Ser-yik-pa* (གསེར་ཡིག་པ་ "golden-letter bearer"): name given to special envoy of the Emperor of China or of the Dalai Lama, bearing presents and formal greetings between the two Courts.

*Ṭulku:* any incarnate lama, *i. e.*, a lama holding in his personality the spirit of some departed saint.

*Kusho* (སྐུ་གཞོགས་) : title of honour placed before the personal name of a person of position, lay or clerical, male or female.

*Rimpochhe :* "most precious;" title added after the names of Incarnate lamas and heads of important Gompas; sometimes appended to official designation, sometimes to personal name.

*Lhá* and *Kusho* are frequently used in first addressing persons as we should say "Sir" and "My Lord."

*Pömbo :* also *Pömbo Rimpochhe :* "Officer!" "most precious chief;" forms of address to Government officials.

*Lhácham* ལྷ་ལྕམ་ : female title like our "Lady." It is affixed to the names of the wives and widows of lay notables. Often also used alone when speaking of or to such ladies.

*Cham Kusho :* honorific female title, but inferior to *lhácham.*

*Cham-chhung :* unmarried ladies' title answering to our "Miss" or perhaps rather "Hon'ble Miss;" as it is only applied to the upper classes.

*Lha-yum Kusho :* lady dowager.

*Khempo* (མཁན་པོ་) : abbot or head of the larger monasteries; but said to be a Degree attaching personally and not necessarily to the holders of particular offices; perhaps like our D.D.

*De-pa* (སྡེ་པ་) : territorial chiefs having feudal authority, but without prejudice to the paramount claims of the Tibetan Government; a common title in Eastern districts where sounded *Deba.*

*T'so-pön* (ཚོགས་དཔོན་) : president of the headmen of a set or "circle" of villages, elected by his brother headmen to control the whole *khor* or circle in its relations with other village circles.

*Pi-pön* (སྤྱི་དཔོན་) : ordinary headman of a single village.

*Gen-po* or *Gen-sum :* village elders who (as in Russia) elect the *Pi-pön.*

*Gerpa :* zemindar or land-owner

*Mi-ser*: tenants of small-holdings, held from monasteries or noblemen or direct from Crown. A numerous class answering to the small farmers in Ireland or crofters in Scotland; but subjected to considerable taxation of produce and with heavy liabilities of personal service (*tá-ū* and *ū-lák*).

*P'á-pün* and *P'á-ts'en*: in a village, those denizens of it having the same *lha* or household god.

*Ts'e-yok*: "life-servants" or slaves, reduced to that condition through gambling or debts, and, occasionally, by capture and purchase.

---

## RELIGIOUS EDIFICES; AND ADJUNCTS THEREOF.

*Ling*: a large collegiate monastery analogous to the Christian abbey.

*Chhoidé*: a lamasery where Tantrik and occult studies are specially followed.

*Gömpa* (often *Gömba*): any ordinary lamasery, large or small.

*Shigön*: small village gompa with only 3 or 4 inmates in adjacent huts.

*Tá-ts'ang*: special schools or "chairs" established within the larger monasteries, for the teaching of particular doctrines and generally endowed with property, land, &c.

*P'uk*: a recluse's cave, often inaccessible to outsiders, and usually such caverns are found together in a colony styled *Ri-ṭ'oi*. Name also given to any set of hermits' cells, not necessarily caverns.

*Ri-ṭ'oi-ba*: the dwellers in the *P'uk*.

*Chhörten*: cenotaphs of stone, built upon a series of square steps, and often containing a saint's relics. They follow one general pattern capable of certain modifications and are of all sizes; being mostly small solid masses of masonry; yet in some cases exaggerated into huge structures 8 or 9 storeys high, containing chapels, shrines, images, and relics, as in the fine chhörtens at Gyangtse and Jhampa Ling.

*Mendang*: long narrow heap of inscribed stones banked-up betwixt two low lenthy parallel walls. Sometimes, as in one example at Leh, more than a mile long, and is formed by degrees from every pious traveller, as he passes, depositing a slab inscribed with sacred formulæ.

*Máni Khorlo* (or simply *khorlo*): prayer cylinders, both the portable ones worked in the hand like a child's rattle and the large barrels fixed on pivots. Those worked by running streams are styled *Chhu-khor.*

*Máni Lhákhang:* shed or house sheltering series of prayer-barrels arranged like a system of huge bobbins; so named when isolated from any religious edifice.

*Tsuk-lá-khang:* the temple attached to large monastery.

*Lhá-khang:* ordinary temple isolated from any monastery.

*Du-khang:* worship-hall of a Gompa.

*Ts'o-khang:* general congregation-hall in large Gompas where public ceremonials are held.

*Gong-khang:* chapel in temple wherein the images of demons and "terrific deities" are segregated.

*Gyá-p'ik*; or *Gep'i:* a cube-shaped structure with concave sides, being a wooden framework covered with gilded metal plates, and placed as a dome on temples.

*Láb-ding:* enclosure where travellers can pitch tents.

*Sung-bum:* conical stone oven outside houses in which juniper is burnt as offering to propitiate evil spirits.

*Lū-ku:* metal images.

*Dempa:* large erect figure of any deity.

*Nyák lu-ku:* licentiously-posed figures.

*Dün-chok:* offering-table for flowers.

*Shu-mar:* chief lamp before the larger images.

*Mar-me:* small lamps burning before deities; and used in large numbers at *kangsha* rites. They are small brass bowls of butter with floating wicks.

*Chhö' kyok:* libation-bowl; sometimes made of skull with gilded metal cover and with stand beautifully chased and ornamented. Frequently known as *ts'e ghi bhumpa.*

*Mé-long:* convex mirror of oval shape over which, in forecasts, holy water is poured.

*Damaru:* small drum composed of two skull-tops fastened back to back, the opening on either side being covered with prepared fish-skin;

sometimes having pendant tassels of bunches of human hair.

*Dorje :* sacred implement held in the hand during ceremonials and shaped like very small hand-dumbells with open-work knob at each end. Originally meant to represent a thunderbolt.

*P'ur-bhu :* ornamental-headed brass javelin with three-sided spike, used by priests during exorcisms against demons. The original *p'urbhu* is in Seṛa Gompa, Lhása.

*Kang-dhung :* long thin trumpet made of hollow human thigh-bone ; sometimes the joint-end has a piece of human skin very neatly sewn round it, or a thong-like piece hanging to it. Used in temple ceremonial.

*Ḍhilbhu :* small brass bell with elaborate handle.

*Dhung-kar :* Conch-shells, blown as interludes in congregational book recitals.

*Dhung-chhen :* great copper trumpet, about 8 feet long, blown at 3 a. m. to summon inmates of gompas to the morning rites in the *du-khang*. Requires two men to hold it up.

*Yai-khyil Dhung-kar :* white conch-shell with whorl twisting to right, very rare and when of large size, almost priceless. Used in monasteries as calling horns.

*Gyá-ling :* long cornet-like trumpet with holes and stops.

*Rá-dung :* copper trumpet or horn without side-holes or stops.

*Roi-ma* (འརོས་མ་) small brass cymbals in pairs.

*Si-nyen* (བསིལ་སྙན་) cymbals of better tone and with cloth pad to hold with on either side.

*Ngá :* large drums with long handles placed in temples and often taken out for ceremonies in houses.

*Ghang-ngá :* large heavy metal gong.

*Yáng-yik :* music-score used in more elaborate temple-music for trumpets and conches.

*Bụmpa :* flagon for holy-water, with a lid and long spout, and with holes at top for tall bunch of peacock-feathers.

*T'ü-bum* (ཁྲུས་འབུམ་) one of the varieties of *Bumpa ;* a small teapot-like vessel clad in red *nabša* and with peacock feather in hole at top. Often of silver.

*Chhάb-bum :* much larger variety like a tea-urn with spout and with receptacle in lid for flowers. Sometimes termed *Jhya-ma-bum.*

*Shön-ḍhö* (བཤོས་དོད་) or *Shön-ṭong:* a tall open copper vessel.

*Nabšá:* wrappings of coloured silk or satin put on idols, books, bowls, &c., and regarded as the "clothes" of such implements.

*Torma:* many kinds of sacrificial offering are thus styled; but name usually applied to small effigies of butter stamped with various sacred devices, or else to pieces of wood or moulded clay, coloured, on which are plastered small slabs and medals made of butter.

*Pöi-rengbu:* incense-tapers, very thin and generally coloured pink, burning rapidly and emitting slight odour; used by visitors to shrines who light them at lamp burning before image they would honour.

*Mendré:* small cone, bee-hive-shaped, stuck all over with raw rice, with dabs of paint here and there, and placed near the *Shu-már.* A hole in the apex serves as a receptacle or vase for unused and partly-burnt incense-tapers.

*Bák:* masks for use in devils' dance on the Guru Pema festival. When not in use are hung up on the walls of temples, with coloured robes and sleeves draped beneath to represent body of face depicted by mask.

*Kyilkhor:* framework or shelves on which series of images are grouped; also any sacred diagram on floor (*maṇḍal.*)

*Gyen-ts'en* (རྒྱལ་མཚན་): the Buddhist "flag of victory." Seen in two styles: (1) a tall cylinder of black felt with a white line or insertion encircling it near lower end, and two vertical lines of white running from top to bottom at right-angles to other white band. Closed in at top where it narrows so as to be often almost like a shut umbrella, and sometimes surmounted by metal trident. (2) Also, made up of three colours, red, yellow, and blue, arranged flounce-like one above the other, with a white flounce between each colour; and placed on tops of poles which are planted in the ground near temples and chhörtens. The first kind decorate the eaves of gompas and palaces.

*Dár-chho* and *Lungtá*: flags inscribed with mystic formula and strips of coloured cloth fastened to tall poles; the wind fluttering the flags and so uttering the prayers printed thereon. *Lung-tá* signifies "airy horse."

*Lü'* (གླུད་) or ལྡོ་ *Dö* (in Sikkim): reeds or very thin straight twigs about 2 feet in height, strung with yarn of various colours and bits of stick,-in close likeness to the yards and rigging on a ship's mast. When anyone is sick, these are made and planted beside the path nearest to the house. As they are supposed to resemble the natural dwelling of demons which cause sickness, the demons are presumed to be enticed therein out of the sick man's body.

*Shol-dum*: gauze cylinder placed over lamp; at top a metal rod, projecting therefrom, holds another smaller cylinder of paper inscribed with prayers above the lamp-flame; and, being freely suspended, the draught from the flame causes it to revolve

## TIBETAN MYTHOLOGY.

The following are the colloquial designations of the more popular deities, saints, &c., whose effigies are to be seen in Tibetan temples :—

SANG-GYE SHÁKYA T'UBPA; or JHO-O RIMPOCHHE: Buddha Shakyamuni, the Buddha who last appeared on earth; known also as *Chomdendai*, and familiarly as "the Jho." There are said to be three original or "self-sprung" images of the Jho: one in the Jho-khang at Lhásá, representing him as a boy of 12; one in the Chan-than-sze temple at Peking, as an adult; and a third in the golden temple of Kumbum, near Koko Nur, as an old man. Copies in bronze of these three occur in the chief Tibetan temples.

| | |
|---|---|
| JHAMPA (བྱམས་པ་); or JHAMPA GOMPO: | the Buddha to come (Sansk: *Maitreya*), generally pourtrayed as seated European-fashion and not as other deities. Many gigantic figures exist; one 70 feet high at Potala; another 180 feet high in Jhampa Bum-ling temple in Amdo; others in the Rong Jhamchhen Gompa in Tsang and in Daipung Monastery. These huge images are styled *Jhamchhen*. |
| WÖ'PÁKME'; or TS'E-PÁKME': | the Sanskrit *Amitabha* the Dhyani Buddha from whom emanated the famous Chenraisi. He is incarnated in the successive Panchhen Rimpochhe of Ṭashilhümpo, who is thus spiritual father of the Grand Lama of Lhásá. |
| JHO-O MI-KYÖ' DORJE: | the Dhyani Buddha corresponding to the Sanskrit *Akshobhya*. A gilt image of this being, said to be 1,200 years' old, is the chief treasure in the Ramochhe temple at Lhásá. |
| JHO-O CHEN-RAISI: | the great protecting genius of Tibet, incarnated in the Grand Lama of Lhásá. He is a *Ye-shei Sem-Pa* or Dhyani Sattwa, spiritually emanating from Wö'pákme', though actually born from a lotos. Usually depicted with eleven faces and many arms (properly 1,000) and in the palm of each hand an eye. His full Tibetan name is *Spyan-ras-gzigs Dbang-p'yug* (Sansk: *Avalokiteswara.*) |
| JÁM-YANG; or JÁM-PÁL: | known as the *Shön-nur gyurpa* or Renewer of Youth; a Dhyani Sattwa, in sanctity second only to Chenraisi. He is conrtantly incarnated in the current Head of Sakya Monastery. Appears in temples seated, with crossed in-folded legs and upturned soles, on a large lotos. Brandishes *gadá* or mace in right hand and a dorje in his left. |

Blue lotos sprig is clasped in inner bend of left elbow. Head encircled with high coronet.

DORJE CHHANG: a third Dhyani Sattwa, who was evolved from the Dhyani Buddha *Mi-kyö Dorje.* Chief shrine is in Chakpoiri Medical Monastery at Lhásá. Often figured in his "terrific aspect" with screaming face and dishevelled hair, his body painted scarlet. He flourishes the dorje. In Gyantse Chhörten is a famous golden statue of this guardian of the Gelukpa order. (Sansk: *Vájrapani*).

ZEKZEN: Kashyapa Buddha, or the Atom Eater; a Buddha who lived on earth in a former age. Relics of his corporeal substance seem still plentiful, as they are served up in medical pills obtainable from several Tibetan dignitaries.

LÁKNA DORJE; or CHHYAKDOR: subduer of evil spirits and guardian of the mystic doctrine. Represented with hanging belly and with open mouth displaying three large fangs. Often confounded with Dorje Chhang (also styled Chhyakdor) and also with the next deity.

LAKNA DORJE; or CHHYAKNA DORJE: *De-pön* or Ruler of the Noijin or mountain spirits. He may be distinguished from the just-mentioned deity by his green paint or green clothing. Known in Tantrik ceremonial as "the green-robed Lakna Dorje."

ḌOLMA (སྒྲོལ་མ་); or ṬÖ-MA: "She who delivers;" the chief goddess of Tibet who has ever co-operated with Chenraisi for the good of mortals. Her spirit has disintegrated itself into 21 branch emanations whose images grouped in series are known as a Ḍolma *kyilkhor.*

| | |
|---|---|
| DORJE P'ÁMO; or DORJE NÁLJORMA: | benevolent goddess at one time incarnated in form of a sow, hence her name "The Sow with the Dorje." Often figured in a curious medley of an upright pig backed by one or more females conjoined in one image. Incarnated in lady-abbess of Samding Monastery, Yamdok; but another female incarnation occurs in a community on margin of Namts'o Chhyidmo, a third at Markula in Lahul. The Pig-lady is also specially worshipped at Tsün-mo-t'ang Gompa in North Sikkim. |
| PÁNDEN LHÁMO དཔལ་ལྡན་ལྷ་མོ་ | a ferocious goddess figured in riotous attitude, trampling on the mangled remains of her lovers whom she has decoyed to destruction, and with uplifted bowl from which she is jauntily drinking their blood. Over her arm there dangles a huge rosary of skulls, and she carries both *dorje* and *gada* (club). Known also as *Pánden Mákjorma.* |
| T'O-NYER CHENMA: | another terrifying goddess, "she who is wrinkled with anger," who was at one time incarnated as Zá-khri, Nepalese wife of king Srong-tsan Gampo. |
| TÁMDIN: | a god always painted red and generally in human form, but occasionally appearing with a horse's head and neck but a man's body. Classed as a *t'owo* or wrathful deity, because, though well-disposed to men, he terrifies demons by neighing. |
| SHINJE; or DORJE JIK-JHYE': | the Lord of Death, figured with sword and many faces, but has several distinct forms represented. His coercion is one of the chief feats of the Ngák-pa or Tantrik priests who then make use of rosaries formed of discs of human skull or of ele- |

phant stomach-stone. *Shinje* is sometimes figured presiding over a cauldron in which he is boiling the heads of the doomed.

NAM-SE; or NAM-T'OI SHRE: God of Riches, said to be the same as Kuwera, but title really means "Son of the listening ears." Usually depicted with retinue of aerial sprites; and he is always painted either yellow or else black.

ZAMBHÁLA: a Ngák lü' or Tantrik deity, often confounded with Nam-se, and usually figured clasping to his breast with lustful gestures some female deity.

ME'-LHÁ-YI GYA-PO: king of the fire-spirits, endowed with power to purge from consequences of sin those souls in the Bardo whose form of rebirth is so far undetermined. Figured sometimes as seated astride a red ram, sometimes as perched on a huge lotos beneath an umbrella.

PE'-HAR; or CHHOI-KYONG: king of the astrologers, represented in Gompas as a king riding on a yellow or white lion, and robed in tiger-skin. He is the *yidam* or tutelary deity of the professional astrologers attached to the Ramochhe temple at Lhásá who, as a body, are likewise known by his name. However, the chief of the class, the incarnation of Pe-har himself, resides at Ná-chhung grove near Lhásá. This personage is styled Náchhung Chhoikyong, is treated with divine honours, and he it is who forecasts, on a vacancy, the characteristics whereby the new Grand Lama of Lhásá may be identified.

GOMA SHI; or CHHOI-KYONG SHI; or JIK-TEN-KYI GYAL-CHHEN SHI; or the "Dik Rajas:" synonyms for the four terrific doorkeepers or guardians of the doctrine, and in Buddhist literature described as four kings dwelling on the edges of the top of Mount Meru to protect the 33 greater gods. They usually seem to be painted on the outside walls of the Gongkhang and the monastery treasure chamber, where they are represented as reeking with gore, wreathed in skulls, and of hideous aspect. Of the four, one carries a hook, another a chain, a third a snare, and the fourth a bell; each bearing in the right hand a bowl, representative of the world. Flames surround the figures together with a retinue of animal-headed demons.

TSONG-KHAPA; or; JE RIMPOCHHE: deified hero; the great Buddhist reformer and founder of the Gelukpa school. Died 1440 A.D. Life-sized figures and relics of him abound everywhere; the most costly effigies being set up in the Galden and Kumbum monasteries which he founded.

PEMA JUNG-NAI; or GURU RIMPOCHHE: the well-known Padma Sambhawa, deviser of much eclectic ceremonial and jugglery, founder of the Urgyenpa sect, and everywhere popular, especially in Derge, Tsang, and Sikkim. Grottoes where the saint lived are shewn in all parts, in some of which refuse of his food in the shape of a reddish dust is still sold. His sayings as contained in his "Lotos Picture-writings" are universally quoted. Other names popularly designating the saint are *Urgyen Pema* and *Guru Pema*. In Tantrik rites he is held to assume a terrific as well as a mild aspect and is then styled *Dorje Dholöt.*

P'UL JHUNG; or JHO-O ATISHA: the famous Bengal paṇḍit, Atisha, otherwise Dipankara Buddha, who came from Magadha as a missionary to Tibet for the revivification of Buddhism. Labouring for 17 years, he died 1053 A.D. at Nyet'ang near Lhásá. Deified and greatly revered.

DOM RIMPOCHHE: bromston, .pupil of Atisha, and founder of Kadampa sect. Built Rading Gompa, to the north of Lhásá, and there a huge effigy of the saint is worshipped. His tomb is shewn in Jhang Taklung Gompa, 35 miles N.N.E. of Lhásá.

LHACHAM MANDARAWA: wife of Guru Rimpochhe! Her shrine is at Ribo Tagzang near Mount Everest.

SÁKYÁ PANDITA: the famous teacher who founded the sect whose head-quarters continue still at Sá-kyá Monastery (50 miles due north of Mount Everest). Died circa 1245 A.D.

SO'NG-TSEN GÁMPO (སྲོང་བཙན་སྒམ་པོ་) or JE GÁMPO: the king of Tibet who introduced learning and therewith the beginnings of the Buddhist faith into Tibet, circa 680 A.D. His effigy and those of his two wives, the Chinese and Nipalese princesses, have been set up in almost every monastery in the land. The most highly reverenced images of the trio, into which it is said their essences were absorbed, are those preserved in the Jho-khang, Lhásá.

LOMPO GAR: prime minister of foregoing king, incarnate, now-a-days in abbots of Tengyai Ling, Lhásá.

T'ANG-TONG GYALPO: a lama of piety and engineering skill who built eight chain bridges over the Yeru Tsangpo, 250 years ago. An amusing anecdote of the saint's birth is given in the *Nineteenth Century*, October 1889.

SHÁBDUNG NGAKWANG NAMGYAL: a saint of literary and engineering skill. He built, 200 years ago, chain bridges over rivers on the Bhutanese border, and is held to be still incarnate in the successive heads of Ṭashichhoidzong Monastery, the chief lamasery of Bhutan.

CHHOI-GYAL TERDAK LINGPA: a deified hero who has appeared on earth so far 17 times; incarnate in the successive heads of Mindol Ling.

LAMA JE P'AKMODUP: known also as Situ Gyalpo, a saintly Tibetan king—the first to gain sway over the whole country, built many forts and monasteries; died 1372 A.D. His image and the tombs of the 18 kings of the dynasty he founded exist at Densat'il, a ruinous gompa on the left bank of the Yeru, 15 miles east of Tse-t'ang.

---

Subjoined are the colloquial designations of the different classes of lesser deities, demons, and other supernatural orders :—

*Rik-zin:* the 8 sages expert in Tantrik arts, of whom the chief is styled Lo-pön Hum-kara (*i. e.*, Pema Jung-nai.)

*Lhá:* any minor god, including local deities and all Brahmins.

*Lhá-min:* an order of beings ever at war, through spiritual rivalry, with the *lhá.*

*Shrimpo* and *Shrin-mo:* male and female monsters, hostile to man, dwelling under huge boulders in valleys. They devour travellers unprotected by greater deities whose aids against *shrimpo* should be propitiated before starting on a journey. Correspond to the Rakshása and Rakshási of Sanskrit mythology.

*Yidák:* lost souls in goblin bodies of stupendous size, often several miles in height, but with tiny mouths which prevent eating aught save the smallest crumbs. They groan terribly with hunger and cause earthquakes.

*Noi-jin:* mountain-gods haunting peaks and passes. Many mountain ranges in Tibet are named after them with varying appendix names; *e. g.*, Noi-jin T'ang-la range S.E., of Tengri Nur, the summits of which are said to be embodiments of the Noi-jin king and 360 of his attendants. *Namt'oi-shre*, god of riches, is called by many the Noi-jin king, and in this last character is sometimes styled *Muk-dzin*: "holder of the mist."

*Lhánḍé:* imps of demoniac character dwelling underground during the day, and at night-time amusing themselves by riding on the backs of foxes, the yelping of which beasts is caused by the blows of the goblins. They carry as their cudgels the huge flowering stems of the greater mullein, which plant is therefore styled in Tibet *Lhanḍe berka*. The *Jhánḍé* is a variety endowed with wings.

*Lu:* deities in the form of water-serpents inhabiting lakes, rivers, and wells. Benignant towards man, they construct at the bottom of lakes gorgeous palaces wherein they watch over great treasures as well as the lives of fish which have been restored to the water as propitiatory sacrifices after being caught. They are of four varieties, a sacred pond to the N. of Potala in Lhásá, for example, being reserved by law for piebald *Lu*. When provoked the Lu cause damage by hail and floods; but payment of *sur-ṭ'al* or "hail tax" to a Tantrik lama insures your property against such injury.

*Támchho':* a fabulous horse whose mouth forms the source of the great Yeru river.

*Dri-ŝa:* sprites inhabiting the air, of fairy-like form, who divert themselves by playing on *ko-p'ong* or guitars. They subsist solely on odours: consuming the sweetest scents of flowers as well as the foulest stenches from privies and slaughter-houses. Butchers burn offal of beasts on pedestals to propitiate these beings, who are often said to be incarnated as bees, wasps, &c.

*Khá-ḍoma:* witches of vast form under five queens, whose spirits now dwell in costly figures which have been set up to their honour in Rámochhe Temple, Lhásá, where their powerful aid to mortals may be duly invoked.

*Má-mo*: other female spirits, but of a mischievous disposition.

*Shib-dák*: the particular god of the soil in each village with the surrounding country appertaining thereto. The number of *Shib-dák* is accordingly great; and every traveller arriving within the boundaries of a fresh place will do well to propitiate the local gods of its soil. Incarnated, at times, as monkeys, they ride upon hares, bearing bows and arrows of straw and shields fashioned from huge toadstools.

*T'áb-lhá*: god of the domestic hearth, invoked after pollutions caused by the boiling over of milk, &c.

*Tsen*: solitary demons haunting particular mountain-paths, but possessed of the habit and power of entering the bodily frame of a human being and causing him to be afflicted with fever and divers other special diseases.

*Dön-chhen*: evil spirits which enter the body in bevies of 15 or 18 occasioning either death by apoplexy or violent attacks of epilepsy and lock-jaw. The rainbow is deemed to be caused by these spirits coming down in troops to drink.

*Dü'* (bdud): is held to be the nearest equivalent to our Satan. In later days many devils or *dü'po* have, however, been developed; and the female devils or *dü'mo* haunt lakes for the purpose of feeding on the bodies of monks thrown in as food for fish.

*Gong-po* and *Gong-mo*: are demons inspiring jealousy, desire for money, cowardice, and licentiousness.

*Gék*: subtle inhabitants of the valleys who put obstacles in the way of travellers to sacred spots and hinder those engaged in the erection of *lhákhang* (temples) and chhorten. The Hindu god Ganesa is regarded by Tibetans as the "King of the Gék" and "Remover" of these obstacles.

*Khyung*: a monster bird akin to the *roc* of the Arabs and the Garuda bird of Hindu literature. He does the bidding of Dorje Chhang, the Boddhisattwa. The Bön priests or sorcerers of Tibet, who are anti-Buddhists, regard him as their protector, and most of the *Bön-pa* religious houses are dedicated in name to the *Khyung*.

*Ḍhul-bhum-mo*: female satyrs with poisonous horns.

*Pung-shri* and *má-ki-shri*: underground demons of the gnome type, who devour children; taking also possession of the hearth after broth and milk have boiled over, unless ceremonial cleansing is performed.

---

## BUDDHIST SECTS.

[The Buddhists of Tibet are split up into about 18 different schools or sects, several of which, however, are not bitterly opposed to one another. There are two great divisions or classes of these sects, namely, the *Nyingma* or ancient schools, and the *Sarma* or new schools. Besides the general division named *Nyingma*, one sect of this class is likewise particularly denominated the *Nyingma* sect. The *Nyingma* votaries are chiefly distinguished for their practice of magic ceremonial; consequently members of the chief *Sarma* sect, the Gelukpa, often resort to *Nyingma* lamas on special occasions].

GELUKPA (དགེ་ལུགས་པ་): The most popular of all the sects; the established church of Tibetan Buddhism; a reformed development set afloat by Tsong-khapa in the 14th century. The Dalai Lama of Lhásá, the Panchhen Rimpochhe of Táshilümpo, and their establishments, together with all the leading monasteries in the province of Ui, hold Gelukpa tenets. Their chief lamaseries are Gálden, Samye, Daipung, Sera, and the Four Lings of Lhásá, in Ui; Táshilhümpo, Gyángtse, Dongtse, &c., in Tsáng; Kumbum near Koko Nur; together with hosts of other large establishments in Khams; also many in Ladak, of which the principal are Pi-tuk, Samtan Ling, and Likir. The gelongs of this sect wear red clothing, but a cap and sacred pouch of amber-coloured cloth; hence their designation "Yellow-hat" Buddhist. The Mongol and Spiti Gelukpa wear yellow robes as well as yellow caps.

**Kádampa** (བཀའ་གདམས་པ་): A school, the result of the first reformation of Tibetan Buddhism under the Indian paṇḍit Atisha in the 11th century, its tenets being eventually shaped by Bromston, strictly upon Maháyana lines. Now closely allied to the Gelukpa school, which has acquired possession of its head centre Rading Gompa. Most of the Kádampa establishments are in P'anyul district, N.-E. of Lhásá; but they are now nearly all in ruinous condition.

**Kágyü'pa** (བཀའ་བརྒྱུད་པ་): One of the leading *Nyingma* or "Red Cap" sects, originally started in opposition to the reforms of Bromston. Its votaries profess acquaintance with the deepest subtleties of Tantrik learning and meditative science. The, presiding deity of the sect is Lagna Dorje, otherwise Dorje Chhang. Most of the so-called Dukpa monasteries in Tibet, such as Dorje-ták on the Yeru Tsangpo, belong to it. In Ladak a most powerful body, the principal establishments of that country, such as Hémis, Karzog, Hanlé, Chhimré, owning allegiance to its tenets.

**Nyingmapa** (རྙིང་མ་པ་): Professedly the most venerable of the schools and governed by the precepts of the Yogacharya system. The head centre is Mindol Ling, a very ancient monastery some 45 miles S.-E. of Lhásá. Its gompas may be known by the red and blue stripes decorating the outer walls. The monks wear red robes with red hat and red pouch.

**Lho-Dukpa** (ལྷོ་འབྲུག་པ་): The prevailing sect in Bhutan, with head-quarters at Ṭáshichhoidzong, under the Dharma Raja. Branches of the sect exist in Tibet, *e. g.*, at Rálung, Dechhen Dzong, &c.; whilst, curious to relate, all the monasteries built round Mount Kailasa near Lake Map'ang (Manasarowar) are peopled by its votaries, the establishments being exclusively under lamas who have been trained at Ṭáshichhoi-dzong.

KARMAPA (ཀ་རྨ་པ་): A sect much followed in Nipal, professing to be deeply versed in the forecasting of *karma*. Samding monastery on Lake Yamdok belongs to this communion. The dress is red with black cap and black pouch.

DZOK-CHHEMPA (རྫོགས་ཆེན་པ་): The sect most predominent in Sikkim, professing Atiyoga doctrine and regarding Padma Jungnai (Padma Sambhava) as their founder. Pemayangtse (Pemiongchi) monastery in Sikkim is head centre of the "Urgyenpa," as the adherents of the school are often styled. In professed imitation of their founder, who is allotted a wife named Mandarawa, many lamas marry or have loose ideas concerning female society, and differ from other Buddhists in the important particular of slaying animals in sacrifice. The dress is a dark red robe with brown cap and pouch. Extensive colonies of this sect exist in Dergé and Zokchhen in Eastern Tibet, the latter district deriving its name therefrom.

SÁ-KYÁPA (ས་སྐྱ་པ་): Formerly a powerful body, the successive chief lamas of the famous Sá-kya monastery having at one period (1270–1340 A.D.) governed the whole kingdom of Tibet. Sá-kya Gompa (Lat. 28° 54′ 30 N. Long. 87° 56′ E.) is still the seat of this once august Red-cap community; and other Sá-kyápa lamaseries continue to flourish, *e. g.*, P'enyul Nalendra, Gong-kar Chhoide, Ngor Gompa, Kyisho Rawana, &c., &c.

JO-NANGPA (ཇོ་མོ་སྣང་པ་): A modern or *Sarma* sect of Yellow Caps which originated in P'unts'o Ling under Kun-khyen Jowo Nang with peculiar dogmas said to be akin to the Gelukpa. Its adherents profess much asceticism, study the Dulwa texts, and are less idolatrous than other Buddhists.

DI-KHUNGPA (འབྲི་ཁུང་པ་) or Ḍi-gumpa: An ancient body, formerly of immense influence, being rivals of the Sá-kyápa; with several large establishments still kept up both in Ui and in Ladak. Lama Yuru, Sháchhugul, Yangḍi Karpo (near Lhásá) and Ḍi-khung Ts'al Gompa all belong to this sect. At the last-named, which stands 70 miles N. E. of Lhásá, resides the incarnation of Ḍi-khung Chhoije Kyobpa, the founder of the sect.

TÁKLUNGPA (སྟག་ལུང་པ་):

YE-ṬAK-PA (ཡྲེ་བྲག་པ་):

CHHAK-GYÁ-PA (ཕྱག་རྒྱས་པ་):

Three Red Cap sects; the last-named being the body predominent in Spiti. Riwo-chhe on the Ngul Chhu is an important Táklungpa monastery.

SHI-JHE'PA (ཞི་བྱེད་པ་): A community differentiated as the result of the labours of the Hindu Buddhist missionary, P'ákpa P'á Tampa Sang-gye; boasting a small following in Khams, as well as in Dengri district where P'a Tampa lies buried.

KUN-CHHOI-TSANGPA (ཀུན་ཆོས་གཙང་པ་): A sect with a few monasteries in the districts bordering on Yunnan.

BHÖN or PÖN-PO (བོན་པ་): These are professedly anti-Buddhists and represent the ancient religious cult of the land, correspondent with the Shámans of Mongolia. Their priests are of both sexes, females being preferred, and deal largely in sorcery and animal sacrifices. Their services are in constant requisition especially among the Himalayan tribes and in remote districts of Eastern Tibet. Their mode of

27

circumambulation is with the left side turned to the object concerned—the exact converse of the Buddhist method. Several Bhön monasteries exist in the Khyungpo district, W. of Chhamdo. The Pön-po themselves are often designated *Khyungpo* after their guardian the Khyung bird. In Sikkim the Lepchas and Limbus follow the Bhön cult.

---

## ETYMOLOGY OF PLACE NAMES IN TIBET.

As in India and elsewhere certain terms are constantly to be found as part of the names of places, &c., in Tibet. The following are the syllables most frequently recurring, with their significations :—

ḌONG (གྲོང་) a town; as in *Ḍong-tse, Ṭashiḍong, Karḍong.*

DONG (གདོང་) a face; as in *Sing-dong* (really *Seng-ge-dong* "lion's face.")

DZONG or JONG (རྫོང་) a fort; as in *Seng-ge-jong*, &c.

KHAR (མཁར་) a fort; as in *Ḍangkhar* (གྲངས་མཁར་), *Kharsa.*

YÜL and YÜLCHE'R (ཡུལ་ཁྲེར་) a village or hamlet; as in *Sáng-yül.*

YUL a country in general, as in *Lho-yul, Zá-yul, Mön-yul.*

TS'O (ཚོགས་) a community, assemblage; as in *Ts'o-kong.*

Ṭ'OM (ཁྲོམ་) a market; as in *T'om-si-gang.*

P'UNG (ཕུང་པོ་) a heap; as in *Rinchhenp'ung, Marp'ung*; also PUNG (སྤུང་)

LAM (ལམ་) a road; as in *Kho-lam.*

SAM (བསམ་) thought; as in *Samdub Guru; Samye.*

DUNG (གདུང་) an abode, settlement, as in *Dung-nyi* ("the two abodes") in Garhwal.

KHANG (ཁང་) a house; as in *Khang dung.*

TAK (བྲག) a rock; as in *Tak-tsa, Tak-mar, Tak-nang.*

RI, mountain; as in *Ri-gön, Palri.*

SAM (ཟམ་པ་) a bridge; as in *Chákšam, Pášamkha,*

GANG, hill-spur; as in *Ṭashigang, Námo-gang, Norbu-gang.*

BYÁR, (བྱར་) hill (in Balti only).

KANG (really sounded "Ghang"), ice, snow; as in *Kang-gar-ra, Kangchhendzönga* (or "*Kinchinjunga.*")

NONG (སྣོང་) ridge (in Bhutan), as in.

DONG (འབྲོང་) a yak; as in *Dong-khya* (*La*); but occurs rarely.

LÁ, a pass; but in Balti we have *Náshek,* a pass.

SHING (ཞིང་) a field; as in *Kyo-shing, Si-shing-shi-khá* (in Bhutan).

GYANG, a wall; as in *Gyáng-tse, Dá-gyáng, Gyángdo, Gyángmo-chhe.*

CHHU, river, waters; as in *Rong Chhu, Nyang Chhu, Shang Chhu,* &c.

CHHU-TS'EN, a hot-spring; as in *Lang-pák-chhuts'en* and many others.

LUNG (ཀླུང་) large river; as in *Tö-lung.*

SHONG, deep valley or gorge; as in *Kyi-shong, Shong-go.*

TSANG-PO (གཙང་པོ་) a river; as in *Lhobra Tsangpo, Yeru Tsangpo, Chhiblung Tsangpo.*

SHI (གཞི་) a site or foundation; as in *Shimong*, &c.

PEMÁ (Padmá) a lotos; as in *Pemá-yangtse* (commonly *Pemiongchi*), *Pemáling*, *Pemakoichhen* (really *Pád-magoschhen* "*Great lotos robes.*")

CHHUNG, small; as in *Pemakoichhung*, &c.

PHRA (or Ṭ'á) small, slender; as in *Ṭ'ámo-ling*.

SE—a crest, hump, knob.

YANG (གཡང་) precipice; as in *Yangma*.

NAK (ནགས་) a forest; when used as prefix (*Nákts'ál*, &c.); but as affix, another word (ནག་) = "black."

CHHEN, great; common affix in place-names.

KAR, white; as in *Gong-kar*, *She-kar Gompa*, *Dongkar*, *Dzá-kar La*, *Ts'o yu-karpa* ("white turquoise lake.")

RING, long, distant.

GYÁL (in Tsang; "Gye"), royal, chief, victorious; as in *Gyal-t'ang*, *Gyal-chhentse*.

SHAM the under part; as in *Shám-gyá*.

SHAR; east; as in *Sharp'en-lung*, *Gyál-ts'o Shar*.

TSE (རྩེ་) summit, peak; as in *Sog-tse*, *Gyángtse*, *Dongtse*, *Shigátse*, &c.

DO (རྡོ་) a stone; as in *Do-tsuk*, *Nangdo*; and especially in names of places near Tengri Nur.

ṬASHI (བཀྲ་ཤིས་) lucky, blessed: as in *Ṭashi-lhumpo*, *Ṭashisudong* (བཀྲ་ཤིས་ཆོས་སྒྲོང་) *Ṭashiding*, *Ṭashi-chhoi*.

GAR (སྒར་) a camp, as in *Gart'ok* (སྒར་ཐོག་), *Gye-gar*.

RÁ; an enclosure; also "a horn;" as in *Ra-lung*, *Ramochhe*, *Rading*

LONG (ཀློང་) a mass, as in *Dolong Karpo* ("white mass of snow"), the name of a rocky sand-bank in the Khánu Lungwa River in Balti.

P'UG a cavern; as in *Du-p'uk.*

GUR, a tent, as in *Gurlá* in Ngari Khorsum.

TSÁ, grass, grassy, as in *Ṭak-tsá, Tsá-sum, Tsá-gang.*

LUNG, a valley; as in *Ṛá-lung, Khu-lung, Tib-lung*; *Nye-má-lung, Chhiblung* ("valley of horses.")

RONG, a defile or gorge; as in *Khyi-rong,* due north of Nipal; *Rong-chhá-khá.*

TÖ, or TOD or TET, (སྟོད་) the upper part: in *Tö-lung,* &c.

MÁT or ME' (སྨད་) the lower part: in Central Tibet pronounced *Má,* or *Me'*; in Ladak, &c., *Mát.* This and the foregoing chiefly attached as affix to names of districts as in *Po-töd, Po-me',* and many others.

OG and YOK: lower; as in *Wur-og, Ambiyok.*

LING (གླིང་) isolated spot: as in *Ḍarjiling, Mart'oling.*

SHOL or SHO, town appendent to a monastery; as in *Tamshol, Chhushol.*

DING (ལྡིངས་) a hollow; as in *Ton-dub-ding, Yon-chhoi-ding, Samding.*

PANG (སྤང་) a bog, or usually, a grassy bog or swamp; as in *Pang-kong* Lake, *Pang-mik, Pang-pochhe.* A syllable generally occurring in the names of lake-side places

YAR, upper (used in Balti place-names), as in *Yarkhor, Yarmichhu.*

T'ANG, a plain, as in *Yang-t'ang, Zé'-t'ang* (བཟེད་ཐང་), &c.

# PART III.

## VOCABULARY.

- LAḌAKI.
- CENTRAL TIBETAN.
- LITERARY TIBETAN.

# VOCABULARY.

## ENGLISH—LÁDAKI—CENTRAL TIBETAN COLLOQUIAL —LITERARY TIBETAN.

The verbs appear here in the infinitive form, though they rarely occur thus in practice. The verbal root alone is generally used; or else the root with some affix annexed indicative of tense, such as *yin*, *re'*, *du'*, *jhung*. *yong*, &c.

The Ládaki words are in large part current in Rudok and Western Tibet. In Balti the dialect is slightly different, the letters *s* and *r* occurring more frequently as the first letter in a word, while the infinitive affix is changed to *chas*. In Tsang, Kirong, and Sikkim this affix becomes *she*, and in parts of Sikkim and Bhutan, *nyi*.

*N. B.*—Before using this Vocabulary, the Notes on Pronunciation on page 131 should be referred to.

| English. | Ládaki. | Central Tibetan. | Literary Tibetan. |
|---|---|---|---|
| Able, to be | *t'upche*; *ngobche* | *chokpa*; *t'up-pa*; and (occasionally) *nüi-pa* | ལྕོག་པ། ནུས་པ་ |
| Able, shall you be | *é t'upin?* | *t'u'-yong-ngá* | |
| Above (*adv.*) | *yar*; *gong-la* | *yar*; *yen-la* | ཐོག་ཏུ། ཡན་ཆད་ལ་ |

| ENGLISH. | LÁDAKI. | CENTRAL TIBETAN. | LITERARY TÍBETAN. |
|---|---|---|---|
| Above (*prep.*) | *lták ; gong-na* | *tang-la ; t'ö* ཐོད་ | གོང་དུ། སྟེང་ལ་ |
| About (concerning) | *p'ila* (with accus.) | *kor* (with genit.) | སྐོར་ལ་ |
| About (*adv.*) | | *tsam-la* | ཙམ་ལ་ |
| Abuse, to | *má-báp kalche* | *lap-she tangwa* | སྨོད་པ་ (with ལ་) |
| Accept, to | *námche* | *lempa* | ལེན་པ་ |
| Accident (mishap.) | *jhur ; jūs* | *jhur* བྱུར་ | རྐྱེན་ |
| Accompany, to | *skyelche* | *nyampo ḍo-wa ; dong-te ḍo-wa* | སྐྱེལ་བ་ |
| Accomplish, to | *chhom yinche* | *ḍup-pa ; ts'ar-wa* | འགྲུབ་པ་ |
| Accord, of its own | *rang shuk-la* | *rang-šhin* | |
| According to | *nang-tár : ts'irla* | *nang-šhin* | ལྟ་བུ། བཞིན་ |

| | | | |
|---|---|---|---|
| Account of, on | *p'ila* | *tön-la; chhirtu* | བཞིན་དུ། ཕྱིར་དུ་ |
| Accuse, to | *kal tangche*<br>*khá-lok tangche* | *kál gyap-pa* | འགེལ་བ་ |
| Accustomed to | *gom* (with *dang* added to object) | *ghom* (with *dhang*) | གོམས་པ་ |
| Across | *t'edla* | *t'é-la* | ཕྱེད་ལ་ |
| Add, to | *nánche* | *nönpa* | སྣོན་པ་ |
| Admittance, to grant (audience) | *jálkhá tángche* | *jálkhá nangwa* | མཇལ་ཁ་གཏོང་བ་ |
| Admittance, to refuse | *jálkhá kákche* | *jálkhá mi nangwa* | |
| Advance (of pay), an | | *ngáchhi* | སྔ་ཕྱི་ |
| Advantage | *dom* | *dhön* | དོན་ |
| Advantage of, to gain | *gyál-khá choche* | *khyer-so zin-pa* | དོན་བྱེད་པ་ |
| Advice: | *dámska* | *khádam* | འདམས་པ་ |

| English. | Ládaki. | Central Tibetan. | Literary Tibetan. |
|---|---|---|---|
| Advise, to | *dámska tangche* | *düm-ma nangwa* | གདམས་པ་ |
| Afraid, to be | *jig rágche* | *šhe'-pa* ཞེད་པ་ | འཇིགས་སྐྲག་པ་ |
| Afraid, he was | *jig song* | *jig-ṭág jhung ; šhe'-pa-yin* | དངངས་སྐྲགས་པ་ཡིན་ |
| After (*prep.*) | *tingla ; yokla* | *jé-la ; šhuk-la ; gáp* (with genit.) | རྗེས་སུ། མཐར། འོག་ལ་ |
| Afterwards | *tingné ; yokla* | *larné ; jé-la* | སླད་ནས། ཕྱིན་ཆད་ |
| Afternoon | *p'it'ok* | *gung-lön* | དགུང་ལོན་ |
| Again | *lokté* | *ŷang-kyár ; lokné* | ཡང་། ཕྱིར་ |
| Age | *náso* | *náts'o* | ན་ཚོད་ |
| Aged | *chenmo* | *genpo* | རྒད་པ་ |
| Agree, to | *rikche* | *chhampa* | མཐུན་པ་ |

| | | | |
|---|---|---|---|
| Agreement, to make an | *kháchhad zumche* | *chhé-zim jhyé-pa* | ཆད་འཛིན་པ་ |
| Agreement, written | *gámgyá* | *ghen-gyá ; ŷig-zin* | ཆད་ཡིག་ |
| Air | *ngárá ; lhungspo* | *ngárá ; nam* | རླུང་མ་ |
| Alight, to | *bápche* | *shö'du bap-pa* | འབབ་པ་ |
| Alive (he is)—living. | *sonte* | *sömpo* | གསོན་པོ་ |
| Alike (are) | *ts'ok-se* | *ḍá-te* | འདྲས་ |
| All (*adj.*) | *kop ; lib* | *kün* | ཀུན་ |
| All (*pron.*) | *ts'angma ; lib* | *t'ámche ; ts'angma* | ཐམས་ཅད་ |
| Alone | *chik-chik* | *shráng-shráng-la* | གཅིག་པོར་ |
| Also | *yang* | *ŷang-kyár* | ཡང་སྐྱར་ |
| Alter, to (anything) | *spoche* | *gyur-wa* | སྒྱུར་བ་ |

| ENGLISH. | LÁDAKI. | CENTRAL TIBETAN. | LITERARY TIBETAN. |
|---|---|---|---|
| Altered, is | *gyur song* | *gyur yö' ; ḍo-wa jhe'* | འགྱུར་བར་སོང་ |
| Altogether (quite) | *lding-se ; yongsu* | *ŷongsu* | ཡོངས་སུ་ |
| Altogether (in a body) | *sag ; kod* | *lhengyé-la ; hlenchi* | ལྷན་གཅིག་ཏུ |
| Always | *námsang* | *dhui-gyün ; tákpa-réshi* | རྟག་ཏུ། རྒྱུན་དུ་ |
| Almost | *ts'á-bhikma* ཚ་བིག་མ་ | *chhálam* | ཧ་ལམ་ |
| Among | *nángnángna* | *nangne* | ནང་ནས་ |
| And | *dhárung* | *dhang* | ཡང་། དང་ |
| Anger | *shro* | *ṭ'ó* | ཁྲོ་བ |
| Angry, to be | *shro chháche* | *ṭ'o-wa lang-wa* | ཞེ་སྡང་བ |
| Animal | *duḍḍo* | *dū-wa ; tünḍo* | དུད་འགྲོ་བ |

| | | | |
|---|---|---|---|
| Animal (of prey) | | *chen-šen* | གཅན་གཟན |
| Another (one) | *dákméd* | *dákme'* བདག་མེད | གཞན |
| Anxiety | *sem-ts'er* | *khok-t'uk* | མཆོར་ས |
| Any, anything | *su-zhik ; chi-tong* | *chi-yang ;* *ḍá* (as an adj.) | ཅི་འང |
| Appear to, (become visible) | *jungche* | *jhungwa* | འབྱུང་བ |
| Apple | *kúshu* | *li ; debu* | སླི |
| Apply one'self, to | *bádche* | *lhur lenpa* | འབད་པ |
| Appoint, to (to any post) | *kálche ; sko-che* | *chuk-pa* | འཆོལ་བ། འཛུག་པ |
| Approach, to | *sar chħáche* | *tá nye-po ḍo-wa ; khe-pa* | ཉེ་བར་འབྱུང་བ |
| Arm | *lakpa* | *l̂akpa* | ལག་པ |
| Arms, in (your) | *pang-la* | *pang khar* | པང་པར |

| ENGLISH. | LÁDAKI. | CENTRAL TIBETAN. | LITERARY TIBETAN. |
|---|---|---|---|
| Army | *mák-ts'ok* | *máa-pung* | དམག་དཔུང་ |
| Arrow | *dá* | *dá* | མདའ་ |
| Arrive, to | *lebche* | *lebpa ; chhinpa* | སླེབ་པ་ |
| Arrive, shall | *leb zin* | *lep yong* | ཕྱིན་ཡོང་ |
| Arrived, has he | *p'in-ná ?* | *lep jhung-ngá ?* | ཕྱིན་བྱུང་ངམ་ |
| As (prep.) | *ts'okse ; zuk* | *ḍe ; nangšhin* | འདྲས་ |
| As far as (up to) | *ts'ukpa* | *t'ukpa* | ཚམ་དུ་ |
| As—as | *tsam* | *t'uk* | ཚམ་ |
| Aside | *zurna* | *l̂ok-la* | ལོགས་ལ་ |
| Ask, to | *ḍiche* (with *nás*) | *šhu-wa* ཞུ་བ་ | འདྲི་བ་ |

| | | | |
|---|---|---|---|
| Ask a favour, to | *zhuwa p'ulche* | *zhuwa ulwa ; solwa* | |
| Ass | *wong-bu* | *wong-gu* | བོང་བུ |
| At | *la* | *la ; tsáne* | ལ་ |
| At once | | *lamsang* | |
| Attack, to | *rubche* | *rub-rup gyákpa* | རུབ་པ་ |
| Attain, to | *t'opche* | *nye'-pa* | ཐོབ་པ། སྒྲུབ་པ་ |
| Attend (at *or* before), to | | *jár-wa* (with *la* or *dün-la*) | འབྱོར་བ་ |
| Attend, will (be present) | | *jár-gyu yin* | |
| Attend to, to | *ngára choche ; sem zhung-che* | *cháng rik jhe'pa* | གཉེར་བ་ |
| Avalanche | *khárud* | *khárü'* | ཁ་རུད་ |
| Avoid, to | *dzurche* | *yolwa* | སྤྱོང་བ་ |
| Autumn | *ston-chhoks* | *tönká* | སྟོན་ཀ་ |

29

| English. | Ládaki. | Central Tịbetan. | Literary Tibetan. |
|---|---|---|---|
| Averse to, is | *mi t'ádkhan duk* | *—yol yin* | |
| Away | *p'ár* | *há-la* ཧ་ལ་ | ཕར་ |
| Axe | *stari* | *tá-ḍhi ; tepo* | སྟེ་པོ་ |
| Baby | *ómt'ung* | *p'ugu* | ཕྲུ་གུ་ |
| Back, the | *gyáp* | *gyáp* | རྒྱབ་ |
| Back (*adv.*) | *lokte* | *lokné* | ཕྱིར་ |
| Backside (posteriors) | *p'ump'um ; spi* | *t'umṭ'um ; kup* | |
| Backwards | *p'i-lok-la* | *gyap-lok-la* | རྒྱབ་ལོག་ |
| Bad | *sokpo* | *ñgempo ; ákpo* | ངན་པོ་ |
| Bakshish | *nángshyin* | *so're ; náng-jyin* | གནང་སྦྱིན་ |

| | | | |
|---|---|---|---|
| Ball (musket) | *rindri* | *dé-u ; dikril* | རྡེའུ་ |
| Bandage | *rást'ák* | *lept'ák* | ལེབ་ཐགས་ |
| Bank (of river) | *tsangs-t'á* | *ḍám.* | འགྲམ་ |
| Banker | *bundák* | *bundák* | བུན་བདག་ |
| Baptise, to | *ṭ'us solche* | *ṭ'ü solwa* | ཁྲུས་གསོལ་བ་ |
| Barber | *ḍeg-khan* | *ḍek-khen* | འབྲེག་མཁན་ |
| Barley-flour | *sá-tu* | *tsampa* | རྩམ་པ་ |
| Barley | *nás* | *ne* | ནས་ |
| Basin (eating) | *shing-kor ; kóre* | *p'orpa* | ཕོར་པ་ |
| Basin or bowl | *kaṭora* | *dhungpen* | |
| Basket | *tselpo* | *nyuktse ; le-po* | ཚེལ་པོ་ |
| Basket (covered) | *kundúm* | *še'ma* | གཟེད་མ་ |

| English. | Ládaki. | Central Tibetan. | Literary Tibetan. |
|---|---|---|---|
| Bat | *ts'anbi* | *p'áwang* | ཕ་ཝང་ |
| Bathe, to | *ṭ'uche* | *ṭ'uwa* | འཁྲུ་བ་ |
| Bear, a | *ḍenmo* | *ḍhemong* | དྲེད་མོ་ |
| Bear, to (carry) | *khurche* | *k̄hyer-wa* | འཁྱེར་བ་ |
| Bear, to (suffer) | *shranche* | *sö'pa ; p'am khur-wa* | བཟོད་པ་ |
| Beat, to | *rdungche* | *chák gyákpa* | རྡུང་བ་ |
| Beautiful | *démo* | *l̂épo ; nying-che'po* | སྙིང་རྗེད་པོ་ |
| Becoming, it is | | *chhak-ghi-du'* | |
| Bedstead | *nyal-ṭ'i* | *m̂ál-ṭ'i* | ཉལ་ཁྲི་ |
| Bedding | *mál-tán* | *m̂ál-chhe ; m̂álting* | མལ་བཏིང་ |

| | | | |
|---|---|---|---|
| Bedskins | *zim-t'ul* | *m̂al t'ulpo* | |
| Bee | *rang-zi bu* | *ḍángma* | འབྲང་བུ |
| Beef | | *lang-shá* | |
| Beer | *chháng* | *né-chháng* | ཆང་ |
| Been, has | *song ; yód-pen* | *chhyin-pa'-in* | ཕྱིན་པ་ཡིན |
| Beer shop | *chháng-sá* | *chháng-khang* | ཆང་ཁང་ |
| Beer drinker | *chháng dádchan* | *chháng t'ung-khen* | ཆང་ཐུང་ཁན |
| Beer, small | *ûksing* | — | |
| Beetle | *burpa* | *burpa* | སྦུར་པ |
| Before (*adv.* previously) | *shngáma ; goma* | *ngar* | སྔར་ |
| Before (*adv.* in front) | *ngun-la* | *dong-la ; ngön-la* | སྔོན་དུ |
| Before (*prep.*) | *dun-la* (with gen.) | *dün-la* | དྲུང་དུ |

| ENGLISH. | LÁDAKI. | CENTRAL TIBETAN. | LITERARY TIBETAN. |
|---|---|---|---|
| Began to, he | *go-zuk yot-pen* | *dzuk jhung*<br>*tsuk jhung* | |
| Beggar | *shṛangpo* | *pang-go* | སྤྲང་པོ་ |
| Begin to, to | *tsukche* | *go-dzukpa* | འཛུགས་པ་ |
| Beginning, the | *góma* | *góma* | མགོ་མ་ |
| Begun, was | *tsugspen* | *tsom jhung; go-dzuk-jhung* | རྩོམ་པ་ཡིན་ |
| Behind (*adv.*) | *p'ina* | *jé-la; chhyi* | ཕྱི་ |
| Behind (*prep.*) | *sting-la* | *ŝhug-la* (with gen.) | རྗེས་སུ་ |
| Believe, to | *den chhéche* | *ŷi' dhe'pa; lo chhé-pa* | དད་པ་ |
| Bell | *dri-lu* | *ḍhilbu* | དྲིལ་བུ་ |
| Bell, to ring | *trolche* | *ṭolwa; tsing-tsingpa* | འཁྲོལ་བ་ |

| | | | |
|---|---|---|---|
| Bellows | *bud-khan* | *bi-pa* | སྦུད་པ་ |
| Belly | *drodpa* | *dhö'pa* | གྲོད་པ་ |
| Belonging to | *chan* (affixed to owner) | *chen* (ditto) | དང་ལྡན་པ་ |
| Belongs to, it | *t'es duk* (with *la*) | *t'i-te-yö* (with *la* of possessor) | གཏོགས་པ་ཡིན |
| Below ; beneath (*prep.*) | *yok-la* (with gen.)<br>*yok* (with accus.) | *khá-wák* ;<br>*wok* (with genit.) | འོག་ཏུ་ |
| Beneath, from | *yok-nás* | *wok-né* | འོག་ནས |
| Bend, to | *kug-kuk choche* | *kug-kuk jhe'pa* | |
| Benefit | *p'ánpa* | *p'empa* | ཕན་པ |
| Bent | *kug-kuk* | *khumpo ; kuk* | |
| Best, the | *chhok* | *chhok ; ṭak-shö* | མཆོག་ |
| Best, one's (utmost) | *chi t'up khan* | *ghang shé-pa* | |
| α β<br>Better than | β α<br>*sang gyalla* | β α<br>*lé...yák-ka* | ལས་ . . བཟང་ |

| ENGLISH. | LÁDAKI. | CENTRAL TIBETAN. | LITERARY TIBETAN. |
|---|---|---|---|
| Between | *zhung-la* | *seb-lu ; bhar-la* | བར་ན་ |
| Beyond (*prep.*) | *p'ar-la ; p'i-loks* | *p'ár-tsam* | ཕ་རོལ་ན་ |
| Bhutan | *Druk-yul* | *Ḍuk-yul* | འབྲུག་པ་ |
| Bind, to | *chhingche* | *khyikpa* | འཆིང་བ་ |
| Bird | *chi-pa* | *jhyá ; p'yá* (iu Sikkim) | བྱ་ |
| Bird's nest | *ts'ángs* | *jhyá-ts'ang* | བྱ་ཚང་ |
| Birth (also *re-birth*) | *skye-sa* | *kye-wa* | སྐྱེ་བ་ |
| Birthplace | *p'á-yul* | *kye-sá* | སྐྱེ་གནས་ |
| Bits, in—Bits, to | *dumbur* | *chhák ṭum la ; longlong* | ཆག་ཀྲུམ་ལ་ |
| Bit, a little | *ts'ábik ; nyung-ngá-rik* | *énts'am chik ; ṭ'embhu chik* | |

| | | | |
|---|---|---|---|
| Bit (horse's) | *shrápchak* | *sápchak* | སྲབ་ལྕགས་ |
| Bite, to | *so tábche* | *mukpa* | རྨུག་པ་ |
| Bitter | *khánte ; gho* | *khápo* | ཁ་བ་ |
| Black | *nákpo* | *nákpo* | ནག་པོ་ |
| Blame, to | *skyon takche* | *chyo-wa* | སྐྱོད་པ་ |
| Blanket | *shápos* | *chhâli ; má.én* | |
| Bleed, to (*intr. verb*) | *t'ák tangche* | *t'ák p'owa* | |
| Blind | *mikzhar* | *mik-shar ; long-wa* | ལྡོང་བ་ |
| Blocks up | *kák duk* | *chur-kin-du'* | འགགས་འདུག་ |
| Blocked up, is | *kák song* | *chur jhung* | |
| Blood | *t'ák* | *t'ák* | ཁྲག་ |
| Bloody | *t'ákchan* | *t'ákchen* | ཁྲག་ཅན་ |
| Blow, to | *p'uche* | *p'u-wa* | འབུད་པ་ |

| English. | Ládaki. | Central Tibetan. | Literary Tibetan. |
|---|---|---|---|
| Blow, a | *dámchák* | *dzok* | |
| Blue | *sngon-po* | *ngön-po* | སྔོན་པོ་ |
| Blunt | *tultul* | *nóme'* | རྟུལ་པོ་ |
| Board, a | *spanglep* | *ándár; shinglep* | ཤིང་ལེབ་ |
| Boards (for book) | *leks-shing* | *lek-shing* | གླེགས་ཤིང་ |
| Boat | *gru-chhung* | *ḍhu; nyen* | གྲུ་ |
| Boat (of hide) | | *ko-ḍhu; ko-á* | |
| Boatman | *gru-khán* | *ko-khen; ḍhu-pa* | གྲུ་པ་ |
| Body | *go̤-po* | *šúkpo; p'ungpo* | ལུས། གཟུགས་པོ་ |
| Boil, to make | *skolche* | *tso tang-wa* | སྐོལ་བ། འཚོད་པ་ |
| Boil, to let | *skol chukche* | *kol chukpa* | |
| Boil over, don't let | *lud ma chuk* | *lü' ma chuk* | |

| | | | |
|---|---|---|---|
| Boiled-meat | | *shá tso-pa* | |
| Bolt, a door | *si-ri* | *ya* | གཡའ། སྒྲུར་ |
| Bolt, to | *siri chukche* | *yá gyakpa* | |
| Bone | *ruspa* | *rui ; dung* | རུས་པ་ |
| Book | *spéchhá* | *péchha* | དཔེ་ཆ་ |
| Booklet | *spé-ka* | *po-ti* | |
| Boot | *kapshá lám* | *lham* | ལྷམ་ |
| Boot (with woollen tops and leg) | *cháruk* | *ke'pa* | ཀྲད་པ་ |
| Born, to be | *skyeche* | *kye-wa* | སྐྱེ་བ་ |
| Borrow, to | *yarche* | *kyin-kyiwa* | སྐྱི་བ་ |
| Bosom | *pang-pa* | *ámbák* | པང་པ་ |
| Bottle | *shelbum* | *bumpa ; potál* | བུམ་པ་ |
| Bottom | *lting* | *ting* | གཏིང་ |
| Boulder | *p'á-long* | *ṭak·pong* | བྲག་བོང་ |

| ENGLISH. | LÁDAKI. | CENTRAL TIBETAN. | LITERARY TIBETAN. |
| --- | --- | --- | --- |
| Bow, a | *zhu* | *zhu (šhu)* | གཞུ་ |
| Bow (salute) | *chhák* | *chál-chhág* | ཕྱག་ |
| Bowl (food) | *ko-re* | *shingkor ; p'urpa* | ཕོར་པ་ |
| Boy | *búts-ha ; bu* | *chi'pa ; potso* | བྱིས་པ། ཁྱེའུ་ |
| Branch | *yálga* | *ŷá'ga* | ཡལ་ག་ |
| Brandy (barley-spirit) | *donrak* | *árák* | ཨ་རག་ |
| Brass | *rágan* | *rágan* | རག་ |
| Brave | *nyingchan* | *ngingchen ; pá-o* | དཔའ་བ་ |
| Bravery, | *hampa* | *nyingtop* | སྙིང་སྟོབས་ |
| Breach of law | | *t'im-dhang-gál* | |

| | | | |
|---|---|---|---|
| Bread | *tágir* | *pá'lep* | བག་ལེབ་ |
| Breadth | *zháng* | *ŝheng-khá* | ཞེང་ |
| Break, to | *chágche* | *chhákpa* | གཅོག་པ་ |
| Breakfast | *tsalma* | *ḍho ; ŝhok-to* | གྲོ་ |
| Breast-pocket (bosom) | | *ámbák* | |
| Breathe, to | *úg tonche* | *ú' jungwa ; ngampa* | དབུགས་འབྱུང་བ་ |
| Breath | *hu ; uk* | *ū' ; ug* | དབུགས་ |
| Bribe, a | *p'aksup* | *p'ák-suk* | |
| Brick | *pá-u* | *pák ; sá-lep* | པག་ |
| Bridge | *zámpa* | *ŝampa* | ཟམ་པ་ |
| Bridge of tree-boughs | *sá-zám* | *chúk-ŝam* | ལྕུག་ཟམ་ |

| ENGLISH. | LÁDAKI. | CENTRAL TIBETAN. | LITERARY TIBETAN. |
|---|---|---|---|
| Bridle | *shráp* | *sáp* | སྲབ་ |
| Bring ! | *khyong !* | *khur shok !* | འཁུར་ཤོག་ |
| | | *khyer shok !* | |
| Bring, to | *khyongche* | *kyálwa ; khur-wa* | སྐྱེལ་བ། འཁྱེར་བ་ |
| Bring, shall I | *khyong yin-ná ; khyers'in-ná ?* | *khur ŷong-gyu-yimpa ; kyal ŷong-gá ? khur lep yong-ngá ?* | |
| Brought, has been | *khyerspen* འཁྱེརས་པ་ཡིན་ | *khur ŷong-wa-yin* or *khur lep du'* | |
| Brought, has | | *khur lep song* | ཁུར་སླེབས་སོང་ |
| Broad : | *zhangchan* | *ŝhengchen* | ཞེང་ཅན་ |

| | | | |
|---|---|---|---|
| Broken, is | *chák song* | *chhák jhung* | འཆགས་སོང་ |
| Broom | *ong-mól* | *chhyák-ma* | ཕྱགས་མ་ |
| Brother (when used of or to an elder brother) | *á-cho* | *á-jho ; jho-jho* | ཨ་ཇོ་ |
| Brother (speaking of or to a younger brother) | *no* | *ñuwo ; chungpo* (hon.) | ནུ་བོ་ |
| Brothers (general term) | *spunla* སྤུན་ཟླ་ | *pün* | སྤུན་ |
| Bruised, is | | *dab jhung* | བརྡབས་བྱུང་ |
| Brush (for painting) | *p'akzet* | *yuk-pir* | ཕྱུག་པིར་ |
| Bucket (of wood) with lid | *zo-wa* | *chhušom* | ཆུ་བཟོམ་ |
| Bug | *chári* | *ḍe-shik* | འདྲེ་ཤིག་ |
| Buddhist | *nang-pa* | *ñang-pa* | ནང་པ་ |
| Build, to | *sikche* | *tsik-pa* | [illegible] |

| ENGLISH. | LÁDAKI. | CENTRAL TIBETAN. | LITERARY TIBETAN. |
|---|---|---|---|
| Bundle (hand) | *lák-kod* | *pömpo* ཕོན་པོ་ | ཨལ་ཧྲིང་ |
| Burn, to (anything) | *duk tangche ; shrakche* | *dhuk-pa* | དགུས་པ། སྦར་བ་ |
| Burn, to (*intrans.*) | *tsikche* | *ts'ikpa* | འཚིག་པ། འབར་བ། |
| Burnt, has been | *tsikspen* | *ts'ik jhung* | |
| Bury, to (anything) | *kungche* | *kung-wa* | སྐྲུང་བ་ |
| Business (affairs) | *ḍelwa* | *dhön ; l̂e-ka* | དོན་ |
| Busy (I am) | (*ngá-la*) *ḍelwa duk* | (*ngárang-la*) *ḍhelwa re'* | བྲེལ་བ་ |
| But | *a-ma* | *ŷin-kyang; ŷinna ŷang* | འོན་ཀྱང་ |
| Butcher | *sháp ts'ongkhen* | *shempa ;* or *dikchen shem-pa* | ཤན་པ་ |

| | | | |
|---|---|---|---|
| Butterfly | *p'e-lebsé* | *chhye-má-lep* | ཕྱེ་མ་ལེབ་ |
| Butter | *már* | *m̃ár* | མར་ |
| 31 Button | *tobchi* | *t'ebji ; t'ole* | |
| Buy, to | *nyoche* | *nyo-wa* | ཉོ་བ |
| y (beside) | *ḍamdu* | *dün-la* | མདུན་དུ་ ... |
| Calf | *béto* | *bhe-to; bhemo* (*fem,*) (often *pe-u*) | བེའུ་ |
| Call, to (to a person) | *kad gyapche ; bótche* | *ke' gyakpa* | འབོད་པ་ |
| Camel | *shngábong* | *ngámong* | ང་བོང་ |
| Came ; has come | *yongspen* | *yong-pa-yö' or p'ep jhung* | འོང་བ་སོང་ |
| Camp | *drangsá* | *ḍángsa* | སྒར་ |
| Camp, to pitch | *gur langche* | *u-ghur langwa* | དབུ་གུར་ལང་བ་ |

| ENGLISH. | LÁDAKI. | CENTRAL TIBETAN. | LITERARY TIBETAN. |
|---|---|---|---|
| Cane-bridge | *sá-zám* | *pá-ŝampa* or *ts'á-ŝam* | སྦྲ་ཟམ། ཚགས་ཟམ་ |
| Cap | *tibi* | *ŝhámbu* | ཞྭ་དབུ་ |
| Cap, Chinese | | *mok-ri* | |
| Care, take | *kadarcho!* | *rikpa ḍhim!*<br>*nyar goi!*<br>*rikpa jhyi!* | ཉ་ར་བྱེད་དགོས་ |
| Careful | *ts'anáchan* | *chag-gha dákpo* | |
| Careless | *zon-me'; lélochan* | *hámákho* | ཟོན་མེད་ |
| Carry, to | *khyerche* | *khurwa* | འཁུར་བ་ |
| Cart, a | *shing-sta* | *shing-tá* | ཤིང་རྟ་ |
| Cast away, to | *p'ángte borche* | *yukle ŝhakpa* | འདོར་བ་ |

| | | | |
|---|---|---|---|
| Cat, | *pishi* | *ŝhumbu, ŝhimmi* | བྱི་ལ་ |
| Catch hold of, to | *zumche* | *pàr-dzin t'empa* | འཛིན་པ་ |
| Caught, to be | *khat-che* | *kharwa* | འཁད་པ་ |
| Cause | *zhi ; gyu-tsan* | *gyu ; ŝhi* | གཞི། རྒྱུན་ |
| Cave | *p'ukpa* | *ṭak-p'uk ; bup* | ཕུག་པ་རྫ་ སྦུབས། |
| Cease, to | *zhiche* | *chhe'pa* | འཆད་པ་ |
| Ceiling | *yá-t'ok* | — | |
| Centre | *te-wa* | *te-wa ; t'il* | ལྟེ་བ་ |
| Centipede | *láre* | — | |
| Certain (sure) | *ngó-tok* | *t'ákchhö* | ངེས་པ་ |
| Certainly | *ṅanchhak* | *nenten* | ནན་ཆག་ |

| ENGLISH. | LÁDAKI. | CENTRAL TIBETAN. | LITERARY TIBETAN. |
|---|---|---|---|
| Chair, European | *ṭ'i-shing* | *gyá-ṭ'i ; shuṭ'i* | ཁྲི་ |
| Chair, sedan | *khyok-pang* | *p'epchang* | ཁྱོགས་དཔྱང་ |
| Change, to (*trans.*) | *spo-che* | *je-wa ; she-wa* | རྗེ་བ་ |
| Changed, is | *p'o song ; rdepspen* | *gyur jhung* | གྱུར་ནས་སོང་ |
| Character | | *shi-gyü'* | གཤིས་རྒྱུད་ |
| Charcoal | *solnák* | *solnák* | སོལ་ནག་ |
| Charge, to (accuse) | *kál tangche* | *gol-wa ; ts'ang dru-wa* | རྒོལ་བ་ |
| Charge, to (price) | *rin nenche* | *rin chö'pa* | |
| Cheap | *khye-mo* | *kye-po* | |
| Cheapen, to (in bargaining) | *rin p'ábche* | *khéru ḍo-wa* | རིན་འབེབས་པ་ |

| | | | |
|---|---|---|---|
| Cheat, to | *gop-skorche* | *go-jhömpa* | མགོ་འཇོམས་པ་ |
| Cheek | *khurts'ok* | *dempü* | ལྡན་བུ་ |
| Cheerful | *gámschan* | *t'ulpo* | ཁྲལ་པོ་ |
| Cheese | *t'ud* | *wo-t'ü'* | འོ་ཐུད་ |
| Chest (of the body) | *ḍáng* | *ḍháng* | བྲང་ |
| Child | *ṭúgu* | *ṭ'ugu ; p'ugu* | ཕྲུ་གུ་ |
| Chilly | *drangmo* | *ḍhang-mo* | གྲང་མོ་ |
| Chimney (smoke hole) | | *kyámtong* | |
| Chin | *má-le* | *ōku* ཨོས་ཀླུ | ཞལ་ཀོ་ |
| China | *Gyá-nák* | *Mahátsin* | མ་ཧ་ཙིན་ |
| Chinaman | *Gyá-mi* | *Gyá-mi* | རྒྱ་མི་ |

| ENGLISH. | LÁDAKI. | CENTRAL TIBETAN. | LITERARY TIBETAN. |
|---|---|---|---|
| Choke, to *tr. v.* | *snangche* | *khyömpa* | གྲེ་བར་སྡོང་བ་ |
| *intrans.* | *ske dámche* | *kye khyikpa* | |
| Cholera | *bokshi* | *nyálok* | |
| Choose, to | *damste khyerche* | *dám-pa* | འདམ་པ་ |
| Chopsticks | *t'u-máng* | *t'urma* | ཐུར་མ་ |
| Chop up, to | *stupche* | *tsap-pa* | འཐུབ་པ་ |
| Christ | *Máshika* | *Máshika* | མ་ཤི་ཀ་ |
| Circumstances | *náts'ul* | *ḍo-go ; sel-chha* | གསལ་ཆ་ |
| Circle | *gort'ik* | *kyir-kyír ; kinkhor* | དཀྱིལ་འཁོར་ |
| City | *gyálsá* | *ḍhong-khyer* | གྲོང་ཁྱེར་ |

| | | | |
|---|---|---|---|
| Claw | *barmo* | *parmo ; der-khyu* | སྦར་མོ་ |
| Clay | *zhápák ; kálak* | *jimpa* | འཇིམ་པ་ |
| Clean, to (*trans.*) | *lákmo choche* | *le-mo zo-wa ; sáng-wa* | འཚང་བ། འདག་པ་ |
| Cleaned, is | *sáng chospen* | *sáng jhung* | |
| Clean (*adj.*) | *lákmo ; sáng* | *tsangwa* | |
| Clear | *sing-mo ; wá-le* | *sálpo ; hleng* | མངོན་པ། ལྷ་ལི་ |
| Clearly | *sálpo* | *sálte* | དྭངས་པོར། ལྷང་ངེ་ |
| Clever | *shang-po* | *t'áb-chen ; khé-t'a* | མཁས་པ་ |
| Climb, to | *dzekche* | *dzek-pa* | འཛེག་པ་ |
| Cloak | *yang-luk* | *bhi* | བེར་ |
| Clock | *chhutshod* | *chhú-ts'ö* | ཆུ་ཚོད |

| English. | Ládaki. | Central Tibetan. | Literary Tibetan. |
|---|---|---|---|
| Close by | *nye-mo* | *ṭ'i-na* | ཉེར། འཁྲིས་ན་ |
| Clotted milk | *chhurp'e* | *so-ŝho* | ཆུར་བ། གསོལ་ཞོ་ |
| Cloth | *rás ; go-nam* | *rái ; ré-ga* | རས་ |
| Clothing | *gón-chhé* | *ko-lák ; nabšá* (hon.) | གོས་ |
| Cloud | *shrin* | *ṭin* | སྤྲིན་ |
| Coat | *gonchhé* | *kwa-tse ; tŭk-po* | གོས། དུག་པོ་ |
| Cock (gun) | *me-kám* | *t'o-chhung* | |
| Coil, to | *ril-che* | *ḍil-wa* | སྒྲིལ་བ་ |
| Ccld | *ḍhang-mo* | *ḍhang-ghi ; ḍhang-mo* | གྲང་མོ་ |
| Cold, a | *yáma* | *lo-ts'am ; năchham* | ཆམ་པ་ |

| | | | |
|---|---|---|---|
| Collect, to | *sduche* | *dŭi-pa* | སྡུད་པ |
| Collection | *dūs-pa* | *ts'o* | མཚོགས་ |
| Collar | *gong-gá* | *kong-ge* | གོང་བ |
| Colour | *ts'on ; ts'ós* | *dok ; khá-dok* | མདོག |
| Comb | *so-mang* | *ṭá-skĕ* | སྐྲ་བཤེད |
| Come, to | *yongche* | *ŷong-wa ; p'ep-pa* (hon.) | འོང་བ། འཕེབས་པ |
| Come here ! | *iru shok !* | *diru shok !* | ཚུར་བྱོན་ཤོག |
| Come, has he ? | *leb-song-ngá* | *kho p'ep-sám ?* | ཁོ་ཕེབས་སམ |
| Come, will | *yong yin ; leb-yin.* | *ŷong-gyu-yin* | འོང་བར་གྱུར་ |
| Come back ! | *lok shok !* | *lókne shok !* | ཕྱིར་ཤོག |
| Come before, to (to appear before) | *chharche* | *jár-wa* | དྲུང་དུ་འབྱིན་པ་ |

| ENGLISH. | LÁDAKI. | CENTRAL TIBETAN. | LITERARY TIBETAN. |
|---|---|---|---|
| Coming, he is | *kho-rang yong-gin duk* | *kho ŷong-gi-du'˙* | ཁོ་འོང་ |
| Come, has | *yongpen* | *yong-pa yin ; jár jhung* | འབྱོར་བྱུང་ |
| Comfortable | *zhi-wa* | *n̂yamgá* | ཉམས་དགའ་ |
| Comet | *ghu-tsiks* | *ring-skár* | རིང་སྐར་མ་ |
| Common (ordinary) | *t'un-mong* | *t'ünmong ; kyui-ma* | ཐལ་པ། དཀྱུས་མ་ |
| Companion—comrade | *yádo* | *ŝádá ; rōk* | གྲོགས། ཟླ་བོ་ |
| Compare with, to | *sdur choche* (with *la*) | *durwa jhye'pa* (with *la*) | སྡུར་བ། འགྲན་པ་ |
| Complain of, to | *kal tangche* | *shu-lok gyakpa* | |
| Complete | *tandu* | *ŷé-dzok* | |
| Condemn, to | *t'im tangche* | *ŝhalchhe chö'pa* | |

| | | | |
|---|---|---|---|
| Confusion, in | *ṭ'ál-ṭ'ul* | *ṭ'ál-ṭ'ul* | འཁྲུལ་འཁྲུལ |
| Conscience | *shés-zhin* | *jhai-chhoi ; jhai-le* | བྱས་ཆོས་ |
| Consequence of, in | | *ten-nai* (with *la*) | རྐྱེན་ནས་ |
| Consumed, is | *ts'arte song* | *ŝin yö' ; ts'ar song* | |
| Contented | *ts'imba* | *ŷi' ts'impo* | ཚིམ་པ |
| Continual, is | *zháktang duk* | *nyukchen du'* | |
| Continually | *gyundu* | *gyündhu ; námzhák* | རྒྱུན་དུ་ |
| Contract, a | *dzin* | *dumṭ'á* | |
| Convenient | *óshán* | *oi-pa ; rungchen* | རུང་བ། འོས་པ |
| Cook, a | *jánma* | *t'áp-yok* | གསོལ་དཔོན་ |
| Cook, to | *ts'oche* | *ts'ö'pa* | འཚོད་པ |

| English. | Ládaki. | Central Tibetan. | Literary Tibetan. |
|---|---|---|---|
| Coolie | *khurupa ; bé-garpa* | *bák-khen ;* | |
| Copper | *zang* | *ŝang* | ཟངས་ |
| Cork | *khádik* | *khádik* | ཁ་འདིག་ |
| Corpse | *ro ; spur* | *ro ; pur* | རོ། སྤུར་ |
| Cotton (raw) | *rás-bal* | *rai-ḅhal* | |
| Cotton-thread | *rás-kut* | *rai-kü'* | རས་སྐུད་ |
| Cough, to | *khogche* | *lo gyakpa* | འཁོགས་པ་ |
| Cough, a | *ldo-khok* | *lo-khok* | གློ་ |
| Country | *yul* | *ŷül* | ཡུལ་ |
| Count, to | *si karche* | *ḍangka gyap-pa* | བགྲང་བ་ |

| | | | |
|---|---|---|---|
| Courage | *nying-rus* | *nying-top ; lo-top* | སྙིང་སྟོབས་ |
| Courtyard | *khyams ; ts'om* | *ts'om-kor* | ཚོམས་ |
| Could, he | *ngob* | *chok yong ; t'up song* | |
| Cover, to | *tumche ; kabche* | *yok-pa ; kóp-pa* | འགེབས་པ |
| Covering, any | *khyeps* | *khebma* | ཁེབ་མ་ |
| Cow | *bá* | *bhá-chu* | བ་ |
| Cracked, has been | *kás song* | *zhák jhung* | |
| Crane | *jhá-trung-trung* | *jhá t'üng-t'üng* | ཁྲུང་ཁྲུང་ |
| Crawl, to | *bá gokche* | *p'e-wa* | འཕྲེ་བ་ |
| Cream | *ó-shri* | *wo-si* | འོ་སྲིས་ |
| Crevice | *seng-bar* | *ser-ká :* སེར་ཀ | གསེང་ |
| Crooked, it is | *khóng chhá dub ; kyok duk* | *gur-gur duk* | ཀྱོག་པོ་ |

| ENGLISH. | LÁDAKI. | CENTRAL TIBETAN. | LITERARY TIBETAN. |
|---|---|---|---|
| Cross over, to | *gál-che ; gyápche* | *gál-wa :* རྒལ་བ་ | འདའ་བ་ |
| Crown of head | *gok-skil* | *gok shün* | མགོ་གཞུན་ |
| Cruel | *nákchán ; támi shébo* | *mi nying-je ; nyemha* | གཉན་པ་ |
| Cup | *ko-re* | *p'or-pa* | ཕོར་པ་ |
| Cup-board | *chhágám* | *gámgomang ; u-páng* | སྒམ་སྒོ་མངས་ |
| Cure, to | *nád pin-che* | *p'en-chukpa* | བཅོས་པ། གསོ་བ་ |
| Cured, is—am | *zhí-song* | *sö jhung* | བསོས་སོང་ |
| Currants | *bá-shoka* | *bá-shoka* | |
| Current (of river) | *ngádchan* | *chhu-gyün* | རྒྱུན་ |
| Curtain | *yóla* | *yol-la ; rai-yol* | ཡོལ་བ་ |

| | | | |
|---|---|---|---|
| Custom (usage) | *shrol* | *ghom-khyé* | སྲོལ་ |
| Custom (revenue) | *sho-gán* | *sho-ṭ'ál* | ཤོ་གམ་ |
| Cut, to | *dé-che ; shnga-che* | *chö'pa ; ḍál-pa* | གཅོད་པ། བྲལ་བ་ |
| Cut off, to | *zhok-che* | *ḍum-pa :* འགུམ་པ་ | འབྲིག་པ་ |
| Daily | *zhák dang zhák* | *ñyin-re šhin* | |
| Dâk-transit | *ulák* | *tá-ŝam* | རྟ་ཟམ་ |
| Dalai Lama | *gyálwá kusho rim-bochhé* | *gyá'wa rimpochhé* | ཏཱ་ལའི་བླ་མ་ |
| Damp | *sher-chan ; hus* | *len-chen* | རླན་ཅན་ |
| Danger | *jig-ri* | *ñyen* | ཉེན་ |
| Dangerous | *nyen-chan* | *ñyen-chen ; m̃i-tenpo* | གདུག་པ་ཅན་ |

| ENGLISH. | LÁDAKI. | CENTRAL TIBETAN. | LITERARY TIBETAN. |
|---|---|---|---|
| Darkness, dark | *mun-dik* | *m̃ün-nák ; m̃ünpa nákpo* | མུན་པ་ |
| Dark, to become | *mun chhá-che* | *m̃ün rib-pa* | འགྲིབ་པ། འཐིབས་པ་ |
| Date | *ts'es* | *ts'e'-tang* | ཚེས་གྲངས་ |
| Daughter | *bo-mo* | *pumo ; pum* | བུ་མོ་ |
| Dawn | *skyá-ód* | *nám lang* | ནམ་ལངས་ |
| Day | *nyin-mo ; nyi-ma* | *ñyin-mo ; ŝhák* | ཉིན། ཉི་མ། ཞག་ |
| Day, all | *nyin kob ; nyi-ma ltang* | *ñyin-t'ág-t'ok* | ཉིན་ཚང་མ |
| Dead, is | *shi-song* | *shi song jhe* | |
| Dead one, the | *shí-khan* | *shi-khen* | ཤི་མཁན་ |
| Deaf | *gud-nák* | *wömpa* | འོན་པ་ |

| | | | |
|---|---|---|---|
| **Dear (costly)** | *rin-t'os* | *ghū-po ; kyongpo* | རིན་ཅན་ |
| **Debt** | *bulon* | *bhulön* | བུ་ལོན་ |
| **Deed** | *le-ka* | *lai-ka ; jhá-wa* | ལས། བྱ་བ་ |
| **Deep** | *lting-mo ; dongpo* | *tingchen ; ŝábsáp* | ཟབ་མོ་ |
| **Degrees, by** | *rémos rémos* | *rim-rim* | རིམ་གྲིས་ |
| **Delay, to cause** | | *gyang jhe'pa* | |
| **Demon** | *lánde ; don* | *de ; gék* | འདྲེ། བགེགས་ |
| **Deny, to** | *zim zerche* | *m̃i t'olwa* | མི་མཐོལ་བ་ |
| **Depend upon, to** | *lo kyelche* (with *la*) | *lo-dang khelwa* (with *la*) | བློ་སྐྱེལ་བ་ |
| **Depth** | *lting ; kongto* | *ting ; ŝab-khye* | གཏིང་ |
| **Descend, to** | *bápche* | *t'eng-la gyu-wa ; shö-dhu bab-pa* | འབབ་པ་ |

| ENGLISH. | LÁDAKI. | CENTRAL TIBETAN. | LITERARY TIBETAN. |
|---|---|---|---|
| Describe, to | *shadche* | *tönpa ; ṭalwa* | སྟོན་པ་ |
| Desert, a | *brok* | *ḍok tong ; wen-sá* | འབྲོག་སྟོང་ |
| Deserted, it is | *tong-pa-duk* | *wem-pa re'* | དབེན་པ་འདུག |
| Determined, I am | *t'ádpa yong-spen* | *t'ákchho' be'chho'* | ཐག་ཆོད་བྱེད་ཆོད་ཡིན་ |
| Devour, to | *midche* | *hăb-háb ŝá-wa* | |
| Dew | *silchhu* | *ŝilpa* | ཟིལ་པ་ |
| Diarrhœa | *shál* | *ṭ'u-ne'* | འཁྲུ་བ |
| Die, to | *shiche* | *shi-wa ; shi-p'owa* | འཆི་བ་ |
| Difference, the | *khyad* | *khye'par ; zolts'o* | ཁྱད། བྱེ་བྲག |
| Different (various) | *so-so* | *so-so ; mi-chik* | སོ་སོ་ |

| | | | |
|---|---|---|---|
| **Different, is** | *mi ḍáchan* | *m̃i ḍá-wa* | ཐ་དད་པ |
| **Difficult** | *gágspo* | *khákpo ; ká-le* | དཀའ་བོ |
| **Dig, to** | *ḍuche* | *ko-wa* | རྐོ་བ |
| **Dirt** | *ḍima* | *ḍhima ; ḍhékpa* | དྲི་མ། དྲེག་པ |
| **Dirty** | *ts'idu ; ts'ichan* | *tsok ; ts'ichen* | བཙོག་པ |
| **Dirty, to make** | *ḍima p'okche* | *ts'ichen gyakpa* | ཚི་ཅན་གྱུག་པ |
| **Disease** | *nád* | *ne'* | ནད |
| **Dish (flat)** | *gráti* | *gugushá ; soldér* | སྡེར་མ |
| **Dismiss, to** | *tangche* | *gong-p'ok terwa* | དགོངས་པ་སྟེར་བ |
| **Distance** | *p'á-zad ; nyé-lot* | *t'ák ring-t'ung* | ཐྲུང་མ |
| **Distribute! (divide them!)** | *gos tong !* | *shā-shā-su go !* | |

| ENGLISH. | LÁDAKI. | CENTRAL TIBETAN. | LITERARY TIBETAN. |
|---|---|---|---|
| Distress | *dukngál* | *ká-duk* དཀའ་སྡུག་ | སྡུག་བསྔལ་ |
| Do, to | *choche* | *jhye'pa; dze'-pa (hon.)* | བྱེད་པ། མཛད་པ་ |
| Doctor | *ám-chhi* | *ám-chhi* ཨམ་ཆི་ | སྨན་པ་ |
| Doing, is | *cho-khen duk* | *jhe'-ghi-re' (chyin-ki-re')* | བྱེད་ཀྱིན་འདུག་ |
| Do, that will | *dá ḍik!* | *dhá-ta ḍikpa* | |
| Dog | *khyi* | *khyi* | ཁྱི་ |
| Done, has been | *chhoms song* | *jhyá song* | བྱས་སོ་ |
| Door | *go* | *go* | སྒོ་ |
| Door-post | *lok-ré* | *go-ru* | |
| Door-frame | *yáre-máre* | *gonḍik* | སྒོ་འདྲིག་ |

| | | | |
|---|---|---|---|
| Double | *nyil--dab* | *len-nyi* | ལན་གཉིས་ |
| Downwards | *t'ur-la* | *shödhu* ཤོད་དུ་ *t'eng-la* | ཐེང་དུ་ |
| Drag, to | *t'enche* | *ḍü'pa* | འདྲུད་པ་ |
| Dress, to | *ghonche* | *könpa ; ghoi-lák ghön-pa* | གོན་པ་ |
| Drink, to | *t'ungche* | *t'ungwa* | འཐུང་བ་ |
| Drowned, be | *chhu khyer song* | *ts'upte shi* | འཚུབ་པ་ |
| Drum | *den jáng* | *ngá* | ང་ |
| Drum, brass | *dolti* | | |
| Drunk, to get | *rárospa yongche* | *ráro-wa* | ར་རོ་བ་ |
| Drunk, is | *sichan song* | *ráro jhung* | ར་རོ་འབྱུང་ |
| Drunkard | *ráros-khán* | *ráro-wa-pa* | |

| ENGLISH. | LÁDAKI. | CENTRAL TIBETAN. | LITERARY TIBETAN. |
|---|---|---|---|
| Dry | *skámpo* | *kámpo* | སྐམ་པོ་ |
| Dry, to | *skemche* | *kám jhe'pa* | སྐེམ་པ |
| Duck | *ngurwa* | *yá-tse* | ངང་པ་ |
| Due, is | | *jal goi-gyu* | |
| During | *nam—zána* | *ts'e-na* (after verb) | |
| Dust | *t'álwa* | *dul* | རྡུལ་ |
| Dung | *lchá* | *ḍhün* | བྲུན |
| Duty | *khák* | *ts'ul-ṭ'im* | ཚུལ་ཁྲིམས |
| Duty (tax) | *sho-gám ; tot* | *sho-ṭ'ál* | ཤོ་འཕྲལ |
| Dwell, to | *dukche* | *nái-pa* (*né-pa*) | གནས་པ |

| | | | |
|---|---|---|---|
| Dye, to | *ts'os gyápche* | *ts'oi gyákpa* | ཚོས་རྒྱག་པ |
| Eagle | *lák-khyi* | *jhá-lák* | གླག |
| Ear | *nám-chhok* | *ámchho'* | རྣ་བ |
| Ear-ring | *álong ; chhá-bu* | *e'-kor* ཨེས་སྐོར་ | རྣ་རྒྱན |
| Early | *ngá-mo* | *ngámo* | སྔ་མོ |
| Earnest, in | *don-drám* | *nén--ten* | ནན་ཏན |
| Earth (ground) | *sá-zhi* | *sá* | ས |
| Easy (not difficult) | *lá-mo ; démo* | *le-lá-po* | སླ་བ |
| Easily | | *le-lá-po-la* | |
| Eat, to | *zá-che* | *to sá-wa* ལྟོ་ཟ་བ | ཟ་བ |

| English. |Ládaki. | Central Tibetan. | Literary Tibetan. |
|---|---|---|---|
| Eaten, has been | *zas song* | *to ŝai song du'* | ཟོས་སོང་ |
| Eatable | *zá-chhok* | *ŝá-nyen* | ཟ་རུང་བ་ |
| Edge, at the | *zur-la* | *ŝur-la* | ཟུར་དུ། ཆ་ག་པ་ |
| Egg | *t'ul ; go-lo* | *góng-do* | སྒོང་ང་ |
| Eight | *gyád* | *gye'* | བརྒྱད་ |
| Emerald | *márgád* | *márgát.* | ཨཤྨ་གརྦ |
| Employ, to | *chodche* | *chö'pa* | སྤྱོད་པ་ |
| Empty, to | *shráche* | *p'o-wa* | |
| Empty | *stong* | *ku-tong-pa* | སྟོང་པ་ |
| End | *jukma* | *t'á-má* | མཐའ |

| | | | |
|---|---|---|---|
| **Engage, to** | *dznn-che* | *dzin-ŝhákpa* | |
| **Enlargen, to** | *pelche* | *p'el-wa* | རྒྱས་པར་བྱེད་པ་ |
| **Enough** | *ḍik* | *yong-nge ; khyé yin* | ཚོག་པ་ |
| **Euter, to** | *zhuk-che* | *ŝhug-pa* | འཛུག་པ་ |
| **Entrails** | *long-khá* | *gyu-ma* | རྒྱུ་མ་ |
| **Entrust, to** | *chhol-tangche* | *chhol-wa* | གཏོད་པ་ |
| **Escape, to** | *shorche* | *ḍoipa* | འབྲོས་པ་ |
| **Even (flat)** | *nyampo* | *ȋep-ȋep* | ལེབ་མོ་ |
| **Evening** | *p'i-tok* | *gong-tá* | ནུབ་མོ་ |
| **Every** | *re* **repeated after the noun twice said** | *re-re* | རེ་......རེ་ |
| **Every day** | *zhák dang zhák* | *nyin re ; nyima tákpa* | ཉི་མ་རེ་བཞིན་ |

| ENGLISH. | LÁDAKI. | CENTRAL TIBETAN. | LITERARY TIBETAN. |
|---|---|---|---|
| Every where | *kobtu* | *tsangmá-la* | ཀུན་དུ་ |
| Exactly | *ṇgótok ; zhibchhá* | *kho-né ; ŝhib* | ཁོ་ན་ |
| Examine, I will | *ngá-is ts'od tá yin* | *ngárang-ghi ts'ö tá ŷong* | རྟོག་པར་གྱུར་ |
| Except (*prep.*) | *mankhán* | *m̃empá* | མིན་པ་ |
| Exert yourself ! | *strád-strád tong ! hád-hád-tong !* | *tsön-dü jhyi ; hur-hur tong* | |
| Explain, to | *shádche* | *she'-pa ; ṭálwa* | འཆད་པ་ |
| Expenses (Hind : *kharach.*) | | *ḍo-go* | |
| Extinguish, to | *sodche* | *sö'pa* | གསོད་པ་ |
| Eye | *mik* | *m̃ik* | མིག་ |
| Eye-ball | | *m̃i' do* | མིག་རྡོ་ |

| | | | |
|---|---|---|---|
| **Eye-lid** | *mik-pák* | *mik-pág* | མིག་ལྤགས་ |
| **Face** | *dóng* | *dóng ; kyé-go* | གདོང་ |
| **Facing (anything)** | *dóng-tád* | *p'árkhá* (preceded by genitive of object) | |
| **Fable** | *shrúngs* | *dum* | སྒྲུངས་ |
| **Fade, to** | *kyukche* | *nyi-pa* | བརྙིད་པ་ |
| **Faint, I am** | *ngál song* | *chhong jhung* | |
| **Faith** | *dádpé sem* | *de'pe yi' ; de'pe sem* | དད་པའི་སེམས་ |
| **Faithful** | *dang-pa-chan ; zhabstokpa* | *lo-dengpa* | བློ་གདེངས་པ་ |
| **Fail, to** | *búd chukche ; or mi t'eb-che* | *mi khĕipa* | མི་ཁེས་པ་ |
| **Fall ! don't** | | *ma ri' ; ma śák !* | མ་ཟག |

| English. | Ládaki. | Central Tibetan. | Literary tibetan. |
|---|---|---|---|
| Fall, to | *gyelche* | *gyelwa* འགྱེལ་བ་ : *ri-pa* | ལྷུང་བ་ |
| Fall down, to | | *mar zák-pa* | |
| Family (lineage) | *ruspa* | *rui* | རིགས་པ |
| Famous | *rág-chan.* | *ḍák-chen* | གྲགས་ཅན |
| Fan | *rang-yáb* | *ḍeng-yáb* | ..................... |
| Far, how | | *t'á-ring-lü ; ká-ts'é !* | ཐག་རིང་པོ་ཅི་ཚད་ |
| Fasten ! | *rel tong !* | *ták chik* | ཐོགས་ཤིག |
| Fasten, to | *relche* | *ták-pa ; dom-pa* | འདོགས་པ |
| Fat (*adj.*) | *rompo ; ts'onpo* | *gyák-shè' ; ts'ömpo* | རྒྱས་པ |
| Fat (of meat), the | *ts'il* | *ts'il* | ཚིལ |

| | | | |
|---|---|---|---|
| Father | *á-p'á* | *á-p'á*; *yáp* (honorific) | ཕ། ཡབ་ |
| Fault | *shnongs* | *kyön*; *nong-pa* | སྐྱོན། ནོངས་པ་ |
| Fear | *jig-ri* | *jig-ṭák* | འཇིགས་སྐྲག་ |
| Fearless | | *min-ji-pa* | མི་འཇིགས་པ་ |
| Fear, to | *jigche* (with "*la*" of the object) | *ŝhe'pa* ཞེད་པ་ | འཇིགས་པ། དངང་བ་ |
| Feeble | *hál-med* | *kyar-kyor* | ཞན་པ་ |
| Feel, to (touch) | *nyuk-che* | *t'uk-pa* | ཐུག་པ་ |
| Feel, to (be sensible of) | *rag-che* | *rig-pa* | ཚོར་བ་ |
| Female (of an animal) | | *á-che* | |
| Fence | *ribma* | *rau-á*; *ḍibma* | འགྲིབ་མ་ |
| Fern | *skyé-ma* | *kyé-ma* | སྐྲུས་མ་ |

| ENGLISH. | LÁDAKI. | CENTRAL TIBETAN. | LITERARY TIBETAN. |
|---|---|---|---|
| Ferry-man | *ḍhu-shang-pa* | *ḍhu-pa* | གྲུ་པ་ |
| Fever | *ts'an-zuk* | *ts'e'-pe ne'* | ཚད་པའི་ནད་ |
| Few, a | *njung ngárig* | *re-gá ; la-la ŝhik* | འགའ་ |
| Fifty | *ngábchu* | *ngábchu* | ལྔ་བཅུ་ |
| Fight, to | *t'abmo choche ; nolche* | *t'áb-mo jhe'pa* | འཐབ་པ་ |
| Figure (form) | *yib ; zo* | *yib ; ŝū* | དབྱིབས་ |
| Fill, to | *kang-che* | *kong-wa* | འགེངས་པ་ |
| Find, to | *t'obche* (with dative of finder) | *nye'pa* | རྙེད་པ་ |
| Finger | *dzug-gu* | *sér-mo* | མཛུབ་མོ་ |
| Finger-nail | *sen-mo* | *chhă' sen* | |

| | | | |
|---|---|---|---|
| Fine | | ts'arpo ; ḽe-mo | མཚར་བ་ |
| Finish, to | ts'ar chukche | ḍub-pa ; ts'ar dze'-pa | སྒྲུབ་པ། འཚར་བ་ |
| Finished, it is | chhom song | dzok ts'ar song | རྫོགས་པ་ཡིན་ |
| Fir | som-shing | som-shing | གསོམ་ |
| Fire | mé | m̂é | མེ་ |
| Fire, to | tu-bák gyapche | p'áng-pa | འཕེན་པ་ |
| Firm | shránte ; ts'uk | sár-ten | མཁྲང་། སྲ་བ་ |
| Firmly | stanpo | tempo | བརྟན་པོ་ |
| First (ordinal) | go-ma | ang-ki dhang-po | དང་པོ་ |
| Fish | nyá | n̂yá | ཉ་ |
| Fish, to | nyá zumche | n̂yá ngön-pa | ཉ་འཚོར་བ་ |
| Fish-hook | nyá-kuk | n̂yá-kuk | ཉ་ཁུག་ |

| ENGLISH. | LÁDAKI. | CENTRAL TIBETAN. | LITERARY TIBETAN. |
|---|---|---|---|
| **Fists, to hit with** | *mult'uk gyapche* | *mult'uk gyakpa* | |
| **Flag** | *dar* | *dharchok* | དར་ལྕོག་ |
| **Flame** | *méling* | *m̃élche* | མེ་ལྕེ་ |
| **Flat** | *leb-mo* | *l̂ep-lep* | ལེབ་མོ་ |
| **Flea** | *khyishik* | *khyi-shik* | ཁྱི་ཤིག་ |
| **Flee away, to** | *shorche* | *ḍoi-pa* | |
| **Floor** | *shem* | *ŝhima* | གཞི་མ་ |
| **Flower** | *mintok* | *m̃é-tok* | མེ་ཏོག་ |
| **Fly, to (as a bird)** | *p'urche* | *p'ir-wa* | འཕུར་བ་ |
| **Fog** | *mámún* | *mukpa* | སྨུག་པ་ |

| | | | |
|---|---|---|---|
| Follow, to | *ting-la ḍángche* (with genit.) | *je-la chö'-pa* (with genit.) | རྗེས་སུ་འགྲོ་བ |
| Food | *zá-che* | *to-chhe ; ŝen* | ལྟོ་ཆས། ཟན |
| Foot | *kang-pa* | *kang-pa* | རྐང་པ |
| For (you, it, &c.) | *p'ila* | *chhirtu ; tönla* | ཕྱིར་དུ། དོན་དུ |
| Ford, a | *gál* | *ráb, shenkhá* | རབ |
| Forehead | *shralwa* | *t'ö'-pa :* ཐོད་པ | དཔྲལ་བ |
| Formerly | *ngan-la* | *ngar ; ngönchhe'* | སྔོན་ཆད |
| Fortress | *jong* | *jong ; zum* | རྫོང |
| Forward, to | *kalche* | *dzang-pa* | རྫོང་བ |
| Forward | *shngán-la* | *dong-la* | གདོང་དུ |
| Forget, to | *ṭ'uk yelche* | *je'pa* | རྗེད་པ |

| ENGLISH. | LÁDAKI. | CENTRAL TIBETAN. | LITERARY TIBETAN. |
|---|---|---|---|
| Found, have you | *khyöd t'ob-bá ?* | *khyö-kyī nye'-pa yimpa ?* | |
| Fox | *házé* | *wâ-tsé* | ཝ་ |
| Free, is | *t'arkhan du'* | *ḍhol yö'* | གྲོལ་ཡོད་ |
| Fresh | *sar* | *sarpa* | གསར་པོ་ |
| Friend | *rok ; dzá-o* | *ṭok-pu ; dzá-o* | གྲོགས་ |
| Frighten, to | *jig-ri kúlche* | *jig-ṭák tön-pa* | འཇིགས་པར་བྱེད་པ་ |
| Frightened, are | *jig-rak song* | *ngang-ṭák yö'* | འཇིགས་སྐྲག་བྱུང་ |
| Frog | *sbâl-wa* | *bé-ăp* | སྦལ་བ་ |
| Frozen, is | *p'id song* | *khyak-rum jhung* | ཁྱིད་པར་འགྱུར་ |
| Frost | *kyak* | *se' ; kyak-pa* | ཁྱགས་པ་ |

| | | | |
|---|---|---|---|
| Fruit | *ḍás-bu* | *shing-gi ḍe-wa* | འབྲས་བུ་ |
| Fuel | *budshing ; burtse* | *argol* | ཨ་རྒོལ་ |
| Full | *gáng* | *tem-tem* | གང་བ། ལྟེམ་པོ་ |
| Further | *p'ár-la* | *p'ártsam* | ཕན་ཚད་ |
| Game (wild) | *ridáks* | *ridák* | རི་དྭགས་ |
| Garden | *ts'ás-po* | *ts'ál* | ཚལ་ |
| Garlic | *sgók* | *gok-pa* | |
| Gate | *stágo ; gyásgo* | *gye-go* | རྒྱལ་སྒོ་ |
| Gather, to | *rúkche* | *ts'ok-pa* | འཚོགས་པ་ |
| Gently | *gú-lĕ-lă* | *ká-le* | ག་ལེ་ |

| ENGLISH. | LÁDAKI. | CENTRAL TIBETAN. | LITERARY TIBETAN. |
|---|---|---|---|
| Get it! | *a' t'ob tong* | *dhe khyer shok!* | དེ་ཁྱེར་ཤོག |
| Get, to | *t'obche* | *t'obpa* | ཐོབ་པ |
| Gift | *chhák-ten* | *nang-kye* | ཡོན། ཞུ་རྟེན |
| Ginger | *jásga* | *chá-gá* | ལྕ་སྒ |
| Girl | *bómo* | *pu-mo; menshar* | བུ་མོ |
| Give, me! | *ngá-la tong* | *ngá-la ter-roch!* | ང་ལ་སྟེར་ཅིག |
| Give, to | *tangche* | *ter-pa; nangwa; p'ulwa* (hon.) | སྦྱིན་པ། གནང་བ |
| Give! | *tong; sal* | *ṭö' chik; nang ro nang* | སྤྲོད་ཅིག |
| Give it up! | *spang tong* | *tong chik!* | |
| Give up, to | *spangche* | *pang-pa* | སྤོང་བ (to renounce). |

| | | | |
|---|---|---|---|
| Given, was | *tángspen* | *ter-pa-yin* | |
| Glacier | *gáng* | *g͠hangchen* | གངས་ |
| Glad, I am | *ngá t'ad duk* | *ngárang* [illegible]*s'or jhe* | ང་ལ་དགའ་བདེ་ཡོད་ |
| Glass | *shel* | *shel* | ཤེལ་ |
| Go, to | *chhá-che* | *ḍo-wa ; gyu-wa* | འགྲོ་བ་ |
| Goat | *rá-má* | *rá-t'ong* (masc.) ; *rá-má* (fem.) | ར་མ་ |
| Go away ! | *lon song !* | *há-la gyuk !* | ཕར་བཞུད་ |
| God | *Gónchhok* | *Könchhoa* | དཀོན་མཆོག་ |
| Going, I am | *ngá chhen* | *ngá ḍo-gi-yin* | ང་འགྲོ་ |
| Going to, was | | *ṭap* (added to verb root) | . . . . གྱབ་ |
| Goitre | *bá-wa ; wo-á* | *bá-wa* | ལྦ་བ་ |

| ENGLISH. | LÁDAKI. | CENTRAL TIBETAN. | LITERARY TIBETAN. |
|---|---|---|---|
| Go round, to | *kor-kor chháche* | *kora gyap-pa* | |
| Gold | *ser* | *ser* | གསེར་ |
| Good (well) that is | *de jak-bo* | *dhe yá'po re'* | Hind : *khub.* |
| Good (virtuous) | *zang-ba ; gyálla* | *šang-po* | བཟང་པོ་ |
| Good (of things) | *gyálla* | *yá'po ; gándé* | ལེགས་པ་ |
| Goose | *hang-tse* | *ngang-pa* | |
| Got, I have | *ngá-la t'ob song* | *nge tsar yö'* | ངའི་ཚར་ཡོད་ |
| Govern, to | *wáng cho-che* | *gyur-wa* | སྒྱུར་བ་ |
| Government | *gyálshrid* | *gye'-si* | རྒྱལ་སྲིད་ |
| Grandchild | *memé ts'áwo* | *kuts'á* | ཚ་བོ་ |

| | | | |
|---|---|---|---|
| Grass | *sá* | *tsá* | རྩྭ་ |
| Grasp at, to | *warmo gyapche* | *parmo gyakpa* | སྤར་མོ་རྒྱག་པ་ |
| Grave | *dur* | *dur-khung* | དུར་ |
| Grease | *snum* | *num* | སྣུམ་པ་ |
| Greasy | *numchan* | *numtsi* | སྣུམ་ལྡན་ |
| Great | *chhenmo* | *chhempo* | ཆེན་པོ་ |
| Greedy | *mugéchan* | *hampachen* | ཧམ་པ་ཅན་ |
| Green | *ljang-khu* | *ngo-jang ; jangku* | ལྗང་ཁུ་ |
| Grieve over, to | *ts'erka gyápche* | *duk-ngál jhye'pa* | སྡུག་བསྔལ་བྱེད་པ་ |
| Grind to, (corn, &c.) | *t'ákche* | *t'á-pa* | འཐག་པ་ |
| Grill, to | *shrákche* | *lam-pa* | སླམ་པ་ |

| ENGLISH. | LÁDAKI. | CENTRAL TIBETAN. | LITERARY TIBETAN. |
|---|---|---|---|
| Groan, to | *kong-shuk donche* | *shuk-nar p'ungwa* | ཤུགས་ནར་འབྱིན་པ |
| Groaning, is | *khun gyap-duk* | *shuk-nar gyak-ghin-re'* | ཤུགས་ནར་རྒྱག་གིན་འདུག |
| Groom | *stádzi* | *ìádzi* | རྟ་རྫི |
| Ground | *sá* | *sá ; sáshi* | ས་གཞི |
| Grow, to (of plants) | *ldanche* | *bo-wa ; yá kye-pa* | འབོ་བ |
| Grow bigger, to | *chheru chháche* | *chhe kye-wa* | ཆེ་སྐྱེད་པ |
| Grown, has | *sket song* | *bo jhung* | འབོས |
| Grumble, to | *nyerche* | *dhang khempa* | |
| Guard, to | *shrungche* | *shung-pa ; tá-kor tang-pa* | སྲུང་བ། ལྟ་བསྐོར་བ |
| Guide, a | *ìamkhan* | *îamkhen* | བཤང་བ |

| | | | |
|---|---|---|---|
| Gumlah, a | *chhukar* | *p'ungpa; dzáma* | ལམ་ཁན |
| Gun | *tubák* | *m̃éndá* | མེ་མདའ་ |
| Gunstock | *gundá* | *gumdá* | འགུ་མདའ་ |
| Gunpowder | *smán* | *m̃edzé* | མེ་རྫས་ |
| Had, you | *khyorang-la yodspen* | *khyörang la yö'pa yin-na* | |
| Hail | *serwa* | *serwa* | སེར་བ་ |
| Hair | *shrá; spu* | *ṭá* | སྐྲ་ |
| Hair-plait | *chuti* | *changlo* | ལྕང་ལོ་ |
| Hair-ribbon | *shram-dút* | *pá-lo; tingku* | |
| Half | *p'et* | *chhye'ká* | ཕྱེད་ཀ |

| English. | Ládaki. | Central Tibetan. | Literary Tibetan. |
| --- | --- | --- | --- |
| Hammer | *t'obós* | *t'o-á* | ཐོ་བ |
| Hand | *lákpa* | *lákpa ; chhyák* | ལག་པ། ཕྱག |
| Handful | *warmo* | *par-rá* | |
| Handle, the | *kapzá* | *ŷu-wa* | |
| Hang up, to | *skar tangche ; chhás la borche* | *kar-wa* | འཕྱར་བ |
| Happened, has | *yong song* | *jhung jhe'* | འབྱུང་སོང |
| Hard | *shránte* | *ṭ'ákmo* | སྲ་བ། མཁྲེགས་པ |
| Haste, make | *ts'á ts'á tong !* | *ts'a-ṭák chi shik* | |
| Hasten to, to | *ring-pa tangche* | *turte gyuk-pa* | རྒྱུགས་པ། དུར་བ |
| Hat | *zhá ; zhwá* | *s̄hámo* | ཞྭ |

| | | | |
|---|---|---|---|
| **Hate, to** | *zhé-zdángche* | *shé ḍé-pa* | ཞེ་སྡང་བ་ |
| **Hay** | *sá-hám ; stswáskám* | *tsá-kampo* | རྩྭ་སྐམ་ |
| **Head** | *go* | *go* | མགོ་ |
| **Health, good** | *kham zang-po* | *khəm šángwa* | ཁམས་བཟང་བ་ |
| **Heap up, to** | *pung-che* | *sák-pa ; pung shik-pa* | སྤོག་པ་ |
| **Hear, to** | *ts'orche* | *ñyem-pa ; t'oi-pa* | ཐོས་པ། ཉན་པ་ |
| **Heard** | *ts'orpen* | *ñyen jhung* | |
| **Heart** | *nyingkhá* | *nying ; lo-sem* | སྙིང་ |
| **Hearthstones** | *gyed-po* | *gyea-po* | སྒྱེད་པོ་ |
| **Heat** | *tsánte* | *tsem-mo* | ཚ་བ་ |
| **Heaven** | *námkhá* | *námkhá* | ཕྱི་བ་ |

| ENGLISH. | LÁDAKI. | CENTRAL TIBETAN. | LITERARY TIBETAN. |
|---|---|---|---|
| Heavy | *chinte* | *chi-bu ; jichen* | ལྕི་བ་ |
| Heel | *sting-pa* | *tingpa* | རྟིང་པ་ |
| Help, to | *rám tagche ; yádo choche* | *ro-rám jhye'pa ; kyong-dhál jhye'-pa* | ར་མདའ་བྱེད་པ་ |
| Help him! | *kho-la kyáp tong !* | *rám-tá nang* | སྐྱབས་ཤིག |
| Help (assistance) | *kyáp* | *kyong-dhál* | སྐྱོང་དཔལ་ |
| Hen | *jhámo* | *jhámo* | བྱ་མོ་ |
| Herb | *ts'odmá* | *ngo-tsá* | ཚོད་མ། སྔོ་ |
| Herd, a | *khyu* | *khyu* | ཁྱུ་ |
| Herdsmen | *sok-khan* | *dokpa* | འབྲོག་པ་ |

| | | | |
|---|---|---|---|
| Here | *iru* | *dir; dipa* | འདིར་ |
| Heron | *kyár-mo* | —— | སྐྱར་མོ་ |
| Hew, to | *sákche; zokche* | *tsáb-pa* | བཙབ་པ་ |
| Hide, a | *ko-wa* | *ko-wa* | ཀོ་བ |
| Hide, to (anything) | *gonte borche; wáste borche* | *bá-wa* སྦ་བ་ | སྦེད་པ |
| Hide oneself, to | *ipche* | *yib jhye'pa* | ཡིབ་པ་ |
| Hiding-place | *ipsá* | *yibsá* | ཡིབ་ས་ |
| High | *t'onpo* | *t'ömpo* | མཐོན་པོ་ |
| Hill | *ri-t'ok; ri-ga* | *ri* | རི་ |
| Hill-spur | *ri-bok* | *gángkhá; nágá* | སྒང་ཁ |
| Hill-side | *gad; ri-ngos* | *ri-ngok* | དགག་པ་ |

| English. | Ládaki. | Central Tibetan. | Literary Tibetan. |
|---|---|---|---|
| Hit, to (with a missile) | *khyelche, p'okche* | *khéi-pa* ཁྲིས་པ (with ལ) | འཕོག་པ |
| Hold, to | *zumche* | *dzinpa ; ju-wa* | འཛིན་པ། འཆངས་པ |
| Hold fast! | *tanpo znm tong* | *tempo par zim!* | བརྟན་པོ་སྦྱར་འཛིན་ |
| Hole, a | *bi-áng* | *khung ; bhuga* | ཁུང་ |
| Hole (in clothes) | *shekpa* | *te-khung* | |
| Hollow (in ground) | *ldups* | *bubh* | སྦུབས |
| Home | *khangpa* | *khyim ; nang* | ཁྱིམ |
| Honest | *ḍángpo* | *ts'eden* | དྲང་པོ་ |
| Honey | *rángsi* | *rángtsi* | སྦྲང་རྩི |
| Hope, to | *lo-dang rákche* | *lo-deng dzinpa* | རེ་བ་ |

| | | | |
|---|---|---|---|
| Hoof | *rágo* | *mikpa* | རྨིག་པ་ |
| Horn | *rucho* | *rá* | རྭ་ |
| Horse | *stá* | *tá ; chhip* (hon.) | རྟ། ཆིབས་ |
| Horse-shoe | *mikchák* | *dhákhá* | ད་ཁ་ |
| Horse-dung | *stálbáng* | *tá-yi bang* | རྟའི་སྦང་ |
| Hot | *ts'ánte* | *ts'em-mo ; ts'á-po* | ཚན་མོ། ཚ་བ་ |
| House | *khángpa* | *khang-pa ; dúm pa ; nang* | ཁྱིམ། ཁང་པ་ |
| House-rent | *kháng-lá* | *nái-lá* | གནས་གླ་ |
| How ? | *gházuk* | *ghándé* ག་འདྲས་ | ཇི་ལྟར་ |
| How much ? | *chi tsam ?* | *ghāts'ö ; ghátsam* | ཅི་ཙམ། ག་ཚོད་ |

| ENGLISH. | LÁDAKI. | CENTRAL TIBETAN. | LITERARY TIBETAN. |
|---|---|---|---|
| Hunger | *tokri* | *tokpa* ; *ṭéi-pa* (hon.) | བཀྲེས་པ་ |
| Hungry, I am | *ngá tokri rák* | *ngárang-la ṭéi'pa* ; *tok-gi yin* | ང་རང་ལ་བཀྲེས་པ་ |
| Hunt, to | *ngonche* | *khyira gyakpa* | རྔོན་པ་ |
| Husband | *káyá* ; *ákhu* | *gárok* ; *khyo-po* | དགའ་གྲོགས། ཁྱོ་ |
| Ice | *dár* | *khyá-rum* ; *chhaprom* | ཆབ་བྲོམ་ |
| Ill, to fall | *nád yongche* | *ne'kyī gyákpa* (*lit.*, to throw by illness) | ནད་ཀྱིས་འདེབས་པ་ |
| Ill, I am | *ngá-la nád yong* or *ngá-la nadchan yong duk* | *ngárang ne'kyī gyáp jhung* | ང་ལ་ནད་ཀྱིས་བཏབ་ |

| | | | |
|---|---|---|---|
| Illness, an | *nád* | *ne' ; náts'á* | ནད་ |
| Image (idol) | *skundá* | *kuten, kuts'áb* | སྐུ་རྟེན་ ; བླུགས་སྐུ |
| Immediately | *mát'ok-ts'e ; dáksa* | *t'el-t'el la ; tap-te* | མོད་ལ། དབ་སྟེ་ |
| Important | *khákchen* | *to-gál ; khochen* དོ་གལ་ ; | གལ་ཆེ། འགོས་ཅན་ |
| Impure (religious sense) | *ts'i-du* | *kyuk-dho* | སྐྱུག་བྲོ་ |
| Impure (of milk, &c.) | *sokpo* | *hle'chen ; ma dhák* | སླད་ཅན་ |
| Incense | *kunduru* | *poi, dukpoi* | བདུག་སྤོས་ ; གུ་གུལ་ ; སིལ་ |
| Including (*prep.*) | *ts'un-na* | *ts'ün-la* | |
| Increase, to (*intr. v.*) | *bur-che* | *p'el-wa* | འཕེལ་བ་ |
| Increase, to (*tr. v.*) | *nán-che* | *nön-pa ; nön jhe-pa* | སྤེལ་བ་ ; བསྣན་པ་ |

| ENGLISH. | LÁDAKI. | CENTRAL TIBETAN. | LITERARY TIBETAN. |
| --- | --- | --- | --- |
| India | *Mon-yul* | *Gyá-ghár* | རྒྱ་གར་ |
| Indian (*Hindu*) | *mon* | *mönpa* | རྒྱ་གར་པ་ |
| Inform, to | *hun tangche* | *lön ŝerwa* | སྤྲིན་སྐུར་བ་ |
| Information | *hun* | *lön* ཕྲིན་ | མནངག |
| Injury | *nod-khen* | *nö'-pa* | གནོད་པ་ |
| Injure, to | *duk-ngál tangche* | *dukpo terwa* | |
| Ink | *che-snák* | *nák-ts'á* | སྣག་ |
| Ink-pot | *siril* or *nák-kong* | *nák-pum* | སྣག་བུམ་ |
| Inn | *ts'ug-kháng* | *náts'áng* | མགྲོན་ཁང་ |

| | | | |
|---|---|---|---|
| Inquire, to | *ḍi-che* | *ŝhip-chhá jhye'-pa* (Hind. *daryáft karna*) | འདྲི་བ |
| Insects | *bu-tsik* | *shik* | ཀང་དྲུག་པ |
| Inside | *khog-ma* | *bug-na ; khongla* | ནང་དུ |
| Instead of | *ts'áb-la* | *ts'áp-la* | ཚོད་དུ |
| Intend, to | *chhá-dukche* (to be going *to*) | *dö'-pa* | སྒོམ་པ། འདོད་པ |
| Intention | *kobtá* | *sám-jor* | བསམ་པ ; དགོངས་པ |
| Interference | *khá t'al-khen* | *khá jukpa* | ཁ་འཛུག་པ |
| Interpreter | — | *ke'-pa* | སྐད་པ། ལོ་ཙཱ་བ |
| Intestines | *náng-rol* | *gyu-ma ; nang-rol* | ལོང་ཁ |
| Intoxicated | *rá-ro* | *rá-ro-chen* | ར་རོ་བ |

| English. | Ládaki. | Central Tibetan. | Literary Tibetan. |
|---|---|---|---|
| Invite, to | *chán rang-che* | *chenḍen-pa* | སྤྱན་འདྲེན་པ་ |
| Iron (*adj.*) | *chák* | *chok* (precedes noun) | ལྕགས་ |
| Irritate, to | *gopnon tángche* | *nyám lempa; nyám dru-wa* | ཉམས་འགྲུབ་ |
| Itch | *za-bun* | *ŝá-kong* | ཟ་ཁོང་ |
| Ivory | *báso* | *bháso* | བ་སོ་ |
| Jackal | *khyi-cháng* | *ŵa-chang* | ཝ་སྐྱང་ |
| Jackdaw | — | *chung-ká* | སྐྱུང་ཀ་ |
| Jar (clay *soraï*) | *zá-bum* | *dzáma* | ཛ་མ་ |
| Jesus | Ye-shu | Ye-shu | ཡེ་ཤུ་ |

| | | | |
|---|---|---|---|
| Jewel | *norbu* | *n̂orbhu* | ནོར་བུ |
| Join, to (*tr. v.*) | *zarche* | *ḍik-pa* | སྦྲིག་པ། སྦྱོར་བ |
| Joke | *khá-shák* | *khá-shá* | ཁ་ཤགས། ཀྱལ་ཀ |
| Journey | *lam* | *l̂am* | ལམ |
| Joyful | *gá-mo* | *gá-ts'or* | དགའ་ལྡན། དགའ་བ |
| Juice | *si* | *tsi* | རྩི |
| Jump, to | *chhong-che* | *chhong-wa* | མཆོངས་པ |
| Juniper-tree | *spáma* | *šhuk-pa* | |
| Keep, to (retain) | *stru ng-che* | *kyong-wa* | སྐྱོང་བ། འཆང་བ |
| Kettle | *p'ándil* | *ŝáng-bu ; khok-ti* | ཟངས་བུ |

| ENGLISH. | LÁDAKI. | CENTRAL TIBETAN. | LITERARY TIBETAN. |
|---|---|---|---|
| Key | *ku-lik* (In Balti: *le-mik*) | *de-mik; demak* | ལྡེ་ཆབ |
| Khatmandu (in Nipal) | — | *Kho-bhom* ཁོ་བོམ་ | ཀླུའི་ཕོ་བྲང་ |
| Kick, to | *dog-chong gyap-che* | *tokt'o p'ulwa; dung-gyak shu-wa* | འཕྲབ། བརྡུང་རྒྱགས་ཞུབ |
| Kick, a | *dog-chong* | *t'á-shák* | འཕྲ་ཤག |
| Kill, to | *sád tangche* | *sö'-pa; sok chö'pa* | སོད་པ |
| Killed, are | *sád song* | *se' jhung* | བསད། སྲོག་བཅད |
| Kind (sort) | *ná-so* | *rík; ḍhái* གྲས་ | སྣ་ཚོགས་ |
| Kindle, to | *duk-che* | *bar-wa* | སྦྲོར་བ་ |
| King | *gyál-po* | *gyál-po* (often *gye'po*) | རྒྱལ་པོ |
| Kiss, a | *ü* | *khá-zor* | འོ་ |

| | | | |
|---|---|---|---|
| Kitchen | *t'áb-ts'ang* | *sol-kháng ; yo'-kháng* | གཡོས་ཁང། བཀད་ས |
| Knife | *ḍi ; dri* | *ṭi ; ki-chhung* | གྲི |
| Knot, a | *dudpa* | *ḍü'-pa* | མདུད་པ |
| Know, to | *she-che* | *shei-pa* | ཤེས་པ |
| Know, will | *she' in* | *she-yong* | ཤེས་པར་འགྱུར་ |
| Kunawar | *Khūnu* | *Khūnu* | ཁུ་ནུ |
| Ladder | *sher-ká* | *kenza ; ṭe-ká* | སྐས་ཀ |
| Lady | *shéma* | *lhácham* | ཇོ་མོ། ཇོ་མ་ |
| Lady, young | *shem-chhung* | *cham-chhung* | ལྕམ་ཆུང་ |
| Lake | *chho* | *ts'o* | མཚོ་ |

| ENGLISH. | LÁDAKI. | CENTRAL TIBETAN. | LITERARY TIBETAN. |
|---|---|---|---|
| Lake, salt | *chháka* | *ts'áka* | |
| Lama, Grand | *Gyalwa Rimbochhe* | *Gye-wa Rimpochhe* | རྒྱལ་བ་རིན་པོ་ཆེ་ |
| Lama, head (of larger monasteries) | *khan-po* | *khempo* | མཁན་པོ་ |
| Lamb : | *lugu* | *l̂ugu* | ལུ་གུ་ |
| Lame | *zhá-wo* | *ŝhá-wo* | ཞ་བ་ |
| Lamed (he is) | *zhá-wo cho duk* | *khong-ril jhung* or *kang-dum jhung* | |
| Lamp, lantern | *zim-ting* | *ong-ku, gongŝhu* | སྒྲོན་མ་ |
| Lamp-wick | *sar* | *dong-kang; ong-re* | སྙིང་པོ་ Ka-gyur. § Mdo xxix. |
| Land | *sá* | *sá-chha* | ས་ |

| | | | |
|---|---|---|---|
| Landlord | *blang-pön* | *nái-bo* | གནས་དཔོན་ |
| Landslip | *sá-rud* | *sá-rü'* | ས་རུད་ |
| Language, a | *spé-ra* | *ke' ; khá* | སྐད་ |
| Large | *chhe-wa* | *chhempo* | ཆེན་པོ་ |
| Lark | *chá-chir* | *chokma* | ལྕོག་མ་ |
| Last (*adj.*)—latest | *t'áma* | *ting-juk* | རྟིང་མཇུག་ |
| Last, the | *p'imo* | *angki jema ; angki-jukshö'* | ཕྱི་མ་ |
| Last, at | *t'á na* | *t'ár ; juk-la* | མཐར། མཇུག་ལ་ |
| Last, to | *ts'o-che ; dukche* | *shu-pa* | |
| Last-night | *khá-ts'án* | *dáng-ts'en* | མདངས་ |
| Last year | *ná-ning* | *khá-ning* | |
| Late, (you) are | *gorte duk* | *gor song ; gyang jhe' yö'* | |

| ENGLISH. | LÁDAKI. | CENTRAL TIBETAN. | LITERARY TIBETAN. |
|---|---|---|---|
| Late (it is) | *p'imo song* | *p'imo yong* | |
| Laugh, to | *god-che* | *ke'mo ghe'pa ; gö'-pa* | རྒོད་པ་ |
| Law, a | *ṭ'ims* | *ká-ṭ'im* | ཁྲིམས་ |
| Lawsuit | *shág ; ṭ'im-dzing* | *ṭ'im-shak* | ཁྲིམས་ཞགས་ |
| Lazy | *le-shol* | *le-lo* | ལེ་ལོ་ |
| Lead (metal) | *ránye* | *ŝhánye* | ཞ་ཉེ་ |
| Lead, to | *hrid-che* | *ṭ'i-pa* | ཁྲིད་པ་ |
| Leaf | *loma* | *l̂oma* | ལོ་མ་ |
| Lean (on), to | *nye-che* (with *la*) | *nye-wa* (with *la*) | སྙེ་བ་ |
| Leap, to | *chhong-che* | *chhong-wa* | མཆོངས་པ་ |

| | | | |
|---|---|---|---|
| **Learn, to** | *lab-che* | *löb-pa* | སློབ་པ་ |
| **Learned** | *kháspa* | *khe-pa* | མཁས་པ་ |
| **Leather** | *ko-wa* | *ko-wa* | ཀོ་བ་ |
| **Leather-strap** | *rok-bu* | *ko-t'ák ; ko-rok* | ཀོ་གྲོགས་ |
| **Leave, to (a thing)** | *lus chuk-che* | *yuk-ŝhák-pa* | ལུས་པར་བྱེད་པ་ |
| **Leech,** | *t'ák-t'ung-bu* | *pü-po ; shrimpa* | སྲིན་བུ་པདྨ་ |
| **Left it, he** | *lus chuk song* | *yuk-ŝhak song ; lui jhya song* | དབྱུག་བཞག་ཡོད་ |
| **Left, to the** | *yon ná* | *yön-ngö lá* | གཡོན་དུ་ |
| **Left, has been** | *luspen* | *yuk-ŝhák du' ; lui-pa-re'* | ལུས་སྟེ་ཡོད་ |
| **Leg** | *skang-pa* | *kang-pa* | རྐང་པ་ |
| **Lend, to** | *skyin tsalche ; skyin cho-che* | *kyin nang-wa ; kyin jhepa* | སྐྱིན་གཏང་བ་ |

| ENGLISH. | LÁDAKI. | CENTRAL TIBETAN. | LITERARY TIBETAN. |
|---|---|---|---|
| Let, to (permit) | *tang-che* | *chuk-pa* | |
| Let down, to | *p'ábche* | *t'eng-la náng-wa* | འབེབས་པ་ |
| Letter (epistle) | *yige* | *chhák-ḍhi* | ཡི་གེ། ཕྱག་བྲིས་ |
| Lid | *khá-kyep* | *khá-khep* | ཁ་གབ་ |
| Lie, a | *shab-shob* | *dzün* | རྫུན་ |
| Lie down, to | *nyal-che* | *ñye-wa* | ཉལ་བ་ |
| Lift up, to | *tág-che* | *seng-wa* | སེང་བ་ |
| Light (*subst.*) | *od ; otchan* | *ŵö'-ṭo* | འོད་སྒྲོ་ |
| Light (not dark), it is | *nam t'ang duk* | *t'ang kárpo re'* | |
| Light, to (kindle) | *me dukche* | *par chukpa* | སྦར་བཙུག་པ་ |

| | | | |
|---|---|---|---|
| Light (in weight) | *yang mo* | *ŷang-mo, ŷangke* | ཡང་མོ་ |
| Lightning | *skạm-hlok* | *log-ká* | གློག་ |
| Like (*prep.*) | *zuk ; ts'okse* | *dre ; ḍánḍá-la* | ལྟ་བུ། འདྲས |
| Line, a | *t'ik* | *t'ik* | |
| Lips | *khálpak* | *chhu-t'o* | ཁ་མཆུ་ |
| Listen! | *nyan tạng !* | *nyen chik !* | ཉོན་ཅིག་ |
| Little. | *nyung-ṇgu ; zá-zhik* | *chhung-wa* | ཆུང་བ་ |
| Little, a | *nyung-nga rig ; ts'abik* | *tiktse chik ; énchám* | ཉུང་ཟད་ཅིག་ |
| Live, to (dwell) | *dadche* | *né-pa, de'-pa* | གནས་པ། སྡོད་པ་ |
| Living, is he | *sọnṭe yịn-nam ?* | *sönte ẏö'dhá ?* | གསོན་པོ་ |
| Lizard | *gákchik ; t'ang malala-tse* | *dhá-jhyi* | སྐྱིན་གོར་ |

| English. | Ládaki. | Central Tibetan. | Literary Tibetan. |
|---|---|---|---|
| Load, a | *khal ; khur-ru* | *khurbu ; khal* | དོས། ཁལ། སྒལ |
| Load, to (a gun) | *kongche* | *dze gyang-pa* | |
| Loan | *skyin-po* | *kar-kyin* | སྐྱིན་པ |
| Locket (charm-box) | *shrung-bu* | *sung-bu ; gá-wo* | སྲུང་བུ |
| Lodgings | *ḍáng-sá* | *ná-ts'ang* | བྲང་ས |
| Loiter, to | *gorche* | *gor-wa* | འགོར་བ |
| Long | *ring-mo* | *ring-po* | རིང་པ |
| Look, to | *stáche* | *m̃ik tá-wa* | ལྟ་བ |
| Loose | *lod-po* | *lhö'-lhö' ; yang-hlup* | ལྷོད་པ |
| Loosen, to | *ṭol-che* | *ḍol-wa* | འགྲོལ་བ |

| | | | |
|---|---|---|---|
| **Lose, to** | *stor chuk-che* | *lák-pa* ལྷག་པ | གོད་པ |
| **Loss, to suffer** | *gun p'ok-che* | *ghö'la ḍo-wa ; p'ám ḍo-wa* | གོད་བྱེད་པ |
| **Loss, a** | *gun, gót-ma* | *ghü' ; ghö'-ka* | གོད་ཁ |
| **Lost, is** | *stor yin* | *lák song ; me'-pa la song* | སྟོར་རོ |
| **Love, to** | *yáshá cho-che* | *dzá-o jhye'pa* | ཆགས་པ |
| **Lower down** | *man-chhad* | *men la ; mar la* | སྨད་ལ |
| **Low ground** | *smad sá ; mámo* | *men sá* | |
| **Lucky** | *sodéchan* | *ṭáshi-chen* | བཀྲ་ཤིས་ཀྱི |
| **Lynx** | *yi* or *ī* | *yi* | དབྱི |
| **Mad, is** | *nyo duk* | *nyömpa jhung* | སྨྱོ་བ |

| ENGLISH. | LÁDAKI. | CENTRAL TIBETAN. | LITERARY TIBETAN. |
|---|---|---|---|
| Maidservant | *yok-mo* | *shetáma* | ཞལ་ཏ་མ་ |
| Maitreya (the coming Buddha) | *Byampa* | *Jhám-pa* | བྱམས་པ་ |
| Make, to | *chóche* | *jhye'-pa* (pr. *chyipa*); *šo-wa* | བྱེད་པ་ |
| Man | *mi* | *m̂i*; men: *mindá* | མི་ |
| Many | *mángpo* | *m̂ang-po*; *dúma* | མང་པོ་ |
| Map | *zing-kod* | *sá-ṭ'á* | ས་ཁྲ་ |
| Market-place | *zok-króm* | *ṭ'om* | ཁྲོམ་ |
| Marry, to | *bhákston cho-che*; * *áni khur-che* | *khyo-shuk jhung-wa*; * *chhungrok lenpa* | * spoken only of a man taking a wife. |
| Master | *dákpo* | *pön-po* | དཔོན་པོ་ |

| | | | |
|---|---|---|---|
| Meaning, the | *don* | *dhön* | དོན་ |
| Means | *t'ábs* | *t'áb* | ཐབས། སྐབས་ |
| Measure, to (length) | *ts'od zumche* | *ts'e' jálwa* | འཇལ་བ་ |
| Measure it! (grain, &c.) | *shor tong* | *sher gyop* | གཞོར་ཅིག་ |
| Meat | *shá* | *shá* | ཤ་ |
| Meddle with, to | *drésche* (with *dang* preceding) | *ḍei-pa* (with *dhang*) | འདྲིས་པ་ |
| Meditate, to (religiously) | *sam-lo tangche* | *t'uk gom-pa* | སྒོམ་པ་ |
| Meditation | *sgom ; semgom* | *sam-ten ; teng-ngendzin* | བསམ་གཏན |
| Meet to | *t'ukche* | *jál-ṭ'e' jhye'pa* | འཕྲད་པ་ |
| Mend, to | *lon-pa gyábche* | *lhempa gyakpa* | གློན་པ་ |
| Merchandize | *ts'ong chhálak* | *ts'ong-zok* | |

| ENGLISH. | LÁDAKI. | CENTRAL TIBETAN. | LITERARY TIBETAN. |
| --- | --- | --- | --- |
| Merciful | *nying-je-chen* | *nying-je-chen* | སྙིང་རྗེ་ཅན་ |
| Message | *p'rin ; hun* | *p'in-kur* | ཕྲིན་ |
| Messenger | *hun khyer-khan* | *mi-ná* | ཕོ་ཉ་ |
| Middle, the | *ūs ; gung* | *ŭi* | དབུས་ |
| Middle of, in the | *gung-la* | *kyil-tu* | དཀྱིལ་དུ་ |
| Midnight | *ts'án-p'ét* | *nám-ghung* | མཚན་ཕྱེད་ |
| Midst, in the | *zhung-la* | *k'ong-su ; bug-la* | ཁོངས་སུ། སྦུགས་ལ་ |
| Milk | *óma* | *ŵóma* | འོ་མ་ |
| Milk-vessel or bowl | *ó-zo ; ó-skyan* | *ŵó-nö'* | འོ་སྣོད་ |
| Millet | *tse-tse* | *t'e-tse* | ཁྲེ་ |

| | | | |
|---|---|---|---|
| Miry—boggy | *dámts'ok* | *dám-dzáp ; dám-pak* | འདམ་རྫབ |
| Mischief | *kagma* | *kyön* | སྐྱག |
| Miserable, to be | *duk-ngal rakche* | *duk-ngál širwa* | སྡུག་བསྔལ་སྐྱོང་བ |
| Mist | *khug-ná ; rlángspa* | *mú'-pa ; humpo* | རྨུགས་པ |
| Mistake | *nor-t'rul* | *nor-ṭ'ul* | འཁྲུལ་པ |
| Mistaken, (you) are | *ṭul-pen* | *sem ṭ'ul jhung ; ṭ'ul-pa-re'* | འཁྲུལ་པ་ཡིན |
| Monastery | *gomba* | *gömpa* | དགོན་པ |
| Money | *hmul ; nák* | *ná-kyang* | ནོགས |
| Mongol | *Sokpo* | *Sokpo* | སོག་པོ |
| Monkey | *shrü ; spryu-mo* | *ṭe-ü ; shtrégo* | སྤྲེའུ |
| Month | *ldá-wa* | *dáwa* | ཟླ་བ |

| ENGLISH. | LÁDAKI. | CENTRAL TIBETAN. | LITERARY TIBETAN. |
|---|---|---|---|
| Moon | *lzá* | *dá-wa* | ཟླ་བ་ |
| More (some) | *mang-ngá mang-ngá* | *ŷang-kyár ; dhárung* | |
| More than | *t'okne (t'ognas) ; sang t'os* | *lhák* (with ablat :) | ལྷག |
| Morning, in the | *ngá-mo* | *náng-mo ; ŝho-ge* | སྔ་དྲོ་ |
| Morning, this | *dá-náng* | *dhá-rang ŝho-ge* | ད་ནང་ |
| Morrow, to- | *t'ore* | *sang-nyin* | ཉིན་སང་ |
| Most | *mang-chhé* | *mang-shö* | ཀུན་ལས་ལྷག |
| Mostly | *mang-ngá* | *p'álchher* | མང་པོར་ |
| Moth | *mung-ma* | *m̂úk-ḍáng* | མུག་པ་ |
| Mother | *á-má ; yum* | *m̂á ; ŷúm* (hon.) | མ། ཡུམ་ |

| | | | |
|---|---|---|---|
| Mount, to | *zhonche* | *šhönpa ; chhip-pa* (hon.) | ཞོན་པ་ |
| Mountain | *ri-gá* | *ri* | རི་ |
| Mountain-spur | *gáng-khul* | *gáng* | སྒང་ |
| Mountain-side | *ri-ngok* | *ghăd ; gáng-kňá* | རི་ངོས་ |
| Moustache | | *yartsom ; šhalgyen* (hon.) | |
| Mouth | *khá ; khá-po* | *khá ; khá-ts'ul* ཁ་མཚུལ་ | ཁ། ཞལ་ |
| Move, to (a thing) | *strulche* | *yo-wa* | གཡོ་བ་ |
| Move away, to (*intrans.*) | *gulche ; nurche* | *gul-wa* | སྒུལ་བ་ |
| Moved, it has | *gul-song* | *kyö' jhung ; gul jhung* | གྱོ་བ་འདུག |
| Much | *mang-ngá* | *m̂ang-po* | མང་པོ་ |
| Mud | *ká-lák ; mer-mer* | *nyokma* | འཇིམ་པ་ |

| English. | Ládaki. | Central Tibetan. | Literary Tibetan. |
|---|---|---|---|
| Mule | *dyu ; driu* | *tre-p'o ; t'olok* | དྲེ་པོ་ |
| Mushroom | *mokshá* | *shámo* | |
| Mustard | *nyungskar* | *pe-kăng* | |
| Nail | *zer* | *šeru* | གཟེར་ |
| Naked | *cher-nyál ; chergók* | *mar-rung-pa* | སྐྲེན་མོ་ |
| Name | *ming* | *m̃ing* | མིང་ |
| Named, to be | *ming tagche* | *m̃ing-la tag-pa* | མིང་འདོགས་པ་ |
| Narrow | *zheng-chhungse* | *tokpo ; p'álmé* | དོག་པ། ཞེང་མེད་ |

| | | | |
|---|---|---|---|
| Near (*prep.*) | *ldán-la* | *tsar* | འགྲམ་དུ་ |
| Near (*adv.*) | *nyé-mo* | *tsánăi ; t'á nyé-po* | ཉེ་བར་ |
| Necessary, it is | *go-she yin* | *goi-gyu yö' ; kho-che' re'* | དགོས་པ་ཡོད་ |
| Neck | *skye ; jingpa* | *kyé* | སྐེ། མགྲིན་པ་ |
| Neck-kerchief | *kháshri* | *kokṭi* | དཀྲི་མ |
| Needle | *khábrul* | *ts'em-kháb* | ཁབ |
| Neglect, don't | *shol ma tob !* | *gying ma nang* | གྱིང་མ་བྱེས་ |
| Net | *dol* | *dhol* | དོལ་ |
| Never | *namsang ma* | *See pages : 69, 95* | |
| New | *soma* | *sarpa* | གསར་པ་ |
| News | *hun* | *lön* | ཆ། ཕྲིན། ལོན་ |

| English. | Ládaki. | Central Tibetan. | Literary Tibetan. |
|---|---|---|---|
| Next, the | *stingma* | *n̂ye-shö* | |
| Night | *ts'an* | *ts'en* | མཚན་མོ་ |
| Nine | *gu* | *gu* | དགུ་ |
| Noise | *kuchor* | *ŵür* | འུར་ |
| Noise, to make a | *kuchor gyapche* | *ŵür gyak-pa* | འཁྲོལ་བ་ |
| Noon | *nyimgung* | *gung* | དགུང་། གདུགས་ |
| North | *jang* | *jhang* | བྱང་ |
| Nothing | *chang* (with verb in negat.) | *chang* (with verb in negat.) | ཅང་མི་ |
| Nobody, no one | | *su yang* (with negat.) | |
| Now | *dá ; kabstok* | *tandá* (in Sikkim : *tá-to*) | ད་ལྟ་ |

| | | | |
|---|---|---|---|
| Meaning, the | *don* | *dhön* | དོན་ |
| Means | *t'ábs* | *t'áb* | ཐབས། སྐབས་ |
| Measure, to (length) | *ts'od zumche* | *ts'e' jálwa* | འཇལ་བ་ |
| Measure it! (grain, &c.) | *shor tong* | *sher gyop* | གཞོར་ཅིག་ |
| Meat | *shá* | *shá* | ཤ་ |
| Meddle with, to | *drésche* (with *dang* preceding) | *ḍei-pa* (with *dhang*) | འདྲིས་པ་ |
| Meditate, to (religiously) | *sam-lo tangche* | *t'uk gom-pa* | སྒོམ་པ་ |
| Meditation | *sgom ; semgom* | *sam-ten ; teng-ngendzin* | བསམ་གཏན་ |
| Meet to | *t'ukche* | *jál-ṭ'e' jhye'pa* | འཕྲད་པ་ |
| Mend, to | *lon-pa gyábche* | *lhempa gyakpa* | གློན་པ་ |
| Merchandize | *ts'ong chhálak* | *ts'ong-zok* | |

| ENGLISH. | LÁDAKI. | CENTRAL TIBETAN. | LITERARY TIBETAN. |
|---|---|---|---|
| Merciful | *nying-je-chen* | *nying-je-chen* | སྙིང་རྗེ་ཅན་ |
| Message | *p'rin ; hun* | *p'in-kur* | ཕྲིན་ |
| Messenger | *hun khyer-khan* | *mi-ná* | པོ་ཉ་ |
| Middle, the | *ūs ; gung* | *ŭi* | དབུས་ |
| Middle of, in the | *gung-la* | *kyil-tu* | དཀྱིལ་དུ་ |
| Midnight | *ts'án-p'ét* | *nám-ghung* | མཚན་ཕྱེད་ |
| Midst, in the | *zhung-la* | *k'ong-su ; bug-la* | ཁོངས་སུ། སྦུགས་ལ་ |
| Milk | *óma* | *ŵóma* | འོ་མ་ |
| Milk-vessel or bowl | *ó-zo ; ó-skyan* | *ŵó-nö'* | འོ་སྣོད་ |
| Millet | *tse-tse* | *t'e-tse* | ཁྲེ་ |

| | | | |
|---|---|---|---|
| Open, is | *be-te duk* | *p'e jhung* | |
| Order, to | *molche* | *ká nang-wa* | བསྒོ་བ་ |
| Order, an | *kábsgo ; húkam* | *ká-nen* | བཀའ་ |
| Order to, in | *p'i-la* | *tön-la* or *töndá-la* (with gen. preceding) | ཕྱིར་དུ། ཆེད་དུ་ |
| Other | *yang-chik* | *šhen ; šhenma* | གཞན་ |
| Outside | *p'i-lok ; p'ista* | *chhyi-la ; p'i-la* | ཕྱིན་ |
| Overflowed | *lud song* | *lü lü jhung* | ལུད་ནས་འཁྲིངས་ |
| Overtake, to | *non-che* | *t'álwa* | འཐལ་བ་ |
| Owl | *ukpa* | *wukpa* | འུག་པ་ |
| Ox | *hlángto* | *lang* | གླང་ |

| English. | Ládaki. | Central Tibetan. | Literary Tibetan. |
|---|---|---|---|
| Page (of book) | *shok* | *shók-lo* | ཤོག་ལོགས་ |
| Paid, were | *táng spen* | *ter-ne yö'* | |
| Pain | *zur-mo ; zuk* | *šúk* | གཟུག |
| Pains, to take | *nángsták choche* | *káduk jhe'pa* | དཀའ་སྡུག་བྱེད་པ་ |
| Paint, to | *si kúche* | *tsi gyak-pá* | སྐུད་པ |
| Paper | *shug-gu* | *shók-gu* | གཤོག་བུ |
| Pardon, to beg | *ngo lenche* | *nong-pa solwa* | བཟོད་པར་གསོལ་བ |
| Parsley | *shámīlik* | *šhera* | གཞི་ར་ |
| Partly | *tsápik* | *ghásnáĭ ; la-lá* | ཆ་འབྲ་ཙམ |
| Pass (mountain), a | *lá* | *lâ* | ལ |

| | | | |
|---|---|---|---|
| Pass, way up to a | *lá-yi gyen* | *lâ-yi ghyen* | |
| Pass, descent from | *lá- yi t'ur* | *lâ-yi t'ur* | ལ་ཡི་ཐུར་ |
| Pass, midway up | *lá sked* | *lâ-ke'* | ལ་སྐེད་ |
| Pass, climax of | *lar-se* | *lâptse* | ལ་རྩེ་ |
| Pass, to pass over a | *lá gyápche* | *lâ gálwa* | ལ་རྒལ་བ་ |
| Pattern (example and copy—model) | *má-spe* | *pé ; má-pe* | དཔེ་ |
| Pay, to | *sminche ; tangche* | *ter-wa ; jinpa* | སྦྱིན་པ་ |
| Pay (wages) | *p'óks* | *lá* | གླ་ |
| Pay back, to | *lán choche* | *len jálwa* | འཇལ་བ་ |
| Pea | *stránma ; shenma* | *sem-ma* | སྲན་མ་ |
| Peacock | *mábyá* | *máb-jhá* | རྨ་བྱ་ |

| ENGLISH. | LÁDAKI. | CENTRAL TIBETAN. | LITERARY TIBETAN. |
|---|---|---|---|
| Pear | *nyu-ti ; nyo-ti* | *ñye-ṭi* | |
| Pebble | *delpo ; doi* | *shák-ma* | རྡོའུ་ |
| Peel, to | *shúche* | *shün-pa shu-wa* | ཤུ་བ་ |
| Peg | *p'urchhá* | *shing-šerbu* | ཤིང་གཟེར་ |
| Péking• | | *Táshi-tikur* | |
| Pen | *nyuk-ma* | *nyúgu* | སྨྱུག་གུ་ |
| People | *mang-ricks* | *ñi-ts'o* | དམངས་ |
| Perhaps | •*chi she* (*lit.* "who knows") | *lái-chhe* | |
| Permission, to give | *gongpá tàngche* | *gong-pa nangwa* | དགོངས་པ་གནང་བ་ |
| Permit, to (let) | *chukche* (with supine) | *chukpa* (with verbal root | གཏོང་བ་ |

| | | | |
|---|---|---|---|
| Perspiration | *ngul-chhu* | *ngul-chhu* | རྔུལ་ |
| Persuade, to | *úchuk choche* | *go-chukpa* | |
| Pheasant, Ruddy | *shrákpa* | *shrá-ghá* | སྲེག་པ་ |
| Pheasant, Snow | *ri-já gongmo* | *ghong-shrág* | གོང་སྲེག |
| Picture | *zhál-t'ang ; sku-t'ang* | *ri-mo ; ku-t'ang* | རི་མོ་ |
| Pick up, to | *rukche* | *yá t'ünpa* | སྒྲུག་པ་ |
| Piece, a | *dum* | *chhá-ṭ'um ; ling* | དུམ། ཁྲུམ་ |
| Pieces, in | *dum-dum* | *chhá-ṭ'um-lá* | |
| Pierce, to | *buk-che* | *bik gyakpa* | འབིགས་པ |
| Pig | *p'ákmo* | *p'ákmo* | ཕག་པ་ |
| Pig-tail | *chu-ti* | *ḉhanglo* | ལྕང་ལོ་ |

| ENGLISH. | LÁDAKI. | CENTRAL TIBETAN. | LITERARY TIBETAN. |
|---|---|---|---|
| Pillow | *nyálbos* | *ngé-ten* | སྔས་སྟན་ |
| Pin | *zum-kháp* | *sing-yá* | འཛོན་གཡའ་ |
| Pipe (tobacco) | | *kangŝak* | གང་ཟག་ |
| Place, a | *sákhyád* | *sá-chhá* | གནས་ |
| Place down, to | *borche* | *ŝhák-pa* ཞག་པ་ | འཇོག་པ་ |
| Plain, a | *t'ang* | *t'ang* | ཐང་ |
| Play a game, to | *senjo se-che* | *tse-mo tse-wa* | རྩེད་རྩེ་བ་ |
| Pleasant (it is) | *sem gá rák* | *sem gá-mo* | |
| Pleased with, to be | *sodche* (with *la*) | *gá-ts'or jhe'-pa* (with *la* of object) | དགའ་བ་ |

| | | | |
|---|---|---|---|
| Pledge (money in advance on article as deposit) | *stepa* | *téma* | གཏེ་བ་ |
| Plentiful, is | *mod yin* | *dzom-po mõ'* | འཛོམ་པ་མོད་ |
| Plenty of | *modpo* | *bolpo* | འབོལ་པོ་ |
| Plough, a | *shol* | *sho'-dá* | གཤོལ་ |
| Pluck, to (fowls) | *spu p'inche* | *dro-pu yung-pa* | སྒྲོ་སྤུ་འབྱིན་པ་ |
| Point, the (to be observed, &c.) | | *s̆hi-kho* | |
| Poisonous | *dukchán* | *dhukchen* | དུག་ཅན་ |
| Poker, a | *pang-ka* | *yokshing* | |
| Pool, a | *skyil-ding* | *chhu-khyil ; dzing-wu* | ལྫིང་ཁ། ཛིང་བུ་ |
| Poor (*adj.*) | *ulpo* | *ülpo* (fem. *ülmo*) | དབུལ་བ་ |

| ENGLISH. | LÁDAKI. | CENTRAL TIBETAN. | LITERARY TIBETAN. |
|---|---|---|---|
| Poor (attribute) | *ulpo* | *nyam-shúng ; duk-p'ongpa* | དབུལ་འཕོངས་པ་ |
| Poor (inferior: Hind: *gharib*) | *khásmán* | *khemén* | ཁས་དམན་ |
| Poplar | *yarpa* | *sholpo* | དབྱར་པ་ |
| Porcupine | — | *bidúrma* | བཟིག་མོ་ |
| Possessing | *chán* (formative attached to nouns) | *chen* (ditto) | ཅན་ |
| Post, a | *ká-wá* | *ká-wá* | ཀ་བ་ |
| Post (letter) service | *ulák* | *ulák* | |
| Post, to plant a | *ká-wá borche* | *ká-wá zuk-pa* | ཀ་བ་འཛུགས་པ་ |
| Postpone, to | *p'i sholche* | *p'i shol gyakpa* | ཕྱི་བཤོལ་བ་ |

| | | | |
|---|---|---|---|
| Potato | *álu* | *ŝho-ko* (also *P'iling kyi-u* "English potato") | ཞོ་ཀོག། གྲོ་མ་ |
| Pour out, to | *p'oche* | *bo-wa ; lū-pa* | བླུག་པ་ |
| Pour out! | *p'os tong* | *lū nang !* | བླུགས་ཤིག |
| Power | *stops* | *wáng* | དབང་ |
| Practise, to | *jáng chóche* | *jang jhe-pa* | སྦྱོང་བ་ |
| Praise, to | *todche ; tod p'ulche* | *ngá solwa* | སྟོད་པ་ |
| Prayer | *chhákp'ul* | *mönlam* | སྨོན་ལམ་ |
| Prayer, to utter | *monlám t'ábche* | *mönlam gyap-pa* | སྨོན་ལམ་འདེབས་པ་ |
| Precious | *shé-pá-chán* | *köm-po ; rinchen* | རིན་པོ་ཆེ |
| Pregnant, she is | *skyechéma song* | *kyebuchen jhung* | སེམས་ཅན་དང་ལྡན་པ་ཡིན་ |
| Prepare, to (get ready) | *ṭ'ál-ḍik choche* | *shomrá jhépa* | ཤོམ་པ། གཡོ་བ་ |

| ENGLISH. | LÁDAKI. | CENTRAL TIBETAN. | LITERARY TIBETAN. |
|---|---|---|---|
| Preparing to, I am | *ngás...zhar-ginduk* | *ngā...ḍháp jhé-ghi-du'* | |
| Present, a | *skyes ; já-gá* | *yön ; jhá-gá ; láktá* | སྐྱེས་ |
| Present, to offer | *skyes p'ulche* | *yön nang-wa* (or *ül-wa*) | སྐྱེས་འབུལ་བ་ |
| Press, to | *nanche* | *chhir-wa ; nempa* | འཚིར་བ་ |
| Press, don't! | *má non !* | *nen gyu min !* | མ་ནོན་ཅིག་ |
| Pretty | *chhormo* | *chhormo, dze-po* | མཚོར་བ་ |
| Price | *rin* | *rin ; ghong* | རིན་ |
| Pride | *p'o-so* | *chhe-t'áb* | ཁེངས་སེམས་ |
| Print, to | *pár gyápche* | *pár gyakpa* | པར་དུ་འདེབས་པ་ |
| Printer | *pár-khán* | *pár-pön* | པར་མཁན་ |

| | | | |
|---|---|---|---|
| Prisoner | *tson-pá* | *tsömpá* | བཙོན་པ་ |
| Private | *lkok* | *sáng-wa* | གསང་བ་ |
| Privy (W. C.) | *dé-chod* | *sáng-chö'* | བདེ་སྤྱོད་ |
| Privy, to go to the | *chhágra chháche* | *tsá tang-wa* | |
| Probable is | *ts'odche yin* | *ts'ö yö'* | |
| Profit | *khebéd* | *khé-pōk* | སྐྱེད། ཕྱོགས |
| Promise, to | *chhád-ká choche* | *khá lempa* | ཆད་འཛིན་པ་ |
| Pronunciation | *zer-ts'ul* | *jö' yáng* | བརྗོད་དབྱངས |
| Prop | *sten-shing* | *ten-shing ; ték* | རྟེན་མ |
| Property | *shul* | *khája ;. shul* | ལོངས་སྤྱོད་ |
| Protect, to | *kyob choche* | *kyong jhe'-pa* | སྐྱོང་བ་ |

| ENGLISH. | LÁDAKI. | CENTRAL TIBETAN. | LITERARY TIBETAN. |
|---|---|---|---|
| Proud | *p'o-so-chan* | *chhé-t'ab-chen* | གྲགས་ཅན་ |
| Provisions | *ts'o-gyáks* | *ŝá-ma* | བགྲོགས་ |
| Pull, to. | *ḍudche ; t'enche* | *ḍem-pa* | འདྲེན་པ་ |
| Pull down, to | *stibche* | *nyil t'empa* | སྙིལ་བ་ |
| Pull off ! | *t'en tong !* | *p'ü' chik !* or *shu-ne ḍen* | ཕུ་བ་ |
| Pull out, to | *p'inche* | *tömpa ; yung-pa* | འདོན་པ་ |
| Punish, to | *gá-sir gyápche* | *chhe'pa kgclwa* | ཆད་པས་གཅོད་པ་ |
| Purse | *khu-mák* | *ngul-khuk* | |
| Push, to | *suk gyápche* | *suk gyakpa* | སུག་པ་ |
| Put, did | *bor song* | *ŝhák-pa-yin* | ཞག་ང་ཡིན |

| | | | |
|---|---|---|---|
| Put down, to | *ṭámsche ; borche* | *sá-la ŝhákpa ; m̂ar p'ap-pa* | སར་འཛོག་པ |
| Quarrel, to | *habsá choche ; ḍán-ts'ik cho-che* | *shák gyakpa* | རྩོལ་བ། འགྲན་པ |
| Queen | *gyálmo* | *gyelmo* | བཙུན་མོ་ |
| Question, a | *ḍi-tok* | *ḍhi-tók ; shu-wa* | དྲི་བ་ |
| Quick, Quickly | *gyokpár* | *gyokpo* (gyo'po) | མགྱོགས་པར་ |
| Quick, be ! | *ring-pa tong !* | *ts'á-ḍhák jhyi' shik* | ཚ་དྲག་བྱིས་ |
| Quiet (of horses, &c.) | *t'unchan* | *sümpo ; dhalwa* | སྲུན་པ |
| Quill-pen | *lákshrogi nyugu* | *ḍoi nyu-ghu* | |
| Quite | *lding-se* | *tsá-wa ne* | ཡོངས་སུ་ |
| Race, a | *sun-gyok* | *bháng-chhong* | བང་ |

| ENGLISH. | LÁDAKI. | CENTRAL TIBETAN. | LITERARY TIBETAN. |
| --- | --- | --- | --- |
| Race, to run a | *báng tángche* | *bháng tángwa* | བང་རྒྱུག་པ་ |
| Radish | *lá-p'uk* | *l̂á-p'u* | ལ་ཕུག་ |
| Ragged (worn out) | *shrulpo* | *šempo* | གཟན་པོ་ |
| Rain | *chharpa* | *chhárpa* | ཆབ། ཆར་ |
| Raining, it is | *chhar bap!* | *chhárpa yong-ghi du'* | ཆར་འབབས་ |
| Raise, to | *sáng choche* | *lang-wa* | སློང་བ་ |
| Rat | *bitsé* | *jhi-tsi; chiwa* | བྱི་བ་ |
| Raw | *jen* | *jempo* | རྗེན་པོ་ |
| Ravine | *rong* | *rong* | རོང་ |
| Reach, to (with hand) | *shringche* | *nyop-jhe'pa* | |

| | | | |
|---|---|---|---|
| Read, to | *silche* | *ḍok-pa ; yige lok-pa* | ཀློག་པ |
| Reach, to (attain to) | *t'elche* | *tál-wa* | ཐལ་བ |
| Ready, are you | *ṭ'al-rik yin-ná ?* | *ḍikpa ḍup-pá ?* | སྒྲིག་པ་འགྲུབ་བམ |
| Ready, all's | *lib dik !* | *ts'ang-ḍik yin !* | ཚང་མ་སྒྲིག་ཡིན |
| Receive, to | *lenche* | *l̂enpa ; t'ob-pa* | ལེན་པ |
| Recover, to | *lok t'opche* | *lok-ne lenpa* | ཕྱིར་དུ་འཐོབ་པ |
| Red | *márpo* | *márpo* | དམར་པོ |
| Refuse, to | *mi solwa* | *mi nangwa* | མི་གནང་བ |
| Regarding (with respect to) | *p'i-á* | *kor-la* (with genit.) ; *wáng-la shorná* (with genit.) | དབང་དུ་བྱས་ན |
| Regent of Tibet | *Pót gyálpo* | *Dé-si ; Gye'po* | སྡེ་སྲིད |

| ENGLISH. | LÁDAKI. | CENTRAL TIBETAN. | LITERARY TIBETAN. |
|---|---|---|---|
| Reins (short) | *shrámda* | *sáb-kyok* | སྲབ་སྐྱོགས་ |
| Release, to | *ṭol chukche* | *ṭol chukpa* | འགྲོལ་བ་ |
| Religion | *chhos* | *chhoi* | ཆོས་ |
| Religious | *chhos sem chan* | *chhoichen* | ཆོས་ཅན་ |
| Rely upon, to | *lor-tád kyelche* (with *la*) | *lo-dáng khelwa* (with *la*) | བློ་གདེང་འགེལ་བ་ |
| Remain, to | *lusche* | *lū-pa ; gor-pa* | ལུས་པ་ |
| Remain there ! | *á-ru shring tong !* | *dher gú'ne dö' !* | དེར་སྒུག་ནས་སྡོད་ |
| Remainder, the | *chhilus* | *lhák-lü ; ting-juk* | ལྷག་མ་ |
| Remedy | *nyen* | *nyempo* | གཉེན་པོ་ |
| Remember ! | *yid-la zum !* | *sem-la ñgé-chik !* | སེམས་ལ་ངེས་ཅིག་ |

| | | | |
|---|---|---|---|
| Remember, to | *yid-la yongche* | *sem-la ñgé-pa* | དགོངས་པ་ |
| Rent | *khang-lá* | *ná-lá* | ཁང་གླ་ |
| Repent, to | *gyodche* | *gyö'pa jhe'pa* | འགྱོད་པ་ |
| Repent, regret, I | *gyodpa yongduk* | *ngá la nong-ngo jhung* ; or *gyö'pa jhung* | |
| Reply, to make | *lan zerche* | *khá-len gyákpa* | ལན་འདེབས་པ་ |
| Reply, a (by letter) | *lan-yik* | *len-yik ; sál-len* | གསལ་ལན་ |
| Require, to | *go-she* (for *gosche*) | *goi-pa* (with *la*) | ....ལ་....དགོས་པ་ |
| Required, is | *go-shes yod* | *goi pa yin* | |
| Respect | *yá shá* | *ŝhesá* | ཞེ་ས་ |
| Respects, to pay | *gus-zháp p'ulche* | *kurti jhe'pa ; jhálkha p'ulwa* | མཇལ་བ་ |
| Responsible, are | *khák khyák-pen* | *khák t'eg-te yö'* | ཁག་ཐེག་ཏེ་ཡོད་ |

| English. | Ládaki. | Central Tibetan. | Literary Tibetan. |
|---|---|---|---|
| Rest, to | *ngál soche* | *ti-wa ; ti jhe'pa* | ཐྱི་བ་ |
| Restaurant | — | *ŝá-khang* | |
| Rest-house | *bor-sá* | *gyá-tsuk ; jik-kyop* | གྲུ་གཙུག་ |
| Return, will | *lokte chhá duk* | *lokne lep gyu yin* | ལོག་པ་འགྱུར་བ་ |
| Returned, has | *lok song* | *lokne lep jhung* | ཕྱིར་སླེབས་སོང་ |
| Return for, in | *lan-la* (with gen.) | *l̂en-la* (postp. with gen.) | ལན་དུ་ |
| Revenge, to take | *lan tangche* | *dhuk-len dömpa* | དྲགས་ལན་ལྡོད་པ་ |
| Reward, a | *sngan-pa* | *suk-ngen ; so're* | སྐུག་ |
| Rheumatics | *shá-ḍum* | *zer-ne'* | གྲུམ་ནད་ |
| Rib | *ŝibma* | *tsibma* | ཚིབ་མ་ |

| | | | |
|---|---|---|---|
| Riband | *lep-t'ák* | *l̂ep-chhingma* | |
| Rice | *ḍás* | *ḍe* | འབྲས་ |
| Rich | *nordak* | *chhyukpo* | ཕྱུག་པོ་ |
| Ride, to | *zhónte chháche* | *ŝhön-ne ḍowa* | ཞོན་པ་ |
| Right | *ōs-chán* | *ŵoi-pa* | རིགས་པ་ |
| Right, to the | *yás-la* | *yé-ngö-la* | གཡས་རུ་ |
| Right, quite! | *ts'ang-dik!* | *ḍik ḍik!* or *ḍikpa yin!* | |
| Ring, a | *á-long* | *serdub* | བསོར་གདུབ་ |
| Ripe | *ts'oskhan* | *minpa* | སྨིན་པ་ |
| Rise up, to | *zhángs-che* | *yar lang-wa* | བཞེངས་པ་ |
| River | *tsangspo* | *chhu; tsangpo* | ཆུ་ |

| ENGLISH. | LÁDAKI. | CENTRAL TIBETAN. | LITERARY TIBETAN. |
|---|---|---|---|
| River-bank | *chhü'-t'á* | *chhu-ḍam* | ཆུ་འགྲམ |
| Road way | *lám* | *l̂am* | ལམ་ |
| Roast, to | *shrágche; no-che* | *sák-pa* | སྲེག་པ་ |
| Rob, to | *kokte khyerche* | *kokne khurwa; chák gyakpa* | འཕྲོག་པ་ |
| Robber | *chom-ṭok-khan* | *chákpa* ཇག་པ་ | ཆོམ་པོ་ |
| Rock, a | *trák* | *ḍhak* | བྲག |
| Rocking, it is | *yuk-yuk tang* | *khyom-khyom ḍo-gi-du'* | |
| Roll up, to | *rilche* | *ḍil jhe'pa* | སྒྲིལ་བ |
| Roof | *t'ok* | *yá-t'o* | ཐོག |
| Room | *nangmik* | *nangmik* | ཁང་མིག |

| | | | |
|---|---|---|---|
| Room, to make | *shong-che* | *shong jhe'pa* (or *nangwa*) | ཤོང་བ་ |
| Room, there is no | *déche méd* | *shong min* | |
| Rope | *t'ák-pa* | *rok ; ro-ghu* | ཐག་པ། སྒྲོགས་ |
| Rope (for bridge, &c.) | *p'áng-t'ák* | *cháng-t'ák* | དཔྱང་ཐག |
| Rope-dancer | *t'ák chhám-khán* | *cháng-khempa* | |
| Rough | *sub-mo* | *tsing-ghe* | |
| Round | *kyir-kyir* | *kor-kor* | སྒོར་མོ་ |
| Round, to go | | *khor gyap-pa* | |
| Rub, to | *ḍudche* | *dar-wa* | རྡར་བ་ |
| Rubbish | *ro-to* | *ghál-ro* | གཡལ་རོ་ |
| Rudder | *shrokpa* | *kyá-juk* | སྐྱ་མཇུག |

| ENGLISH. | LÁDAKI. | CENTRAL TIBETAN. | LITERARY TIBETAN. |
|---|---|---|---|
| Rule | *t'ims* | *t'im* | ཁྲིམས་ |
| Rumour | *loplo* | *ŝer-ri ; ŝer-ke'* | གཏམ་ |
| Run, to | *gyukche* | *gyuk-pa ; gyuk-shá lö'pa* | རྒྱུག་པ་ |
| Run away, to | *shorche ; shorte chháche* | *ḍoi-pa* འབྲོས་པ་ | འཆོར་བ་ |
| Runner, a | *gyuk-khan* | *kyu-po* | |
| Run out, to (of water) | *dzák-che* | *dol-wa* | འཛག་པ་ |
| Rupee | *girmo* | *chhi-gor ; gyá-tam* | ཕྱི་གླིང་གི་སྒོར་མོ་ |
| Saddle, a | *stásgá* | *tá-gá* | རྟ་སྒ་ |
| Saddle, to | *stásgá tákche* | *gá ŝhákpa* | སྒ་འཇོག་པ་ |

| | | | |
|---|---|---|---|
| **Safe** | *stánpo* | *sárten* | ངྡེན་ཀ |
| **Salt** | *ts'á* | *ts'á* | ཚྭ་ |
| **Salty** | *ts'áchan* | *ts'áchen* | ཚྭ་ཅན་ |
| **Same, the very** | *de-rang* | *dhe-rang* | དེ་ཁོ་ན་ |
| **Sand** | *bé-ma* | *jhé-ma* | བྱེ་མ་ |
| **Satisfied** | *ḍhang-chen* | *ts'im-ts'im* | ཚིམ་པ་ |
| **Save, to** | *kyápche* | *kyong-wa* | སྐྱོབ་པ་ |
| **Saviour** | *kyap-gon* | *kyap-gön* | སྐྱབས་མགོན་ |
| **Savoury** | *zhimpo* | *dánte* | ཞིམ་པ། བདའ་དེ་ |
| **Saw, a** | *gyá-sok* | *sok-le* | སོག་ལེ་ |
| **Saw, to** | *gyá-sok shrulche* | *sok-lé ḍek-pa* | སོག་ལེས་འབྲིག་པ་ |

| ENGLISH. | LÁDAKI. | CENTRAL TIBETAN. | LITERARY TIBETAN. |
|---|---|---|---|
| Say, to | *zerche ; molche* | *ŝerwa ; sungwa* | སྨྲ་བ། གསུང་བ་ |
| Said, he | *zer song* | *sung-wa yin* | ན་རེ་ |
| Says, he | *zer duk* | *ŝer , sung-gi du'* | |
| Say, will | *zer'in ; lab-bin* | *ŝer-gyu yö'* | ཟེར་གྱུ་ཡོད་ |
| Scales, pair of | *shrang* | *tulā* | |
| Scatter, to | *ṭámche* | *tor-wa ; torné gyap-pa* | གཏོར་བ་ |
| School | *lob-khang* | *lob-ḍá ; lap-ṭá* | སློབ་གྲྭ |
| Scissors | *chhan-pa* | *chemtse ; ḍimtse* | ཆན་པ་ |
| Scorched | | *se-ŝhop-pé* | སེ་ཞོབ་པེ་ |
| Scrape, to | *rádche* | *ḍe'pa* | འབྲད་པ |

| | | | |
|---|---|---|---|
| Sea | *gyáts'o* | *gyáts'o* | རྒྱ་མཚོ་ |
| Seal, to | *dám-khá gyápche* | *dámkhá gyákpa; t'étse gyákpa* | ཐེ་མོ་གཏོན་པ་ |
| Search for it! | *ts'al tong!* | *ts'ál jhyi shik! tsá-chö' jhyi shik* | ཚ་དཔྱོད་ཅིག |
| Sedan-chair | *gyok-chyang* | *p'ep-chyang* | ཁྱོགས་དཔྱང་ |
| See, go and | *song-la tos* | *toi-shok* | ལྟོས་ཤོག་ |
| See, to | *t'ongche; stáche* | *t'ongwa* | མཐོང་བ་ |
| See, will | *t'ongin* | *t'ong-gyu-yin; m̀ik tá yong* | |
| Seed | *brudok* | *sábön* | ས་བོན་ |
| Seen, have | *t'ong-pen; stáspen* | *t'ong-jhung* | |
| Seize, to | *zumche; t'amche* | *su t'op gyap-pa; nampa* | འཆང་བ |

| ENGLISH. | LÁDAKI. | CENTRAL TIBETAN. | LITERARY TIBETAN. |
|---|---|---|---|
| Sell, to | *ts'ongche* | *ts'ong-wa* | འཚོང་བ་ |
| Send, to | *kálche* | *dzang-wa; kur-wa; tangpa* | སྐུར་བ་ |
| Send for, to | *boche* | *guk-pa* | འགུགས་པ་ |
| Send word! | *ṭ'in tong!* | *ṭ'in ṭing!* | ཕྲིན་སྐྱོང་ |
| Sent, was | *khál-song; kalpen* | *tang-pa re'; dzang du'* | སྐུར་སོང་ |
| Sent, will be | *kallin* | *tang-gyu yin* | |
| Separate, to | *gárte borche* | *ghye'-pa; khá ṭ'elwa* | འབྲལ་བ་ |
| Servant | *kholpo; kholmo* | *ŝhál-tápa,; ŝhe-táma* | བྲན་ཁོལ་ |
| Set out, to | *chháche; kyotche* | *ḍul-wa* | བཞུད་པ་ |
| Sew, to | *ts'emche* | *ts'empa* | འཚེམ་པ་ |

| | | | |
|---|---|---|---|
| Shake, to | *shrukche ; gulche* | *zob-zop jhe-pa* | འཛོལ་བ་ |
| Share | *go-kál* | *go-kál ; goké* | བགོ་སྐལ་ |
| Sharp | *nonpo* | *nömpo* | རྣོ་བ་ |
| Shave, to | *brekche* | *s̆har-wa* | བཞར་བ་ |
| Sheep | *luk* | *l̂uk* | ལུག་ |
| Sheep, flock of | *luk-khyu* | *l̂uk-khyu* | ལུག་ཁྱུ་མོ་ |
| Sheep-skin | *luk-lok* | *l̂uk-pák* | ལུག་ལྤགས་ |
| Shelter (any) | *skyip* | *yap-sá ; gyám* | སྐྱིབས་ |
| Shoot, to | *p'angche* | *p'empa ; m̂enda gyap-pa* | འཕེན་པ་ |
| Short | *t'ungse ; t'ungan* | *t'ung-ngu* | ཐུང་བ་ |
| Short cut, a | *t'ung-lám* | *gyok-l̂am* | རྒྱོགས་ལམ་ |

| ENGLISH. | LÁDAKI. | CENTRAL TIBETAN. | LITERARY TIBETAN. |
|---|---|---|---|
| Shoulder | *pungpa* | *t'rakpa* | ཕྲག་པ་ |
| Shout out, to | *bósra tangche* | *boi-ḍá gyakpa ; ke'tangpa* | བོས་སྒྲ་རྒྱབ་པ་ |
| Shovel | *khyem* | *khyem* | ཁྱེམ་ |
| Shut, to | *kagche* | *kák-pa ; ts'umpa* | འགེགས་པ་ |
| Sick, I am—he is— | *nád-kyī zir duk* | *(ngá-la, kho-la) ná-ts'á gyak-ghi yö'* | ང་ལ་ནད་འབྱུང་ |
| Side, the | *ldo* | *lo ; šhō* གཞོགས་ (hon.) | གློ་ |
| Side of, on the | *deb-la* | *der-la* | ལྡེབས་སུ་ |
| Sight, in | *t'ong khor-la* | *t'ong khor-la* | |
| Sikkim | *Ḍás-jong* | *Dénjong* | འབྲས་ལྗོངས་ |

| | | | |
|---|---|---|---|
| Silent | *chhem-chhem* | *chhem-mer* | ཆེམ་མེ་བ་ |
| Silver | *mul* | *ngul* | དངུལ་ |
| Sin | *dikpa* | *dikpa* | སྡིག་པ་ |
| Sin, to be cleansed from | *dikpa salche* | *dikpa salwa—jang-pa* | སྡིག་པ་འབྱང་བ་ |
| Sinful | *dikchán* | *dikchen* | སྡིག་ཅན་ |
| Sink, to | *horche* | *nerwa* | ནུབ་པ། འབྱིང་བ་ |
| Sinner | *dikpá-po* | *dikpo; m̃i dikchen* | སྡིག་པོ་ |
| Sir | *Sáb; á-jo* | *kusho; lhá* | ཨ་ཇོ་ |
| Sister | *shringmo* | *singmo* | སྲིང་མོ་ |
| Sister, elder | *á-she* | *á-chhe* | ཆེ་ཞེ་ |
| Sit, to | *dádche* (impera. *dod.*) *or dukche* | *khar-wa; de'-pa* | སྡོད་པ་ |

| ENGLISH. | LÁDAKI. | CENTRAL TIBETAN. | LITERARY TIBETAN. |
|---|---|---|---|
| Size | *ts'ád* | *chhe-cühung khye* | ཚད་ |
| Sleep, to | *nyid-la cháche* | *nyi-lokpa* | ཉལ་བ་ |
| Slip down, to | *ḍed-de gyelche* | *shorné gyel-wa* | ཤོར་ནས་འགྱེལ་བ་ |
| Slipping, I am | *ḍed-de shor duk* | *ḍe'-ták shor-ghi yin* | འདྲེད་བདག་ཤོར་གིན་ཡིན་ |
| Slope, a | *ngók* | *ghad ; khad-pa* | ངོགས་ |
| Slowly | *gul-gul* | *ngang-ghi ; gor-po* | བུལ་པོ་ |
| Smell, a | *dri* | *ṭi* | དྲི་ |
| Smell, to | *dri snumche* | *ṭi nom-pa* | སྣོམ་པ་ |
| Smoke | *dudpa* | *tu-á ; dhü'pa* | དུད་པ་ |
| Snake | *rul ; sbrul* | *ḍul* | སྦྲུལ་ |

| | | | |
|---|---|---|---|
| Snow | *khá* | *khau-á* | གངས། ཁ་བ་ |
| Snow-storm | *khá-ts'up* | *ghâng-ts'ub* | ཁ་ཚུབ་ |
| So, (*i. e.*, "like that") | *a'zuk* | *dhenḍe* | དེ་འདྲས་ |
| Soap | *sábon* | *shukpa; láng-le'* | གླང་གློད་ |
| Soft | *bólmo* | *bolpo* | འཇམ་པོ་ |
| Softly | *guléla; sámsum* | *ghále; sámsum* | ག་ལེ་ |
| Some (*adj. & pron.*) | *re-sgá* | *khá-she* | རེས་འགའ། འགའ་ |
| Somebody | *chigchik* | *la-la ŝhik; su-ŝhik* | སུ་གང་ |
| Something | *chi-tong* | *chi ŝhik* | ཅི་ཞིག་ |
| Son | *bu-tsá; shrás* | *bhu; se-bhu* | བུ། སྲས |
| Song | *lu* | *lu; lu-yang* | གླུ |

| English. | Ládaki. | Central Tibetan. | Literary Tibetan. |
|---|---|---|---|
| Sorry for, to be | *dukⁿgál yodche* | *sem dukpa* | སེམས་སྡུག་པ |
| Sort, what | *chi náts'ok* | *ghang rik* | ཅི་ལྟ་བུ |
| Soul | *nam-shes* | *sem-nyi ; nam-shei* | ཉམས། ཐུགས |
| Sound | *rá* | *ḍá-ke'* | སྒྲ |
| Speak, to | *zerche* | *lap-pa* | ཟེར་བ |
| Speak of, to (mention) | *zhodche* | *jö'pa* | བརྗོད་པ |
| Spoilt, is | *khákpo song* | *sáng jhung* | |
| Sportsman | *khyi-rá-khán* | *khyi-rá-pa* | ཁྱི་ར་བ |
| Squeeze it ! | *cher cher tong !* | *lem-né cher* | གླེམ་ནས་བཅེར |
| Stand up, to | *láng-te dadche* | *láng-né dö-pa ; kyére sheng-wa.* | འགྲེང་བ |

| | | | |
|---|---|---|---|
| Stag (*Cervus Thoroldi*) | *sha-wa-ru-lep* | *shau-á-ru-chu* | ཤ་བ་རུ་བཅུ་ |
| Steep | *żáng-zong* | *šárpo* | གཟར་པོ་ |
| Step (of ladder) | *shrál-dáng* | *ţe-ká ; t'emso* | སྐས་ལྡན |
| Stick, a | *berka* | *yukpa* | དབྱུག་པ་ |
| Stick, to (of a cart, &c.) | *jarche* | *kharwa* | འཁད་པ་ |
| Stone | *do-wa ; do-á* | *do* | རྡོ་ |
| Stomach | *ḍodpa* | *ţo-ko ; ḍhö'pa* | གྲོད་པ་ |
| Stop, to | *kagche* | *kák-pa* | འགོགས་པ་ |
| Straight (*adj.*) | *ḍang-po* | *ḍong-po ; shrangpo* | དྲང་པོ་ |
| Straight (*adv.*) | *kyang-kyang* | *t'é-kang-la ; khá-du* | |
| Strayed, has | *yan song* | *yaṛ song* | ཡན་སོང་ |

| ENGLISH. | LÁDAKI. | CENTRAL TIBETAN. | LITERARY TIBETAN. |
|---|---|---|---|
| Strong | *rempa ; remrem* | *shegchen ; ŝhe'-mo* | ཤེད་ཅན་ |
| Stupid | *len-nák* | *lempa* | གླེན་པ་ |
| Stupid-fellow | *bong-gutsok* | *hlümpo* | གླེན་པོ་ |
| Such as this | *i-zug-gi* (before noun) | *dindáwe* (before object) | |
| Suddenly | *hurpo* | *har-ghyī ; tap-tap-la* | གློ་བུར་དུ་ |
| Suffer, to | *sir-che ;* | *ŝir-wa ; nárwa* | འཆིར་བ་ |
| Substitute, a (Hind. *badli*) | *ts'áps* | *ts'áp-po* | ཚབ་པོ་ |
| Sugar | *gurám* | *chéma-kára* | ཀར་ |
| Sun | *nyi-ma ; nyóma* | *nyi-ma* | ཉི་མ་ |

| | | | |
|---|---|---|---|
| Support, to | *kyarche* | *kyong-wa* | སྐྱོང་བ་ |
| Sure | *tánpo* | *t'ákchho* | ཐག་ཆོད་ |
| Surface, on the | *khá-la* | *khá-t'ok-la* | |
| Swallow, to | *smidche* | *khyur mi'-pa* | མིད་པ་ |
| Sweep, to | *chhákdar gyapche* | *chhákdar gyakpa* | ཕྱག་དར་བྱེད་པ་ |
| Sweet | *ngármo* | *ngárpo* | མངར་བ་ |
| Sweets | *zhimzák* | *ŝhim-ŝhim* | ཞིམ་ཟས |
| Swim, to | *kyál gyapche* | *kyál gyak-pa* | རྐྱལ་བ་ |
| Sword | *rál-gyi* | *rá-gyi* | རལ་གྲི་ |
| Syllable | *ts'ekwár* | *ts'egblar* | ཚེག་བར་ |
| Syphilis | *p'árang nad* | *rekduk; khúlu* | རེག་གདུག་ |

| ENGLISH. | LÁDAKI. | CENTRAL TIBETAN. | LITERARY TIBETAN. |
|---|---|---|---|
| Table | *choktsé ; sol-stak* | *sol-chok ; t'oktse* | ལྕོག་ཙེ་ |
| Tail | *shngáma* | *ngáma ; ŝhu-gú* | རྔ་མ་ |
| Tailor | *ts'empa ; ts'emkhan* | *ts'empa* | ཚེམ་པ་ |
| Take away, to | *khyerche* | *khur ḍo-wa* | འཁུར་བ་ |
| Take away | *khur khyer !* | *khur song !* | |
| Take, to | *kyelche* | *kyalwa* | སྐྱེལ་བ་ |
| Take off (clothes, &c.), to | *p'udche !* | *p'ü'pa* འཕུད་པ་ | བཤུ་བ་ |
| Take out ! | *p'ings tong* | *yung song !* | ཕྱུང་སོང་ |
| Take out from, to | *tonche* | *tömpa* | འདོན་པ་ |
| Talk (*subst.*) | *spéra* | *jö'pa ; lap-chha* | གཏམ ; ངག་ |

| | | | |
|---|---|---|---|
| Tall | *go-ring* | *ringpo ; jong-jong* | སྒོ་བོ་རིང་མོ་ |
| Taste (flavour) | *dob-lák* | *ḍho-wa* | བྲོད་ |
| Tax | *pyá-t'ang* | *pyá-ṭ'ál* | ཁྲལ་ |
| Tea | *já* | *jhá ; so'-jhá* | ཇ་ |
| Tea-pot | *tibril* | *jhámbing ; khok-t'i* | ཇ་འབིང་ |
| Teach, to | *láb-tangche* | *lob-pa* | སློབ་པ་ |
| Teacher | *láb khán* | *lo-pön* | སློབ་དཔོན་ |
| Tear up, to | *shrálche* | *hrálpa* | འདྲལ་བ་ |
| Tell, to | *shádche* | *she'pa ; tam ŝerwa* | ཤད་པ་ |
| Temple | *lhá-khang* | *lhá-khang* | གཙུག་ལག་ཁང་ |
| Tent | *gur* | *ḍá-ghur* | གུར་ |

| ENGLISH. | LÁDAKI. | CENTRAL TIBETAN. | LITERARY TIBETAN. |
|---|---|---|---|
| Tent-pole | *gur-ber* | *ghur-shing* | གུར་ཤིང་ |
| Terrific deity | *ḍák shed* | *jik-jhe lhá; lhá ṭ'o-wo* | ལྷ་ཁྲོ་བོ་ |
| Than | *sáng* (following word governed) | *le* (ditto) | ལས། ནས་ |
| Thank-you much | *ká-ḍin chhe!* | *t'u'-je-chhe! ká-ḍin-chhe!* | ཐུགས་རྗེ་ཆེ་ |
| Thank, to | *tang-rák p'ulche* | *lésol p'ulwa* | བཀའ་འདྲིན་ཆེ་ |
| Then | *de-la; de-ts'e-la* | *dhe-tsá-na* | དེར། དེ་ནས་ |
| Thick | *rompo* | *bompo* | སྦོམ་པོ་ |
| Thick (of fluids, &c.) | *skánte* | *gárpo; mongpo* (of mist) | སྐ་བ་ |
| Thickness, the | *shrápt'uk* | *sáp-t'uk* | སྲབ་འཐུག |
| Thief | *skunma* | *kümpo; küm-ma* | རྐུན་མ་ |

| | | | |
|---|---|---|---|
| Thigh | *láshá* | *vlá* | བརླ་ |
| Thin | *shráp-mo* | *t'á-mo; simbhu* | སྲབ་པ་ |
| 45 Thin (of fluids, mist, &c.) | *sing-sing; lánte* | *sim-sim; sengpo* | སིངས་པོ་ |
| Thing | *chhá-lák* | *chhá-la; chhá-kha* | ཆ་ |
| Think, to (imagine) | *sámche* | *nyampa; mik-la tangpa* | དམིགས་པ་ |
| Think about, to | *sam-lo tangche* | *sam-lo tangpa* | བསམ་པ་ |
| Thirsty, I am | *ngá-la skom-ri rák* | *ngárang-la kom yö* | སྐོམ་ |
| Throat | *ó-lé* | *wokma* | སྐོག་མ་ |
| Throw, to | *gyapche; tábche* | *yuk-pa; gyak-pa* | དབྱུག་པ། འདེབས་པ |
| Throw away, to | *p'angche; drimche* | *bhor-wa; yung-wa* | འཕེན་པ། འདོར་བ་ |
| Thumb | *t'é-bong* | *t'ebbo; 't'ebchhen* | མཐེ་བོ་ |

| ENGLISH. | LÁDAKI. | CENTRAL TIBETAN. | LITERARY TIBETAN. |
|---|---|---|---|
| Thunder | *bruk ; bluk* | *ḍug-ke'* | འབྲུག་སྐད་ |
| Thus (like this) | *i-zuk* | *dinḍa* འདི་འདྲས | འདི་ལྟར་ |
| Tibet | *Boḋyul* | *Bhö'-yül (Pö'-yül)* | བོད་ཡུལ་ |
| Tibetan, a | *Bod-mi* | *Bhö'pa (Pö'pa) ; Pö'kyi m̂i* | བོད་པ་ |
| Tibetan tongue | *Bodkád ; Bót* | *Bhö'-ke'* | བོད་སྐད་ |
| Tie, to | *chhingche* | *khyik-pa* | འཆིངས་པ་ |
| Tight | *t'ángmo* | *t'ang-t'ang* | དམ་པོ་ |
| Time (period) | *dus ; yun* | *dhü ; dhui* | དུས་ |
| Time, the (for anything) | *skábs* | *ren* རན་ *; kap* | སྐབས་ |
| Tinder | *tsá* | *shrá-wa* | སྤྲ་བ་ |

| | | | |
|---|---|---|---|
| Tired, are you | *khyod-la ngál song?* | *khyörang t'ang chhe'po re'* | ཁྱོད་ངལ་བྱུང་ངམ་ |
| Tobacco-pipe | *gang zák* | *ghang-ŝák* | |
| To-day | *di-ring ; álta* | *dhe-ring* | དེ་རིང་ |
| Toes, the | *kangsor* | *kangsor* | རྐང་སོར་ |
| Tongue | *lche* | *che ; jā* (hon). | ལྕེ། ལྗགས། |
| Too ; too much | *mang-drák* | *háchang ; drakne* | |
| Tooth | *so* | *so ; ts'em* (hon). | སོ་ |
| Torn, has been | *shrál-song* | *rál jhung ; zhák jhung* | ཧྲལ་བྱུང་ |
| Touch, to | *nyukche ; t'ukche* | *ñyukpa ; chhang-pa* | རེག་པ་ |
| Touch, don't | *ma t'uk!* | *ma chhang ; ma ñyuk!* | |
| Towards | *gán-du* | *t'e'-la* | ཐད་ལ་ |

| English. | Ládaki | Central Tibetan. | Literary Tibetan. |
|---|---|---|---|
| Town | *gyál-sá* | *ḍhong-khyer* | གྲོང་ཁྱེར་ |
| Trade, to | *zong gyapche* | *ts'ong gyakpa* | འཚོང་རྒྱག་པ་ |
| Trafficker | *khe-pa* | *khe-ts'ong-pa* | ཁྱེ་པ་ |
| Translate, to | *kád p'ábche* | *ḍá p'ábpa* | སྒྲ་སྒྱུར་བ་ |
| Translation | *gyurwa* | *gyurwa* | སྒྱུར་བ་ |
| Transmigration | *khor-lam* | *khor-wa* | འཁོར་བ་ |
| Trap | *dem ; nying-ngu* | *nyi ; gál* | རྙི་ |
| Tree | *shing* | *shing* (tree-trunk: *shing-*[*dong*) | ཤིང་ |
| Trial of, to make | *ts'od stáche* | *ts'ö' lenpa* | ཚོད་ལྟ་བ་ |
| Trousers | *dorma ; kangsnám* | *dhorma* | དོར་མ་ |

| | | | |
|---|---|---|---|
| True | *rdenpa* | *dempa ; ṅgo-o* | བདེན་པ་ |
| Truth | *denpa* | *dempa ; ṅge-pa* | ངེས་པ་ |
| Try, to (endeavour) | *bádche* | *dhöndhu nyerpa ; tsön-ḍui jhe'pa* | འབད་པ་ |
| Turn, to (to right, left, &c.) | *chhyokche* | *kyokpa* | སྐྱོགས་པ་ |
| Turn over, to (wood, &c.) | *bubche* | *pub-pa ; lok-pa* | སྤུབས་པ་ |
| Turn round, to (wheel, &c.) | *korche* | *kor jhe-'pa ; kor gyappa* | སྐོར་བྱེད་པ་ |
| Turn-by-turn | *rémos chos la* | *ts'irla ; ts'ir ts'ir* | ཚིར་དུ་ |
| Umbrella | *chhar-rib* | *wu-dū* | གདུགས་ |
| Unable, is | *mi nyan duk* | *chok ma re' ; chokpa me'* | ནུས་པ་མེད་ |
| Under | *yok-la* | *ŵok-la ; khá-wak* | འོག་དུ་ |

| English. | Ládaki. | Central Tibetan. | Literary Tibetan. |
|---|---|---|---|
| Understand, to | *há-go-che* | *ŷi'-la zin-pa ; há-gho-wa* | གོ་བ་ |
| Unfinished | *t'é-rel* | *m̂a ts'ang-ma* | |
| Unroll, to | *ṭolche* | *lok ṭil-wa* | བཀྲོལ་བ་ |
| Unripe | *jenpa* | *m̂a ts'oschen* | མི་སྨིན་པ་ |
| Until | *ts'ukpa* | *t'ukpa ; p'en* | བར་དུ་ |
| Up to | *ts'ukpa* | *t'ukpa ; kám-la* | བར་དུ་ |
| Upon | *khá-tod-la ; teng-na* | *tang-la* | སྟེང་དུ་ |
| Upper, the | *gyenchhád* | *yági ; tö'-kyi* | སྟོད། ཐོག་མ་ |
| Upward, Up (*adv.*) | *gyen-la ; yar-la* | *gyen-la ; yár* | ཡར་ |
| Urge on, to | *nanche* | *be'-pa* | ཐེད་པ |

| | | | |
|---|---|---|---|
| **Useful** | *p'andoks* | *p'en-t'o* | ཕན་པ་ |
| **Useless, it is** | *chhon-la duk* | *dhön-me' re'* | ཕན་མེད་ |
| **Use, to** | *lob-khyad choche* | *chyö'-pa ; kyel-wa* | སྤྱོད་པ་ |
| **Usual** | *p'alpe* (before noun) | *t'al ; t'ünm ng* | ཐུན |
| **Usually** | *mangché* | *chyi-la ; tün-chyir* | ཕྱི་ལ་ |
| | | | |
| **Vacant (untenanted)** | *stong* | *yempa* | |
| **Valley** | *lungpa* | *lungpa* | ལུང་པ་ |
| **Valuable** | *konmo* | *kömpa* | དཀོན་པ་ |
| **Very** | *má* | *háchang* (preceding adj.) or *t'ák-chhö* (after it) | ཤིན་ཏུ་ |
| **Vexed, to be** | *zhe-sun rakche* | *gongpa ts'umpa* | དགོངས་པ་ཚུམ་པ་ |

| ENGLISH. | LÁDAKI. | CENTRAL TIBETAN. | LITERARY TIBETAN. |
|---|---|---|---|
| Victorious, to be | *gyalche* | *gye-wa* | རྒྱལ་བ་ |
| Village | *yults'o ; yul* | *ḍhong-gu* | གྲོང་ |
| Virgin | *zhon-numa* | *pumo sarpa ; ménshár* | གཞོན་ནུ་མ་ |
| Vomit, to | *kyukche* | *kyuk-pa* | སྐྱུག་པ་ |
| Wages | *p'oks ; lá-cha* | *p'ok* | གླ་ |
| Walk, to | *ḍulche* | *ḍulwa* | འགྲུལ་བ་ |
| Walk, to take a | *gom tángche* | *ghom ḍowa* | གོམ་ཆགས་པ་ |
| Wall | *siṅk-pa* | *tsikpa ; bharkya* | རྩིགས་པ་ |

| | | | |
|---|---|---|---|
| Want, I | *ngá-la gos* | *ngárang-la kho-jhe yö'* | ང་ལ་དགོས་ |
| Wanted, not | *kho-che met* | *m̃ingo* | མི་དགོས་པ་ཡིན་ |
| Want to (would like to) | *t'ád* (following other verb) | *gá-ki-du'* (ditto) | དགའ་ཀྱིན་འདུག་ |
| War | *rmák-hruk* | *mák-t'áp* | དམག་ཐབ་ |
| Warm one'self, to | *lde-che* | *de-wa* | ལྡེ་བ་ |
| Warm | *ḍon-mo* | *ḍhön-mo* | དྲོ་བ་ |
| Wash, to | *ṭuche* | *ṭ'ui-pa* | འཁྲུ་བ་ |
| Watch, a | | *chhuts'o' khorlo* | ཆུ་ཚོད་འཁོར་ལོ་ |
| Watch, to keep | *gukte dadche* | *shrung-wa ; sorang jhe'pa* | སྲུང་བ་ |
| Water | *chhu* | *chhu ; chháp* (hon.) | ཆུ་ |
| Water-tub | *chhu-zem* | *chhu-shong* | |

| ENGLISH. | LÁDAKI. | CENTRAL TIBETAN. | LITERARY TIBETAN. |
|---|---|---|---|
| Way, the | *lam* | *l̂am* | ལམ་ |
| Way of doing | *shul* | *t'áb ; ts'ül* | ཐབས་ཚུལ་ |
| Way, to open a | *skabs borche* | *t'áb jhye'-pa* | |
| Weak (of soup, wine) | *sing ; lánte* | *la-po* སླ་པོ་ | བཅུད་མེད་ |
| Weak | *shedchhung* | *she-chhung ; kyar-ra-kyor-ré* | ཞན་པ་ |
| Wear, to | *gonche* | *ghön-pa* | གྱོན་པ་ |
| Wear out, to | *gokpo choche* | *šen-pa* | གཟན་པ་ |
| Weary, to feel | *sunna rakche* | *süm-po širwa* | སུན་པ་ |
| Wearied of, am | *sunna rak song* | *sem sün jhung* | སྐྱོས་འབྱུང་ |

| | | | |
|---|---|---|---|
| Weary, to | *ngal chukche* | *sün jhe'pa* | ངལ་བྲེད་པ་ |
| Weigh, to | *chalche* | *shrang-la jálwa ; tulá tek-pa* | གཞལ་བ་ |
| Weight, the | *shráng ts'ád* | *shrang-ts'ö ; dek-khá* | སྲང་ཚད་ |
| Well, a | *khronpa* | *chhu-m̃ik* | ཆུ་མིག |
| Well (properly) | *lák-mo ; nantán* | *î̂e-mo* | ལེགས་པར་ |
| Well ! very | *ḍik ḍik !* | *yá'po !* | |
| West, the | *nup* | *nup* | ནུབ་ |
| Wet | *rlánchan* | *sherpo ; sher* | གཤེར་བ་ |
| What | *chi ?* | *ghang ?* | ཅི་ |
| Wheat | *dro* | *ḍho* | གྲོ་ |
| Wheel | *khorlo* | *khorlo* | འཁོར་ལོ་ |

| English. | Ládaki. | Central Tibetan. | Literary Tibetan. |
|---|---|---|---|
| While | *zána* (after verb of sentence) | *la-la* (after verb of sentence | |
| Whip | *chák* | *tá-chák* | ལྕག་ |
| Whistle, a | *shug-ra* | *shuk-ḍa* | ཤུགས་སྒྲ་ |
| Whistle, give a | *hu hu tong !* | *shuk-ḍa gyak !* | |
| White | *kárpo* | *kárpo* | དཀར་པོ་ |
| White wash, to | *márkarlága tangche* | *kartsi gyakpa* | དཀར་རྩིས་གཏོང་བ་ |
| Whose | *su-i* | *so-kyi* | སུ་ཡི་ |
| Whole, the | *ts'angpo* | *ts'angma ; l̂ip* | ཚང་བ་ |
| Whole (undivided) | *son-te* | *lingpo ; ghángmo* | གང་བ་ |
| Whole day, the | *nyin t'ák-t'ok* | *n̂yin ghang* | |

| | | | |
|---|---|---|---|
| Why | *chi-la ? or chi-p'i-á ?* | *ghang-gi tön-la ?* | གང་ལ |
| Wide | *zhang-zhang ; hel-hel* | *ŷáng-po ; sheng-chen* | ཡངས་པ། ཞེང་ཅན |
| Width | *zhangts'ad* | *sheng-khá* | ཞེང་ཁ |
| Wife | *áne ; chhungma* | *kyemen ; nangma ; chhung-ḍi* | ཆུང་མ། ཁབ |
| Wild | *rgod* | *ngarma ; gö'* | རྒོད་ |
| Willing, are you | *khyod t'ádkhan yin-na ?* | *gong-pa nang-ngá* | དགོངས་པ་གནང་ངམ་ |
| Wind, the | *lungpo* | *lung ; hlakva* | རླུང་ |
| Window | *kárkhung* | *gyá-kar ; gi-khung* | རྒྱལ་དཀར་ |
| Wing | *shokma* | *shokma* | གཤོག་མ |
| Winter | *gunkhá* | *günka* | དགུན་ཀ |
| Wish, to | *t'ádche* | *dö'-pa ; ts'alwa* | འདོད་པ |

| ENGLISH. | LÁDAKI. | CENTRAL TIBETAN. | LITERARY TIBETAN. |
|---|---|---|---|
| Witch | *kháḍoma* | *kháḍhoma* | མཁའ་འགྲོ་མ་ |
| Witness (in law-court) | *mir-páng* | *mi-páng* | མི་དཔང་ |
| Wolf | *shangku* | *chyang-ku* | སྤྱང་ཀུ་ |
| Woman | *bomo* | *bhü-me' ; kye-men* | བུད་མེད། སྐྱེས་དམན་ |
| Wonderful | *yáts'amchan* | *ŷáts'empo* | ཡ་མཚན་གྱི་ |
| Wood | *shing* | *shing* | ཤིང་ |
| Wool | *bál* | *bhál* | བལ་ |
| Woollen | *bálchan* | *bhálchen* | བལ་གྱི་ |
| Word | *ts'ik* | *ts'ik* | ཚིག་ |
| Work (labour) | *le-ká* | *l̂e-ká ; šo* | ལས་ |

| | | | |
|---|---|---|---|
| Work, to | *le-ká choche* | *ĩeka jhe'pa; šo-wa* | ལས་བྱེད་པ་ |
| Work, the (manufacture) | *zo* | *šo* | བཟོ་ |
| World | *jik-ten* | *jikten* | འཇིག་རྟེན་ |
| Worth, what is it | *ri-che chi yinná* | *khoská ghá ts'o ?* | རི་བ་ག་ཚོད་ |
| Wound, a | *smá-khá* | *má* | རྨ་ |
| Wrap up, to | *rilche* | *shub-su dilwa* | སྒྲིལ་བ་ |
| Write, to | *driche* | *ŷige di-wa* | འབྲི་བ་ |
| Writing materials | | *di-we yo-che'* | འབྲི་བའི་ཡོ་བྱད་ |
| Written, have | *drispen* | *dī jhung* | བྲིས་པ་ཡིན་ |
| Written, anything | *yi-ge* | *ŷi-ge* | ཡི་གེ་ |
| Wrong | *ósmed* | *woi-min; m̃i-oi-pa* | མ་རིགས་པ་ |

| ENGLISH. | LÁDAKI. | CENTRAL TIBETAN. | LITERARY TIBETAN. |
|---|---|---|---|
| **Yak, wild** | *ḍong* | *ḍong* | འབྲོང་ |
| **Year** | *l o* | *l̂o* | ལོ་ |
| **Yeast** | *sábs ; skyūr* | *p'áp* | ཕབས་ |
| **Yellow** | *ser-mo* | *serpo* | སེར་པོ་ |
| **Yes** | *o-oh ; ó-ná* | *yá-yă* | དེ་ཀ་ཡིན་ |
| **Yesterday** | *dáng* | *khá-tsang* | མདང་ |
| **Young** | *zhonma* | *shömpa ; lo-nyung* | གཞོན་པ་ |

# APPENDIX.

## MONGOL-TARTAR WORDS AND PHRASES.

[Mongol traders and pilgrims are constantly encountered in N.-E. Tibet and at Lhásá. These mostly speak Tibetan, but give to many letters a peculiar pronunciation. Thus *gy* is usually sounded *j*, and *khy* and *ky* as *chh* and *ch*; while *d* and *t*, *ts* and *ch* are often interchanged. It was probably this distorted pronunciation which influenced the American traveller, Mr. Rockhill, to adopt his extraordinary system of transliteration for Tibetan place-names in his, otherwise, most reliable narrative of exploration. The lama who taught Mr. Rockhill at Peking was evidently a Mongol; and the curious syllabary in his Appendix, wherein he sets forth the phonics of Lhásá, was plainly founded on Mongol information. As a possible aid to travellers, I have thought it well to annex a few useful words and phrases in Mongolized Tibetan as well as in the genuine Mongol language, the latter the colloquial idiom of the South. *N. B.*—In Mongol words, the vowels marked long, thus *ā*, *ū*, &c., have a greatly prolonged and somewhat guttural intonation, being sounded deep in the throat. The *h* is likewise guttural, being identic with the Persian خ in such words as *khabar*, *Khuda*, &c. The Mongol adjective, unlike the Tibetan, precedes its noun.]

| ENGLISH. | MONGOL-TIBETAN. | MONGOL-TARTAR. |
|---|---|---|
| Good | *jág-po* | *sain* |
| Bad | *ṅág-po* | *mágo* (often *mō*) |
| Not good | *ma le-mo* | *sain bishi* |
| Great | *chhembo* | *iké* |
| Small | *chhung* | *bhága* |
| Much | *mangbo* | *olon* |
| Little | *alich* | *utsün* |
| All; the whole | *kun gangmo* | *kámuk*; *bü-hül* |
| Thin | *t'ámo* | *nárin* |
| Strong | *she'mo* | *hūtsün* |
| Good enough | —— | *saishik* |
| New | *surba* | *shiné* |
| North | *chang* | *buguk* |
| South | *lho* | *barōn* |
| East | *shar* | *jün* |
| White | *kárbo* | *tsághán* |

| English. | Mongol-Tibetan. | Mongol-Tartar. |
|---|---|---|
| Black | *nágpo* | *hára* |
| Red | *márbo* | *uláng* |
| Blue | *ömbo* | *kö-kö* |
| Yellow | *serbo* | *shára* |
| Man | *mi-bo* | *kümün ; ere* |
| Woman, wife | *pü'me'* | *eme* |
| Boy | *potso* | *hübün* |
| House | *nang ; khim* | *ger* |
| Tree | *shing* | *modo* |
| Road ; path | *lam* | *jám ; mür* |
| Land | *sáchhá* | *gádzar* |
| Ground, the | *sá* | *shéré* |
| Stone | *do* | *chulün* |
| Town | *dron-chher* | *hoton* |
| River | *sangpo* | *gul* |
| Mountain | *ri* | *ūla* |
| Lake | *chho* | *nūr* |
| Plain | *t'ang* | *tála* |
| Mountain Pass | *la* | *hutul* |
| Wood | *shing* | *modo* |
| Fire | *mé* | *gál* |
| Water | *chhu* | *ossu* |
| Sand | *jéma* | *elesün* |
| Salt | *ts'á* | *tábsun* |
| Butter | *már* | *tosun* |
| Milk | *homa* | *sága* |
| Bird | *syá* | *shubūn* |
| Marmot | *chhipi* | *tarbága* |
| Sheep | *luk* | *huni* |
| Ox | *hláng* | *imé* |
| Camel | *ngámong* | *temēn* |
| Horse | *tápo* | *morin* |
| Horses, herd of | *tá-chhö* (or *tá-khyö*) | *ádün* |
| Dog | *chhi* | *nohói* |
| Bear | *demo* | *ötögö* |
| Old man | *gánbo* | *öbgön* |
| One—two—three | *chig—nyi—sum* | *nige—khojár—gurbán* |
| Four—five—six | *zhi—gá—druk* | *dörbön—tábun—zhörgön* |
| Seven—eight—nine | *dün—gyát—gu* | *tolōn—naimán—yissün* |
| Ten—hundred | *chu-tamba—gyá* | *arbán—dzūn* |
| Which ?—What ?—Who ? | *kang ?—kang ?—su ?* | *ali ?—jün ?—ken ?* |

| English. | Mongol-Tibetan. | Mongol-Tartar. |
|---|---|---|
| Eternal life | *ts'e t'á-ye* | *möng-hö ámın* |
| Come here | *diru shok!* | *entur irten!* |
| Go further off | *p'árchham song!* | *kholo yábu!* |
| Begin this | *dika go-dzuk!* | *ene ögöskhö* |
| Clean that | *dhega tsangwa chi!* | *tere archi!* |
| Get up | *langne dod!* | *bostŭn!* |
| Run away | *há-la gyuk* | *niss yábu* |
| Take it to them | *de-ts'o-la di khur song!* | *ene teden-tur bári!* |
| Go inside the tent | *gur nangdu song* | *kabidka-in dotoro yábu* |
| He took it | *kho len-pa-re'* | *tere ene ábá* |
| Come in five days | *shak ngá shuk-la shok* | *tábun ödür khoino irten* |
| Write a letter | *yige dri chik* | *bichik bichi* |
| Lift the pack on the horse | ——— | *morin dero achā dā* |
| Go after the goats | ——— | *yámān-u arda dága* |
| The man has come | *mibo lep-pa-re'* | *Kümün irdzü* |
| Your camels have gone | ——— | *tánu temén yábulái* |
| This was given me | ——— | *ene nádur ügküksen bui* |
| Give me water | *ngá-la chhu nang chik* | *ossu nádur ük* |
| Speak to them | *de-ts'o-la ke lap* | *teden-tur ügüle* |
| Dig the ground here | ——— | *gádzar-dur ende erü* |
| Cut up the sheep | *luk tub chik* | *hunin ánzhála* |
| I will taste the butter | *ngá már dho-wa tá yong* | *bá tosun-i ámkurku bo* |
| Are you at peace? | ——— | *amur bhaino?* |
| Reverence be (to you) | *sollo!* | *mandū!* |
| Are your herds well? | *khyod-kyi khyö le-sam?* | *tánu sürük sain bhaino* |
| Remain in peace | *kále zhu!* | *amurli!* |
| Is there tranquility in your country: | ——— | *tánu gádza-dur ámuguláng bhaino?* |
| Is the grass plentiful there: | ——— | *tende ebüsün olon bü-ü?* |
| Have you seen our horses: | ——— | *tán-anu mánu morid-i ödzön?* |
| Who is this man: | ——— | *ene kumün ken bui?* |
| He is my elder brother: | ——— | *ene minu akhá bui.* |

## ERRATA AND ADDENDA.

Page 22, line 24: *lak* should be omitted from list of substantives invariably monosyllabic.

Page 27, lines 7 & 25: *tsána* is correct, but *tsíne* is the usual form.

Page 37, line 8: for *t'o-wa* read *t'o-a*.

„ line 20: for *Dhüd-ḍo* read *Tün-ḍo*.

Page 41, line 30: for *Chupgu* read *Chu-gu*.

Page 44, line 18: for "to arrive" read "to depart."

Page 58, line 9: Tibetan idiom requires that this sentence should be turned "I observed *the body of* the ox dying," *i. e., Nge lang-ghi ro shi-wa t'ong jhung*.

Page 66, lines 3 & 4: *dhön-dhák-la* is ordinarily sounded *tön-dá-la*.

Page 97, line 23: for *toi shik* read *tö shok*.

Page 103, line 13, &c: for *bhámo* read *bháchu*.

Page 119, line 4: for *ŝhák* read *gung-ŝhák*.

Page 131, line 12: for "often as" read "as often as."

„ „ „ 15: for *tāng* read *tang*.

Page 132, line 9: for "is!" read "is?"

„ „ „ 24: for "broad" read "bread."

Page 136, lines 2, 5, 7, 10 & 34: for *ke* and *ké* read *ke'*.

„ „ lines 35 & 36: for *jé* read *je'*.

Page 164: *Tákpa* is the name for *any* white-flowered rhododendron, and *Tákma* for red-flowered varieties: the Tibetan idea being that all the former are male trees and the latter female.

Page 168: To list of deer, add the Cervus Thoroldi; in Tibetan *shau-á-ru-chu* (not *shoa-u-chu*, as in Captain Bower's narrative) meaning "The ten-antlered stag."

Page 171: line 1: for *Ghong-sek* read *Ghong-shág;* and in line 3, omit "*Sekpa:* partridge."

Page 192: another name for a *Mendang* is *Máni-ringpo*.

Page 198: The chief emanations of the goddess Ḍolma are *Ḍol-jang* and *Ḍol-kar*, the Green and the White Ḍolma, respectively.

Page 213, line 3: for "snow" read "stone."

# THE TIBETAN GRAPHIC SYSTEM.

### SIMPLE CHARACTERS.

| *Tenues.* | *High-toned Aspiratæ.* | *Low-toned Aspiratæ.* | *Nasalæ.* |
|---|---|---|---|
| ཀ Ka | ཁ Kha | ག Gha | ང Nga |
| ཅ Cha | ཆ Chha | ཇ Jha | ཉ Nya |
| ཏ Ta | ཐ T'a | ད Dha | ན Na |
| པ Pa | ཕ P'a | བ Bha | མ Ma |
| ཙ Tsa | ཚ T'sa | ཛ Dz'a | ཝ Wa |
| ས Sa | ཤ Sha | ཞ Zha | ཟ Za |
| ར Ra | ལ La | འ Aa | ཡ Ya |
| | | ཧ Ha | ཨ 'a |

Each consonant carries with it the vowel *a*, as indicated above, changed to *e*, *i*, or *o*, according as ◌ེ ◌ི or ◌ོ is marked over the consonant, and into *u*, if ◌ུ is marked underneath.

PREFIXES.—In numerous words, if any one of the five letters, ག ད བ མ or འ, stands first in a syllable, it is termed a Prefix, and is silent, the letter following being sounded as initial. In all syllables comprising three or more characters (reckoning doubles and triplets as one only), *should one of these five stand first* it may be known to be a Prefix. In all two-character syllables the first letter is never a Prefix, except when the second letter bears a vowel mark or is a double or triplet (as in མདོ་ བདེ་ འདི་ བརྟ་, sounded *do*, *de*, *di*, *ta*.) If the letter following a Prefix is a Low-toned Aspirate, then the latter loses its aspiration and becomes an ordinary Medial. Thus, དག sounds *dhag*, but བདག *dag*; གོས་ *ghoi*, but དགོས་ *goi*.

### DUPLEX CHARACTERS.

(The actual pronunciation given in bracketted Italics.)

1. Y subjoined; as ཀྱ Kya (*kya*) ཁྱ Khya (*khya*) གྱ Ghya (*kya*) པྱ Pya (*chya*) ཕྱ P'ya (*chhya*) བྱ Bhya (*jhya*, or *chya*) མྱ Mya (*nya*).

   R subjoined; as ཀྲ Kra (*ṭa*) ཁྲ Khra (*ṭ'a*) གྲ Ghra (*ḍha*) དྲ Dhra (*ḍha*, or *ṭa*) པྲ Pra (*ṭa*) ཕྲ P'ra (*ṭ'a*) བྲ Bhra (*ḍha*, or *ṭa*) མྲ Mra (*mra*, or *ma*) སྲ Sra (*sa*, or *shra*) ཧྲ Hra (*shra*).

   L subjoined; as ཀླ Kla གླ Ghla བླ Bhla ཟླ Zla རླ Rla སླ Sla. All sounded *La*, except ཟླ which makes *Da*.

2. R superscribed; as རྒ (*ga*) རྐ (*ka*) རྔ (*nga*) རྗ (*ja*) རྙ (*nya*) རྟ (*ta*) རྡ (*da*) རྣ (*na*) རྦ (*ba*) རྨ (*ma*) རྩ (*tsa*) རྫ (*dza*).

   L ,, as ལྐ (*ka*) ལྔ (*nga*) ལྕ (*cha*) ལྗ (*ja*) ལྟ (*ta*) ལྡ (*da*) ལྤ (*pa*) ལྷ (*lha*).

   S ,, as སྐ (*ka*) སྒ (*ga*) སྔ (*nga*) སྙ (*nya*) སྟ (*ta*) སྡ (*da*) སྣ (*na*) སྤ (*pa*) སྦ (*ba*) སྨ (*ma*) སྩ (*tsa*).

*Note.*—The superscribing letter is not sounded (at least in Tibet Proper), but where it surmounts a low-toned aspirate, the latter, as will be seen, loses the aspiration.

### TRIPLICATE CHARACTERS.

རྐྱ Rkya (*kya*) རྒྱ Rghya (*gya*) རྨྱ Rmya (*nya*) སྐྱ Skya (*kya*) སྒྱ Sghya (*gya*) སྤྱ Spya (*chya*) སྦྱ (*jya*) སྨྱ Smya (*nya*) སྐྲ Skra (*ṭa*) སྒྲ (*ḍa*) སྡྲ Sdhra (*ḍa*) སྤྲ Spra (*ṭa*) སྦྲ Sbhra (*ḍa*) སྨྲ Smra (*mra*).

Again must be noted that a surmounting letter deprives the low-toned aspirate of its aspiration. Thus རྒ sounds *ḍha*, but སྒྲ sounds *ḍa*.

### FINAL LETTERS; &c.

ས is styled second final after ག ང བ and མ and is then silent; as in སྐབས *kap*, མདངས *dang*.

ས as ordinary final either sounds *i*, or being dropped modifies preceding vowel; as ནས *nai* or *ne*, ཆོས *chhoi*, མདོས *dö*.

ད final is inaudible, but modifies preceding vowel; as ནད་ *ne'*.

ན as final is sounded, but, like ད, modifies *a* into *e*, *o* into *ö*, and *u* into *ü*. ག followed by ས, as second final, is usually dropped prolonging last vowel; as ནགས *nā*, ལྷུགས *lhū*.

The inherent *a* of any final is unheard save in one-character syllables. ག or བ as finals sound *k* or *p* respectively: ལག་པ *lakpa*, སྐྱོབ *gyop*.

Where ད prefix is followed by བ as initial, both are silent; as དབུགས *ū*, དབང *wáng*, དབྱིབས *yib*.

བ as particle sounds *wa*; འ འུ འོ as initials *wā*, *wū*, *wō*.